IBN ʿARABI

The Enlightened are Not Bound by Religion

Kevser Yesiltash

Translated by Pınar Karaman Kaan
Edited by Clare Duman
Designed, Published and Distributed by Bookcity.Co
www.bookcity.co

Bookcity.Co

ISBN: 978-1-912311-01-9

When an enlightened one becomes truly wise, he / she cannot be bound by one belief.

'Feiza kanel arifu arifen hakikaten felem yeterkayyed bimutekadin'

Muhyiddin Ibn 'Arabi

Contents

Preface

The mystical teachings of Ibn 'Arabi, particularly influential in Anatolia, are rooted in a tens-of-thousands-of-years old knowledge attainment and transfer tradition, which is one of the fundamental cornerstones of Sufism.

Through his unique method, Muhyiddin Ibn 'Arabi performed an unparalleled role in conveying the secrets of the Sufi mystical teachings across the generations. The secrets concealed in his teachings are not immediately revealed, and the knowledge they contain is hidden in such language that those who encounter it are often left in a state of shock and bewilderment. Those who strived to understand this language have been able to discover the real meaning hidden within, yet the majority, without making such an effort, took the meaning at face value and accused Ibn 'Arabi of being anti-religious.

The title of this book, *'The Enlightened are Not Bound by Religion'*, is one Arabi's notable sayings, about which alone a whole book could be written; because, to be able to understand just this saying requires knowledge of many subjects of the mystical teachings. In just one word, many layers of mystical secrets are waiting to be revealed.

The saying, 'The enlightened are not bound by religion', *'Feiza kanel arifu arifen hakikaten felem yeter kayyed bimutekadin'*, in other words 'when an enlightened one becomes truly wise, he/she cannot be bound by one belief', is the adapted version for English. This saying conceals important wisdom about religions. As we delve into the meaning of this saying we will perceive that the current form of religions is very different to their pure form. It is for this reason that we've chosen to explore the deep, mystical meaning of this saying as the topic of this book. Because, even today, religious instruction of the masses excludes the inward, mystical aspects of faith and concentrates on its outward form and functions.

Introduction

In Islamic history, Ibn 'Arabi is the sufi whose work was the most harshly debated. His 'divinely inspired' writings gave rise to two opposing groups: those who accepted his work and those who disputed it. His vast knowledge gained him the title Sheikh-i Akbar, meaning 'The Greatest Sheikh', from his admirers, while those who disputed him called him Sheikh-i Kafir, 'The Most Ungodly Sheikh', arguing that the knowledge he attained through inspiration could be incomplete and wrong. One of his most disputed ideas, 'The Infinite Human is Eternal and Permanent in terms of Hadith, Appearance and Essence', attracted immense opposition and many scholars responded by writing works to refute his claims.

In this book, we will attempt to examine the apparent meaning, the mystical meaning and the hidden knowledge about the saying, 'The enlightened are not bound by religion', which made Ibn 'Arabi famous. We will answer questions such as, 'Why is there no religion for the enlightened?' or 'Who are religions for?'

I had the opportunity to examine Ibn 'Arabi's original Arabic texts, which had been brought from Syria. I very much wanted to visit the grave of this expert of spiritual discovery, in the Damascus region of Syria. However, due to the civil war's affect on that region I could not gain permission from the authorities to cross the border. Despite not being able to go physically, in my dreams I visited him and wandered around his grave. When he was alive, Arabi also assigned great importance to the knowledge conveyed by dreams. For this reason, my intuition tells me that the insights and knowledge I have gained through the spiritual journeys of my dreams is the truth. I have sometimes found that the flow of information channeled to me through my dreams, lasting until sunrise, enabled me to fully understand the knowledge found in the texts of Arabi's original work. I have realized, by both witnessing and hearing its cry, that the knowledge of Truth seems complex yet it has a very simple meaning. Experiencing these states helped me to conceive that, in truth, none of the enlightened ones have died and the abandonment of their bodies does not mean that they have stopped existing. I have consulted my master, Mehmet, about my visions, journeys and conversations with the enlightened ones. Mehmet, a graduate of Syrian Higher Islamic Sciences, completed his Ibn 'Arabi training in Syria and has visited Ibn 'Arabi's grave numerous times. His clear answer to me was:

'Not everyone sees them in their dreams and they don't visit everyone's dreams. They are immortal. Know that when you think about them, they are also thinking about you. There are channels and bridges from one spirit to another and being in body is not a barrier to this. In your dreams, you travel towards the mystical and in the mystical world you comfortably attain and understand knowledge, which you cannot attain in the world, and when you wake up you try to remember in the world of appearance and your delusional body, and you translate everything that seems complex into a simple language.' I offer my gratitude again to my master Mehmet and the owner of his heart.

While writing this book, Ibn 'Arabi became my mystical master and friend. He accompanied me on my journey of observation to my Truth. He didn't leave me incomplete in terms of inspiration, intuition, witnessing and enjoying the states for each line. Through divine influence, he conveyed the secrets of his works one-by-one, to my heart and my soul. His immortal soul is still with us; he touches and will continue to touch until eternity, the bodies and souls of those who wish to reach him. He is the master of the Way of Spiritual Discovery. The Way of Spiritual Discovery is the knowledge of Suveyd. It is the witnessing of the invisible world beyond the mystical, in other words the Unknown World. Spiritual Discovery is the knowledge of the Unknown World, the source of wisdom and the knowledge of the divine attributes. He is a Sheikh of Divine Inspiration. He is a genius of the mystery of the letters. As he mentions, 'All of us were High Letters, we descended and became words in the lines of the universe.' We still continue to read the words between those lines. The human being is the greatest book and each one of us is a word. We continue and will continue to read the verses in our cells.

> 'The wise cannot see the Absolute directly, since they witness the infinite manifestations that work as veils hiding the Absolute. What concepts such as Perception or Witnessing try to explain, which may be reminiscent of the ability to connect to the Absolute, do not encompass the Absolute.'
> **Futûhât al-Makkiyya / Muhyiddin Ibn 'Arabi**

This book, *The Enlightened are Not Bound by Religion*, conveys the fact that the enlightened ones are not restricted by one belief. Religions change, however the Truth does not. All teachings on Earth, including firmamental and philosophical religions, are both about and for human beings. Religions have both hidden and apparent aspects; those relating to the internal state and those relating to the road map for the continuation of external life. Rituals and various forms of worship structure and organize external life, using rules that are to be made and abided by. The internal objective, on the other hand, focuses on the importance of humankind by encouraging learning as a way of deepening their self-knowledge and embarking on a quest to seek the reason for their existence. And with the last revealed religion, Islam, the period of religions was closed and the time of prophets came to an end.

The Truth is one and unchanging, it does not deform. However, it cannot be directly transmitted. It can only be conveyed through hidden symbols and inferences. Because no human being, having a physical body, can overtly see or know the Truth. Since one can neither see nor know, one cannot transmit. The knowledge of Truth is very powerful and is only sent to the minds of humankind by way of symbols and interpretations, and with the condition that it remains a secret of the Unknown World that it possesses.

The physical world doesn't have the knowledge of Truth. It has not yet encountered the true reality. The only real knowledge humankind encounters is the knowledge of birth and death. Every human being comes to the world through birth and dies through leaving the physical body. This is humankind's only experience of real knowledge. Humankind has received divine revelations through the religions and esoteric knowledge indicating the Truth via symbols. The enlightened ones visually and openly pointed to the Truth. Nevertheless, whether this knowledge is understood or not, depends entirely on individuals' mentality. Those with the capacity for reason interpreted the truth by following the evidence in the symbols and verses. Those with both physical and spiritual hearts, were able to attain the true meaning of the symbols and verses, but since they could not transmit it, they indicated it using words of wisdom.

The essence of any knowledge becomes comprehensible when one digs deeper; because the knowledge is not outside but inside. For this reason, esoteric teachings purport that nothing is as it seems.

The saying, 'Those who are wise understand', which originates from Sufi teachings and has been adopted by the

Anatolian people, came to be used in relation to this subject. In other words, it means that in order to understand an issue, one must uncover its internal secret just as the wise and those who see with the eye of their hearts do. The meaning of the word 'Arif' also refers to this. The word, 'Arif', takes its roots from Arabic and means 'very understanding, intuitive, knowledgeable, insightful, knowing, wise'.

The Qur'an talks about the existence of *'ulul elbab, lüb'*, meaning those who witnessed the secret and attained knowledge that cannot be attained by reason, but only by the purity of their physical and spiritual hearts. Reason is an infinite gift given to all. However, it is not sufficient to realizing the true meaning of symbols and verses, or for attaining knowledge through exploring their depths. Reason is only sufficient for the visible, physical world, but the Qur'an conveys that the depths of the knowledge of the Unknown World are only accessible the owners of spiritual hearts. And we all have a heart made of flesh and an eye organ located in the skull. They breathe and watch the world. However, only a minority possesses the openness of the spiritual heart and the heart's eye in secret. That which is less is always more precious than that which is more. Because, what's less feeds what's more.

Truth is simple, but only those who see with their hearts can know it is simple. Complication is a construct of the mind. It makes things impossible to resolve by making them complicated. Because, the mind makes interpretations, it sees with assumptions and it evaluates using the knowledge at hand. Humans have made the knowledge of the Truth complicated with their minds; they wanted to understand but they interpreted using their assumptions and got lost in those interpretations.

Truth never dies or becomes extinct. It always continues to exist. There are always those possessing hearts and spiritual hearts to transfer the knowledge of Truth. All teachings containing ancient knowledge have not melted into nothingness over time. They have been uncovered and have reached humankind in all time periods in history. All knowledge that was written, translated incompletely, burned, destroyed or misunderstood has come to light again and again. And the minority, who have had open hearts and heart's eyes, have interpreted that knowledge.

Everyone sleeps but the knowledge, that is always alive and found in places where no sleep can reach, continues to flow to humankind.

There is no religion or wisdom that teaches giving up the physical body. The physical body is the greatest vehicle for understanding the divine order and turning towards the One. What is true is not to give up on the physical body, but to train it.

Each soul, before inhabiting the physical body, defines a form in a registered disk called 'Al-Lawh'l-Mahfuz' and from that form, drop-by-drop, reaches the body, on its journey from Heaven to Earth. In Egyptian initiation, this was described as Thoth's descent from spheres to spheres. And later, this adventure will be completed by elevating to the starting point of descent, just like the saying, 'Our return will be to the One'.

Each human being's secret is registered in that disk. The physical world is a world of forms. Humankind is made captive by the secret of whatever is allocated to its share in that registered disk. This captivity is the spiritual mechanism's rule and possession of the physical body. Our bodies are our graves and in those graves, we have been given life by our soul that is granted to us.

We presume that we believe with our hearts of flesh and that our search is conducted with our reason. What we gain, however, is entirely of appearance; in other words material knowledge. Only those that can open, expand, and wish to expand, the eyes of their hearts can approach the real knowledge of Truth. Belief is not a matter of the heart of flesh or of the brain. It is not reason and it is not mind – these are our self-made assumptions.

For as long as the human being cannot establish order in himself, there will not be order in the world. Humankind is lost in all its assumptions and beliefs and is drowned in all that is matter and material. When one is so deeply stuck, one becomes unable to free oneself. And one will only be able to become free by starting from the point of getting lost. Once one knows where he is lost, one will reach the point of exit. Each human being appeared on Earth with a divine attribute and a high letter and the divine attribute that one carries takes its place in that person's life. The reasonable person, who has the least needs, is as close to the Truth as this and is able to control the material world to this extent.

The meaning conveyed by 'Ulul'elbab' is for those of humankind who are able to open their heart's eye, establish a link between the body and the spirit and using their reason are able to view both their internal and external worlds as a whole. These people are known as the Wise or the Enlightened. The true meaning of the wise is, those who die in their body and find life again in the body. They are truly (spiritually) alive in their physical body. Whereas, each human being is born dead in the body, detached from the Truth, and later reunites with the Truth when they leave their body (die), the wise, are those who are alive in the world of death, without having to leave the body. If you are a prisoner in the body, you cannot know the freedom outside.

When inhabiting the physical body, one is as asleep. When one is asleep, one's knowledge consists of misconceptions. The one who is asleep is the human being, the one who stands against the universe is the human being and the one who denies everything is the human being. To awaken is painful. The most painful of all pains, is the journey towards knowing oneself. The body is not accustomed to this. The body is the place of sleep, and it is programmed that way. To wake up in the body is difficult and almost impossible and for this reason it is a must to die in the body to be able to wake up in the body, as pointed out by all prophets and enlightened ones.

There are no written documents of awakening. All those that are written are merely for appearance sake only. In esoteric knowledge, wisdom and enlightenment are not transmitted in the form of writing. When something is recorded in writing, it is registered. All acts of registration are giving something a form. From then on, all kinds of registered things become shadows, illusions and untruth.

All objects that seem to be solid matter are in frozen form. The body is also a frozen matter. It is the reflection of the Divine Form as a registered disk. When a comment about the body is made with the mind, it is registered and becomes damaged. It is for this reason that esoteric knowledge is not recorded in writing. No information related to the body was cited outside of Truth. The transfer was made verbally. After verbal transfer, the mind would interpret it and would awaken with an understanding in accordance with this interpretation. When written, it would damage the essence of the verbally transferred knowledge.

Inside is an Intelligence that waits to be known, yet Outside is the human being with a frozen intelligence, that damages all that it sees, by registering it.

Hence, humankind, by dividing each moment into attributes, misses the beauty of life and all human beings. To give you a simple example; one can identify some humankind as bad in one's mind and may have the thought that they will be judged one day, one can wait and pray for this, but at the same time another one can pray for the good of the same people; or if you are wishing good things for one person, do not forget another one can be angry with the same person. We make judgments. We live in a world that we create in our minds and this is definitely not a world of Truth. This is a world of imagination and shadows. For this reason, it is necessary to only observe and not make any judgments. This is hidden vanity. It is possible that what is good for us may be bad for another, and what is negative for us may be positive for another. It is true that humankind cannot be truly fair at any given moment. Since assumptions are not just, the decisions will also not be just.

Every manifestation appears with its opposite, becomes visible in expression. Only the One does not appear or is not seen because there is no opposite or duality for the One. The One, which is One, cannot be seen, and if we can see Him, then it means He has appeared as a duality for sure and is witnessed by His opposite. Isn't He the One which enables things to be visible? We love only one of the opposites if it suits us, and we don't love the other because it doesn't suit us, and another person may feel just the opposite. It is hidden vanity to judge these opposites, and favoring cannot produce a fair judgment in the human world. The mind drowns in misconceptions and assumptions. For this reason, we must free ourselves of our worldly assumptions and start constructing the world of Truth. However much duality you possess, you are that far from your Truth. The wise sit at the Pole ('Qutb) and observe the entire universe, its beauty, and the creation that manifests differently at each moment.

Every (moment of every) day, He is in a new manifestation (with all His Attributes and Names as the Divine Being).
Qur'an / Ar-Rahman / 29

Nevertheless, the human inhabits the world, and for this reason, is unaware of and unable to see everything; he interprets life within the limits of his reason. What a great delusion if you are in the world of separation and in perception of separation, as described by İbn 'Arabi. It is said that humankind is ignorant. Being able to establish sameness (pointing to visual connection - Ayn) when in separation… The wise have transferred this knowledge through history: 'Whatever you look for, look for it in yourself and everything is within yourself.'

The only objective of flowing drop-by-drop from Heaven to the Earth, and being wrapped in skin and becoming visible as humankind, was to conceive Oneness in many. The religions came to explain this, however they were never effective. Humankind has become even more buried in material things and fallen into an even deeper sleep. The wise revealed the meanings and increased in depth, yet still could not be understood. Their words of wisdom could not go beyond repetition like tongue twisters. They could not penetrate people's understanding. The message they gave was very clear; they transmitted everything openly and visually with symbols.

Breathe between the world and humankind; know you are inside! There is a Divine Part inside you that knows everything. On the outside there is a body that is asleep. An intelligence that waits to be understood continuously sends signals from inside, yet humankind with their frozen intelligence can never know that. And the human can never wake up since he doesn't love himself. In order to wake up, one must dig inside the grave of the body and reach the light.

The wise are granted the interpretation of the symbols that cannot be seen or understood by everyone. The wise transferred these by witnessing them. Ibn 'Arabi talks about three types of people in his work, *Fusûs al-Hikam* (The Ringstones of Wisdom): 'The wise, the unwise and the ignorant!' In this understanding, he describes the wise one as, 'The one who sees the Truth in the heart of the Absolute with the eye of Absolute'. He describes the unwise, on the other hand, as, 'The ones seeing the Truth, in the Absolute but in its own nafs (ego)'. He describes the ignorant as, 'The one seeing the Truth, neither in the Absolute, nor from the Absolute but believes and hopes that he will see the Absolute in the life to come with the eye of his own nafs'. Because the wise are not bound by any belief or any religious system, they reach the truth and see with the eye of the Absolute. The wise ones add no interpretation to anything and convey in a language of truth and at a level that can be understood by humankind.

Ibn 'Arabi separated the wise and the others in his work, *Mevakıf*: 'The intellectual seeks the evidence of My (The Absolute) existence, however every evidence that it finds points not to Me but to himself; the Wise, on the other hand, seeks with me'

The one who is unwise, interprets to the extent of what he sees and by deforming, registers and damages the truth that he conceives with his reason. In short, the unwise renovates the knowledge of truth.

The ignorant one, on the other hand, has limited comprehension and tries to understand the Absolute through existing teachings and knowledge and ruins his whole life in pursuit of reward and punishment.

The wise one is the one who has reached the Absolute before dying and is visible in the body. He only observes the world of existence and is immersed in the witnessing of creation that manifests itself in a myriad of ways in each moment.

The one who is unwise says, 'If I believe You for Your heaven, keep me away from Your hell. If I believe You with the fear of hell take me to Your hell, and if I only wish to be reunited with You, help me be reunited with You'. Since he is not fully awake, he forgets his secret if he is strongly attached the material world called *masiva* (material); he gives up on the world if he dives into his secret.

The ignorant one on the other hand, spends his life concerned with 'measures and reconciliations' by saying, 'protect me from Your hell, take me to Your heaven'. He is completely worldly. He is obsessed with form. He spends his life keeping account of one more and one less. Yet, Ibn 'Arabi, in his book, *Fusûs al-Hikam*, mentions whatever one does, one does it for the Absolute and The Great Truth of That. He specifically points out, 'Whoever is doing what, in whatever form, is in service of the Absolute.'

The mirrors, mentioned in the original Arabi texts, hold an important place in the knowledge. Despite being misunderstood in society, the correct version is: 'Each human is a mirror of the Absolute and not of each other'. Each human being is a manifestation of the Divine Attributes. In other words, when you look at me, you see a manifestation of an attribute of the Absolute in you, when I look at you I see the manifestation of one of the names of the Absolute. The Truth is the Absolute, humankind is the manifestation of the attributes of the Absolute. Humankind can never be a reflection of each other because humankind is a shadow and is not real. It is frozen material, matter, substance. Frozen materials cannot reflect each other. This incorrect information was too ingrained in society. In short, Divine Attributes are a mirror of the Absolute and humankind is the mirror of the attributes.

In the original *Fusûs al-Hikam*, Arabi mentions, 'The Absolute is your mirror to see yourself. The Divine Attributes are the mirror of the Absolute. You are the mirror of the Absolute in the seeing its attributes and manifestations of the meaning of these names.' In the knowledge of mirrors the Absolute is a mirror, and its divine attributes are the reflection of the Absolute. Since each divine attribute is manifested in humankind, the human must look at the reflection of the Absolute to conceive the manifestation of this divine attribute in himself. In the mirror of the Absolute, one can only find the attribute of the Absolute in oneself. It is this understanding that no longer leaves room for the concept of 'other'. The unity of all humankind is the unity of the manifestation of the divine attributes of the Absolute. When people attain the belief of Unity, the Truth of the Absolute will manifest in the world.

The concepts of 'The Absolute, Allah, Truth' in the book mean the 'virtuous three'. Oneness is the Truth. Anything that exists outside of this virtuous three is a shadow. The three meanings are beyond the infinite and cannot be perceived by the limited human intelligence. They are the truth of the beyond of the beyond. The concept of 'The Absolute' is darkness with no bottom and is a point that will never be known or found by any of creation. With the command of Be! existence comes from nonexistence. And exists with the name of Allah. The meaning of Allah, in esoteric knowledge, is the Only and The Most Beautiful Creator known as 'Rab (Teacher) of All the Worlds'.

> *So Blessed and Supreme is God, the Creator Who creates everything in the best and most appropriate form, and has the ultimate rank of creativity.* **Qur'an / Al-Mu'minun / 14).**

The name Allah, is the Oneness and Unity, where all the divine attributes and forms that will be discussed later in this book are found in unity (kül). We cannot say Allah is One because Allah is Unity itself. We cannot say One because that is Oneness itself. The meaning of Truth, on the other hand, is the last of the virtuous three. It is the manifestation of the name of Allah, which is the Rab of the Universe. Allah is the reality in which all the divine names and attributes that are found in unity in its name are manifested, become 'separate' from each other, disconnected, and called one name, the Truth. The Truth is the general name for all divine names and attributes. Ibn 'Arabi uses Truth for the World, and the World for the Truth. The Absolute is the world in Truth; all the apparent worlds are shadows of the Absolute.

Again, we can describe the concepts that were most frequently referred to in the book; 'Divine Attributes' and 'Divine Forms' as the following: Each 'name' belongs in the unity of the Absolute. Each name and its meanings are expressed in the holy books. These names are categorized into two groups: The Life Giving, The Merciful, The Much-Forgiving, and The Punishing, The Pressuring, The Destroying. Ibn 'Arabi divided these names in two as 'Ones that give existence' and 'Ones that destroy'. There are 99 Divine Names (attributes) that were conveyed to humankind but the true number is infinite. Each of these names is commanding and supreme. In his works, Ibn 'Arabi talks about how each of humankind is embodied under the command of one or more of these divine names.

The divine names take shape in 'Mirror of the Absolute' as divine forms before they give existence to the bodies of humankind. Hence, the place of the true form, the true image of humankind is the divine forms. Each divine form is the image of each divine name that has taken form. Each member of humankind embodies truth in Authority of Truth and Mirror of Truth. In short it has a divine form. Its body that is visible on Earth is only a shadow of its divine form. Ibn 'Arabi says, 'The truth of humankind is found as a form in the Mirror of the Absolute'. Its image on Earth is nothing other than an incidental shadow, in other words a reflection.

In conclusion, each one of us is individually very precious. We are the reflections of the truth written in the mirror of the Absolute. When those reflections enter the body, they fall sleep succumbing to the temptation of the body. Time will pass for them to awaken. However, it must be known that time only exists for us. There is no time that is passing or has passed by. For the human, there is no one closer to him than himself. No one can awaken another. Everyone will awaken through his own individual efforts and via his own route. Everyone is representative of his/her own truth on Earth. The One that talks inside is his/hers truth and humankind will chase duality until they realize 'who' is talking inside. Only then one reaches the realization that one is not separated from the One who talks.

While the entire world is in denial, the Absolute does not send those who reach out for Himself without anything. When one, who is only a delusion and a shadow, reaches out from his body, holds onto His rope and is colored with His color, one acquires a body and becomes a part of the real body. All humankind 'proves the One' with their existence and 'are with the One' in their Nonexistence. Earth is a world of denial. In denial we prove the One, and we are completely with the One when we reach Nonexistence. Everyone has come from the One and will again return to the One.

Lastly, if we return to the Unknown World of the wise ones, the following knowledge echoes in the world of the spiritual heart they have built within them:

'The One said prostrate (Secde) and approach, make two hearts one, you don't exist I am, I don't exist you do. He tied my

tongue in a gordian knot. Opened and melted in its infinity, neither me nor the One is left.

The One said my name is nobody. The One said, only I long for your fragrance, only the One longs for your fragrance, no separate fragrance other than the body of the Absolute. Two longings have become one, did not leave desperate in place of ruins. Each Moment 'I prove the One' with my existence, again each Moment 'I am with the One' in my nonexistence. Such joy the One feels for each one that heads towards Himself, when most try to head towards the opposite. The One has opened His arms saying Come, calls continuously but only a few hear the voice of the One. In the luminosity of the Stars, calls out with one cry His Supreme Body, His Glory, His heart beating in Silence, Come He says Come.

This is a divine surging from yourself to yourself, a journey from self to self. Such a beautiful game this is. I was in need of the One. I found myself when the One was longing for me. Where to without being burned in your hell? Reaching the One but reaching where? When you realize there is no place to reach, becoming a heart beat in the heart of the One. When my soul is strolling in His deserts like a female dervish, what a delusion it is to be in the body. Crowded my mind, so crowded, yet I am alone, in the deepest state of solitude, I'm only with the One in His silence. My soul has become so deep that, I can no longer recognize myself: who am I and where do I belong? When I cannot dock myself anywhere, I ask myself why am I home inside my body. When will I reach Him, while I am swimming with a surge in the vast ocean of the One, when I burn with His divine light, when I gush with the coolness of His water? I am free of all that is 'What', far from all 'To Where'. I couldn't fit in my body, or its world. What kind of pouring out grievance, saying goodbye is this, I found myself again when all my trouble was myself. How beautiful is Your world, take me to Your world, burn me in Your hell for thousands of years, cool me in Your heaven I am willing, if my hope is only to reach You, I am drunk with Your love.

I have reached that edge so many times since past eternity, yet the One behind the door smiling, waited as if saying there is still time.

It was not approached assuming it would be difficult; I was frightened of His greatness, yet the One has made us its sustenance with His mercy. If the One will manifest a mercy, He makes the entire universe sustenance for His creation. Ready He is. The distance of two arches, the distance of a Moment, of a blink of an eye. He waits on, He becomes a visitor for the one who turns a light on his heart, and one knows himself in the One, the One also in the One. While one's soul, like a migrant, seeks for Him in the desserts, sees Him like an oasis, and then looks, the One is everywhere, left His seal in every minute particle. Which eye can see the One, aren't you the One seen in duality with your secrets of Rahman (The Exceedingly Compassionate) and Rahim (The Exceedingly Merciful). You will find your way in His deserts by smelling and smelling.

He has always been with me, always there, in the depths of my heart, caught me like a terrible hunter from my back, established Himself like a life marrow in between my spine, flowing infinitely, taking over my whole body, all my cells. Not just from time to time, I always think of the One, my every moment, my entire mind, all my dreams are entirely full with the One. In service of dedication, only full of the One. I hear that voice with all my existence. But where are my eyes that see? They left me alone. I reached out my hands but no one held them. The wetness of His teardrops wetted my palms. I rubbed them on my face like YOU, as if they were YOU. Why don't you exist? My tears fall on earth, maybe they will become rain and rise to the sky and reach you. I left You like You. Even if I break in parts in every moment, the pain of the far places will still remain with me, in my soul. This is the love of the silence, love of soul. I don't ask anymore. I only wait, hear me! Hear my voice already!'

> *My heart that beats as silent as the stars*
> *Can you feel from there?*
> *Come says Come even closer!*
> *Take I say, Take me near you!..*
> *Make my duality ONE..*
> *Lighten me up in your nights so,*
> *I shall increase in your days*

I

Who is Muhyiddin Ibn 'Arabi?

'All what we have written and have been writing depends on Divine Spelling, Divine Teaching, Divine Breath. Our knowledge is not Words of Revelation but Divine Inspiration.'
Futûhât al-Makkiyya/ Muhyiddin Ibn 'Arabi

Muhyiddin Ibn 'Arabi is a world-renowned sufi with a universal philosophy. He is known for one of his most famous sayings, 'when one gains wisdom of his own Truth, he cannot be bound by any belief', in short meaning, 'The Enlightened are not bound by religion'. Just like Rumi's, 'Come whoever you are', Haji Bektash Veli's, 'Whatever you seek, seek in yourself', and Mansur Al-Hallaj's 'I am the Truth, Ene'l Hakk, Ana'l Haqq' sayings, the saying, 'There is no religion for the wise' has become universal.

There are various associations and institutions organizing activities for Ibn 'Arabi, a master of Sufism in whom the Western world takes close interest. One of these institutions, The Ibn 'Arabi Society Association, organizes an annual 'Ibn 'Arabi Symposium' in Oxford with the objective of translating his work and conveying his opinions to humanity. Also, in San Francisco, US, there is an annual Ibn 'Arabi symposium, and in Scotland, UK, the Beshara School teaches Ibn 'Arabi's works.

The Western world's love of Ibn 'Arabi is an important indication of the universality of his philosophy.

His Life

Ibn 'Arabi was born in 1165 in Murcia, Spain. When he was eight years old, he moved to Sevilla where his first years of schooling took place. During his formative years, he met sufi, Ahmed Ibnul Esiri, and had meetings with him. Later, he also met Ibn Rusd who he frequently mentioned in his works.

When Ibn 'Arabi was around 15 years old, he frequently met and conversed with Rusd. Despite his youth, Arabi detached himself from the world started his journey of self-discovery. Ibn Rusd was a significant influence on Ibn 'Arabi, however, despite his belief that, 'Knowledge is acquired via reason', Ibn 'Arabi conversely believed, as a result of the states that manifested in him, 'True knowledge, in other words Knowledge of Truth, could only be attained via the way of 'discovery of secret knowledge' and not through reason.'

The spiritual expansions of Ibn 'Arabi started at an early age when he attained knowledge via dreams or in the state between sleep and awakening. He reflected this knowledge in his work. He was directed towards Sufism by the recommendation of someone that he saw in a dream.

Later, Ibn 'Arabi met a sheikh called Ureyni, whom he refers to in his works as his first teacher. At the same time, he continued to work with a sheikh called Martili. His first teacher Ureyni had told him, 'Turn only to Allah'. His second teacher Martili, on the other hand, instructed him, 'Turn towards your Nafs, be careful with the subject of your Nafs, and do not listen to it'. Arabi, who had been caught in between these two opinions, asked again for help from his teacher. Martili explained to him that his first teacher's advice was more appropriate and told him to 'turn his face to Allah'. He said that the path Ureyni showed him is the right path with the words, 'Everyone argues for the correctness of their own state. Yet, the heart concentrates on the path that is reasonable.'

Saint Sheikh Akbar was the master of Ibn 'Arabi. His name was Suayb Bin Hassan, and he was also known as Ebu Midyen. He was one of the greatest saints, known as Sheikh-i Mesayih. He died and was buried in Algeria.

Due to his passion for travelling, Ibn 'Arabi found the opportunity to visit many Anatolian cities. After living in the

Malatya area for ten years, he travelled to many Anatolian cities including Sivas, Kayseri, Larende, Karaman, Erzurum and Harran before settling in Konya. He established bases in Konya where he could share his opinions more comfortably. Here he became the master of Sadrettin Konevi, and married his widowed mother. He lived in Konya for a period of time.

On another note, let's share some information about his student Konevi, whose grave is located in Konya. Sadrettin Konevi was Ibn 'Arabi's closest student. Under Arabi's guidance, Konevi learned methods that would be key for him to study, learn and understand all his work. Although he wasn't as knowledgeable as his teacher, he wrote six books and many tracts. At the same time, because he was trained in Arabi's philosophy school, he became well known in his community. The chain that started with Ibn 'Arabi, continued with him.

Konevi's most important contributions to Arabi's teachings were some key arrangements that he made for the transfer of knowledge to make it readable and understandable in all time periods.

Later, Ibn 'Arabi travelled to Egypt. From there he went to Mecca where he stayed for a period of time. In Mecca, he received the knowledge of his works: *Futûhât al-Makkiyya* (The Meccan Openings) and *Fusûs al-Hikam* (The Ringstones of Wisdom). He took orders from the Last Prophet and wrote those works in a style that was revealed to him by the Last Prophet. He discusses this in his work *Futuhatın Sit Fass*.

After completing trips to Baghdad, Aleppo and Konya, he went to Syria where he settled in Damascus. In 1239, he departed from his body and giving his last earthly breath, walked to unite with the Absolute.

His Works

• Futûhât al-Makkiyya fi Esrar-ı Mahkiyye ve l'Mülkiye

This book contains the inspirations about knowing the secrets of property and ownership that came to him during his period in Mecca. The 31-file copy that is written in his own handwriting is located at the Museum of Turkish-Islamic Works, no 1845-1881.

In this work, Ibn 'Arabi reflected all states that he and his students lived. Other than this, he also wrote the dialogues in the form of questions and answers.

Ibn 'Arabi made the following comments about this work and how it was written.

'We wrote this book so that it becomes useful for the public, more correctly not me, but the Absolute did. For that reason, all of it, consists of the inspirational flow that came from the Absolute.' (Futûhât al-Makkiyya, II, 93, IV, 502)

- Fusûs al-Hikam

- Kitabu'l-İsra ilâ Makâmi'l-Esrâ

- Muhadaratü'l-Ebrâr ve Müsameretü'l-Ahyâr

- Kelamu'l-Abâdile

- Tacu'r-Resail ve Minhacu'l-Vesâil

- Mevaqiu'n-Nucûm ve Metali' Ehilletü'l-Esrar ve'l-Ulûm,

- Ruhu'l-Kuds fi Münasahati'n-Nefs

- et-Tenezzulatu'l-Mevsiliya fi Esrâri't-Tahârât ve's Salavât ve'l-Eyyami'l-Asliyye

- Kitabu'l-Esfar,

- el-İsfar an Netaici'l-Esfar

- Divan

- Tercemanu'l-Eşvak

- Kitabu Hidayeti'l-Abdal

- Kitabu Taci't-Terâcim fi İşarati'l-İlm ve Lataifi'l-Fehm

- Kitabu'ş-Şevâhid

- Kitabu İşarati'l-Kur'an fi Âlaimi'l-İnsan

- Kitabu'l-Ba'

- Nisabü'l-Hiraq

- Fazlu Şehâdeti't-Tevhîd ve Vasfu Tevhîdi'l-Mükinîn

- Cevâbü's-Sual

- Kitabu'l-Celal ve hüve Kitabu'l-Ezel

- Ankâu Mu'rib fi marifeti Hatmi'l-Evliya ve Şemsi'l- Mağrib

- Rahmetun-mine'r-Rahman fi Tefsiri ve İşârâti'l-Kur'ân

- Reddu Maani'l-Müteşabihîhât ila Maani'l-Âyâti'l-Muhkemât

- Mişkâtü'l-Envâr

- el'Kur'atü'l-Mübarek

- el'Hucub

- Seceretu'l-Vûcüd ve el-Bahru'l-Mevrûd

- Mevâkiu'n-Nücûm

II

Arabi's Philosophy and Teaching

'Humankind is the spirit and the meaning of the universe.'
Fusûs al-Hikam / Muhyiddin Ibn 'Arabi

In Ibn 'Arabi's philosophy, the first foundational concept is the 'complete person' (Also referred to as the 'perfect person' in some translations). This foundational point is the journey of observation of the complete person, with the descent (nuzul) and ascent (miraj).

Arabi's entire teaching is about the 'complete person' who has first been created as a perfect divine being, then descended to the lowest of the low and will later ascend to the level of the divine being. This is the most foundational principle and knowledge of the law of ascent and descent in esoteric knowledge.

The understanding of 'The Absolute is the Universe, and the Universe is the Absolute' is recognized in all of his works. And again, with a similar proposition, it is said that 'The 'complete person' is the universe, the universe is the 'complete person''. Therefore, it can be concluded that 'The Absolute is the complete person, and the complete person is the Absolute'.

In his works, Ibn 'Arabi says obscure of obscure (enker ennekirat) about the Absolute. The Absolute is the 'Unknown of the Unknown'. He uses the term, 'Unfathomable Darkness', for the Absolute. We will look at the subject of Unfathomable Darkness; in other words, the subject of 'LaTaayun', in more detail later. When the Absolute reflects with love, with divine light, the universe appears like a dream in that divine light. Truth is what manifests as the Absolute in 'unfathomable darkness'. However, the universe appears as a shadow and a dream in His divine light that reflects from unfathomable darkness. Nothing is detached or separate. Each of the worlds that appear with love is a dream, a shadow. The Absolute is what exists in the 'Darkness of the Truth.'

From unfathomable darkness

The divine light of love appears...

... And the worlds,

In the form of dreams and shadows,

Appear in that Divine Light

The light of day, is His Divine Light

The dark of night, is the One Himself.

The universe of existence exists with day and night. The night is the truth of the Absolute, the day is the world of imagination and shadow. 'Hubb', in other words 'Love', is a will. The ones who reach for and attain the love of the Absolute, the One and the Eternal, are those who have made day and night one and became free from the effects of day and night. Hence, the wise become immortal when they completely surrender to the will of love. This is the knowledge Muhyiddin Ibn 'Arabi attained and tried to reflect for us in all his work. Reaching the Absolute is an observation. What is important for the wise is to reach the love of the Absolute. That place is the level of love. And love, for the wise, is only but only a pleasure.

In almost all sections of all his works, Muhyiddin Ibn 'Arabi tried to talk about and to convey the name of 'Allah', the most difficult concept to understand. Specifically, his works *Fusûs al-Hikam* and *Futûhât al-Makkiyya* are the most difficult books to understand and to conceive. It is a commonly held idea that these works will only be understood in future times because Ibn 'Arabi, who was not understood during his own time, made explanations for future generations, but we can only try to understand these using the explanations of our own time. In light of the esoteric knowledge of our time, we wanted to review his works, work on and present his mystical side as well as the subjects he tried to explain in his works both in a hidden and open way.

According to Muhyiddin Ibn 'Arabi, the One, which is the Absolute, is at Ama (Blindness), meaning at a level invisible to all created beings. Only the One sees and knows Oneself. That is at the Level of Blindness for all that is apparent and emerged. The One which creates the 'Whole' as a 'Whole' in one body, embodies its knowledge and commands Existence from Nonexistence with the order 'Be!',

The 'Be!' command of the One, signifies Embodiment, Creative Allah. For this reason, Arabi defines Allah as One, Pure and Unique.

His Oneness indicates there is no other being.

His pureness indicates everything, in all molecular particles visible or invisible, is made of the One. The One is in the Universe, yet in His own hiddenness.

His Uniqueness shows He is not dependent on anything.

Ibn 'Arabi says 'Everything is Him and belongs to Him'.

No definition can be made for the One. Saying 'before' is not sufficient. Because when you say 'before', in other words 'early', it implies a limitation. When you use the word 'last', in other words 'end', again it implies a limitation. When you say 'first' and 'last', this time it will be incomplete since other attributes and names don't have any meaning. In the holy verses, the names and attributes conveyed by numbers are whole. However, the numbers show them separately. Yet, because it is One, Pure and Unique it has not yet been embodied. It is manifested as the Absolute when it is embodied. We will talk about this later in the book as the

Virtuous Three that is The Truth of the Truth according to Ibn 'Arabi:

- **The Absolute, Allah, Haqq**

  The Absolute, is the unknown level of Hiddenness.

  Allah is One, Pure and Unique.

  Haqq, on the other hand is that which is embodied, uniting all the names. Haqq, in our understanding, is Love itself. And to the extent that love allows them, all divine names and attributes, emerge as forms and matter and enable creation. For this reason, Haqq is love by its name; it is the Universe itself; it is the Complete Man himself; it is the grace that wishes to present itself on Earth, and elevates to the level of the wise. Without Haqq's permission, not a single leaf moves. Without Haqq's permission, it is not even possible to mention its name. If the Haqq doesn't will it, nothing emerges, appears or takes form. The meaning of Haqq in Ibn 'Arabi philosophy is:

  'I AM is the apprentice of the road that leads to the One.'

A fundamental reality that Ibn 'Arabi mentions in his works is that; the Universe is composed of a delusion; in other words assumptions. The universe doesn't have a real existence. It is an assumption to think, 'It creates its own self and has formed and is separate from Haqq', because, everything that you discriminate as 'you and me' is a dream. In other words, you yourself are the product of imagination, and the universe that you look with your seeing eyes is also the product of imagination. In other words, you are an imagined 'I' composed of an assumption in an imagined universe. In short, Ibn 'Arabi says 'Humankind is a dream in a dream.'

Everyone is asleep in this life, only wake up when they die. One, who is born in the body, is asleep and only wakes up when he goes back to his own reality. Where is one's own reality? Of course, there is a form of reality for everyone in the Heart of Haqq. The reflection of that form is seen as existence in the universe. It is an image of an existence that has no reality. Its essence is still in the Heart of Haqq, in the silhouette; the shape in the divine mirror. The true shape, the true form is the shape in the divine mirror. The divine thought created by that divine form takes its shape and is reflected in the material plan. This reflection is the reflection of Haqq as a dream in the universe.

> 'The world of Existence and Creation (Vucud and Kevn), is a dream, and the reality is Haqq itself.' **Fusûs al-Hikam – Muhyiddin Ibn 'Arabi**

In Ibn 'Arabi's philosophy, Haqq (Truth) is the only reality. Other than the Truth, anything that can been seen and has limits is temporary, empty, a shadow, unnatural, a game and imagined. The only truth is Haqq. It is the third of the Virtuous Three. The Virtuous Three is 'One' and whole.

The name Haqq is open to the name 'Allah'. The name 'Allah' is secret to the name Haqq and is secret to all existence. The Absolute on the other hand is secret to the name of 'Allah' and the name of 'Haqq' and is the point of hiddenness that is unknown and unfound.

The name Allah, is in the secret of the name Haqq. 'Allah' Loves, when 'Haqq' can't see 'Love' hears. And with that Love, it reveals each reality, each truth that is separated from its Essence. In one moment it creates in all humankind and recreates in all molecular particles. And only the wise one sees this. Because the wise one, having reached the center of Haqq, is in his own center.

In the name 'Allah', all names and attributes are found in 'kül', meaning in whole, pure, single and unique form.

The names that bring 'existence' and the names that bring 'nonexistence' manifest with their dual meanings in the name Haqq. And the meaning of the numerous names that were reported to us are manifest in creation in a single moment. The name 'Allah' expresses itself in 'Haqq'. The name 'Haqq' expresses itself in the divine names, and the divine names make themselves apparent in the divine forms. The divine forms know themselves through the universe. And Haqq knows itself through people. It knows itself by the reflection of divine names and attributes created in each of humankind. If a human refines and cleans his/her heart then it shines like an unpolished mirror and Haqq becomes apparent there. When Haqq is apparent in the hearts of humans, those humans become aware of their own Haqq. When Haqq is apparent in the spiritual heart of humans, the humans recognize the Haqq in their spiritual heart. And this state of mutual seeing, is a state of 'KNOW'ing. When a human knows, he/she elevates to the level of the wise. The names and attributes of existence and nonexistence no longer manifest in the wise one. The wise have freed themselves from duality and are equipped with the Unity of the Haqq. For this reason, the wise start observing humankind, which is in states of existence and nonexistence. The wise observe the universe with Haqq in their hearts, and witness the manifestations of the divine names form within humankind. This is what is called 'observation in observation' which we will mention later in this book.

Humankind witnesses Haqq in line with its own beliefs and knowledge. Let's say, there are a few people who can each see one color but cannot see the other colors. There are thousands of mirrors and there is a form in the middle, and let's assume in those thousands of mirrors thousands of people are reflected in various colors. The humans who can only see the red color, in those thousands of mirrors can only see the humans reflected in the red mirror. Similarly, the humans who can only see the blue color, can only see the human form in the blue mirror. Each human perceives the universe in line with his/her own beliefs and the information he/she was taught or received, and can only perceive one name or attribute of Haqq. For example, if one only looks through the eye of the mind and the conception cannot go beyond this, one can only see in multitude, in other words the physical world, which is a reflection of the 'Apparent' name of Haqq. Because belief and knowledge are limited to that.

We are in Delusion

Everyone witnesses and perceives the creation in relation to his/her own capacity. Even though creation happens at every moment, humankind can only see the apparent divine name and perceives everything as constant instead of being constantly recreated. One is in delusion. Because the physical world that is apparent, is in truth temporary, meaning it came to existence for a limited time. It exists in reality, however it doesn't have a body in its reflection. In truth, it is the 'same' (*ayn*) as the Truth, yet it became 'separate' (*gayr*) in reflection. Since we've mentioned them, let's talk about the words 'same' (ayn) and 'separate' (gayr), which Arabi frequently mentions in his works. These two words are examined in detail in later chapters. Even though Ayn and Gayr seem to be two very simple words, their depths and spiritual meanings are different from their apparent meanings in Turkish. What Ibn 'Arabi tried to convey with these two words, is very different from the meanings they have in our daily terminology.

Ayn, in our language means, 'same, mirror, identical, alike, twin'. Yet, Ibn 'Arabi's 'ayn' is different. It's a word with Arabic roots. Ayn means, 'eye'; 'eye, look, depth, apple of the eye, well, water source, original, essence, self, root, reality'. In his works, Ibn 'Arabi says, 'The One, is the ayn of the universe.' However, in Turkish translations, it is interpreted as Allah is the same as the universe, He is the Universe,

Himself. Yet, what Ibn 'Arabi wanted to say is this: 'The One is the Truth, Essence, Origin of the Universe.' These two meanings are very different from each other and are outside the meanings that are now being widely used. It doesn't mean that The One is the same as the universe, or its identical, or its twin, or its likeness. In Ibn 'Arabi's teaching, when he uses the saying, 'The One is the world of Ayn', He is Gayr from the Universe but He is Ayn to the Universe. In other words, He is not the universe, He is the Truth, the eye, the source, the Self, the Origin of the universe. The One is not in the universe, but is the truth of the universe.

To be ayn in Truth means different entities being complementary to each other, and the other's molecular particles being in each unified entity. Gayr on the other hand emerges as separation. The unified image of the different entities. For example, men and women's bodies are separate. They are different, but in difference they are also unified within their own selves. Yet, they are ayn in Truth, because in every woman's body there is masculine energy and in every man's body there is feminine energy. After this short explanation about ayn and gayr, we will now carry on with our subject.

Our eyes, that are called the mind's eyes, see this finite temporary manifestation and witness that it is constant. They see the physical form of their beliefs. Whatever they hold in their mind as their belief is what they see, and this is limited, because the Truth is beyond all beliefs and faiths. The explanation, 'humankind can only free the Truth of its assumptions' refers to this. Humankind can only interpret the temporary image it sees of the Truth and make an 'assumption' about it. Because in the universe, the Truth is based upon the assumption of its servants. Each interpretation is an assumption. Assumption, on the other hand, is a sign that emerges, appears temporarily. It is not real, it is only shadow. For this reason, the Truth that humankind tries to conceive of in light of its own beliefs is not real, it is a misconception. Beliefs restrict people within a tight framework and do not allow them freedom from it. Sanctions, impositions, limitations and enforcements constitute 'assumptions' one by one, and these assumptions do not lead to the truth about the Truth.

If your aim is to reach the truth of the Truth, you must only wish it from the One. Wishing it from the One means viewing with the heart's eye alone, unrestricted by any beliefs. 'He said you mention me, and I shall mention you'. It is enabling a mutual resonance. Without any restricting belief, thought, separation, detachment, enforcement, imposition or limitation in between, 'mention me, I shall mention you' is formed. Because, what is in the heart is the Truth and it is closer than the jugular vein. The One is a sultan who resides in the spiritual heart, and no bridges or vehicles can come between the Truth and its servant or act as a mediator. For this reason, it is said, 'only a saint is the Truth'. Who is the Truth? It is the Complete Human. It is the oneness and the unity of the whole universe.

The Truth is not found in mental assumptions, it is *mütekadde*. Its definition is this; the Truth is separate from the 'assumptions' formed by beliefs. Mütekadd, on the other hand, is above belief, is a heart-felt faith. Hence, the only way to attain the Truth of the Truth is to understand and see by mütekadd. Mütekadd is understanding the unity of all forms that one sees individually with one look. While some humankind know the Truth with assumptions, some others can know the reflected divine names and attributes. This is an objective perception, thinking outside beliefs. These people are known as experts of self-discovery. By becoming free of the world, even for just a moment, they can leave all their beliefs to one side and reach an understanding of the Truth. Yet, the wise, on the other hand, are those people who have realized that all the divine name and attributes reflect a whole, and hence have reached the Truth.

The only true belief is the belief of the Truth, and it is mütekadd; in other words, it is surrender beyond all beliefs, beyond all assumptions.

According to Ibn 'Arabi, Allah has two manifestations: 'Gayb' (the Unknown World) and 'Sehadet' (Witnessing). 'Gayb' means secret. 'Sehadet' means what is witnessed; in other words what is open.

For Allah, the Truth is Open; in other words apparent. According to the Truth, Allah is hidden; in other words in the Unknown World. (Gayb)

All divine names and attributes are apparent, the Truth is hidden, Allah is hidden.

According to the spiritual realm (*misal alemi* also known as World of Illustration), all divine names and attributes are hidden, the Truth is hidden and Allah is hidden.

The Sehadet (witnessing) or the physical world, material plan, is overt. On the other hand, the hierarchy from the spiritual realm, the divine names and attributes to the Truth and Allah, which all came prior to the physical word, are hidden.

For Allah, the universe is apparent. For the Truth, the entire universe after itself is apparent. For this reason, Allah surrounds and encompasses the entire universe and the Truth observes the entire universe with the 'eye' that is called ayn.

Allah, extends from the entire universe to the physical realm and reaches individuals with the education system called Rab. For this reason, it is said that: 'Allah comes between the individual and its heart.' He can be found between the heart of each individual and the individual itself. This is what Ibn 'Arabi defines as the manifestation of 'witnessing'.

The manifestation of the Unknown World is an unknown and unfound point, as the Absolute Creator, and is beyond our comprehension.

When the wise look at the creation, they witness in every molecule at every moment the divine name and form manifested by the Truth. They see whichever divine name and attribute is manifest in that molecule without being limited by interpretations or assumptions. However, the unwise interpret these manifestations according to their own beliefs and presumptions. This is the difference between them.

The unwise and believers are referred to as, 'ignorant' man; those who are dragged from their foreheads; those who sleep in the cradle of the Earth; and; those who are heedless like the herd because, they act, think and comment based on their 'assumptions'.

For example, when sunlight is reflected on blue glass, humans see it and say 'the sun is blue in color', because they comment based on their assumptions. When the sunlight is reflected on a red surface, humans say 'the sun is red in color' and make this assumption accordingly.

The wise, on the other hand, have the knowledge that 'the sunlight is reflected on blue ground and seems blue, but in truth it is white in color'. Hence Knowing and Asking happen in this way.

Humankind can never know how to know and ask. They only interpret what they see in line with their own knowledge, beliefs and suppositions.

Again, Ibn 'Arabi gives a very good example of this: An elephant is put in a dark room. A few people come into the room and are told the following: 'There is truth inside and know this truth.'

One of these people holds the foot of the elephant and says, 'The Truth is a thick but long thing'. Another holds the trunk of the elephant and says, 'Truth is a thin, long but flexible thing.' Yet another holds the tusk of the elephant and says, 'The Truth is a hard and pointy thing.' One holds the ear of the elephant and says, 'The Truth is a wide, flexible and a large thing.'

In short, none of them knows what they encounter in reality. Whatever they touch in the darkness, they interpret to be the Truth according to their assumptions. Because they cannot see the whole, and because their hearts are blind, they focus on the parts. The parts are merely their assumptions. They are temporary and do not constitute the Truth.

In this example, however, the wise one does the following, 'He sees the Truth with his hearts eye that sees in darkness, looks from the whole to the part and says: 'The Truth is a live elephant.'

In his works, Ibn 'Arabi says, 'don't be mad at time'. Because, the divine name that emerges at that time may seem confusing, negative or ugly according to your assumptions. Yet, the divine name that will manifest in another moment erases all footprints of the previous moment. This time lapse of manifestation between two moments, is a long time period for us, humankind. It may even last for centuries. Yet, at the level of the Truth and the wise, the process is realized in a moment. All creation comes into existence and becomes nonexistent with one divine name. And those two time periods may seem very long for us humans. This idea of a long or short time period is based entirely on our perception. There are such times, when wars, conflicts and massacres do not cease and when natural disasters, deaths, sicknesses are frequent, which may seem to cover a very long time period for humans. In that moment, what is being experienced is a manifestation of one of the divine names. Never be angry with time because that is also a manifestation of one of the divine names of the Truth.

In *Futûhât al-Makkiyya*, Ibn 'Arabi says the following: 'There are such moments that the name Saint manifests yet cannot find Hayy, meaning cannot find life, it only manifests. Yet, there are such moments that, the name Saint is manifested and becomes Life.' This is knowledge that he gives for the whole universe and the world. And he gives the same example for humans saying: 'The name Saint manifests in one person but one doesn't find life with the name Saint, it only manifests. But sometimes, one manifests with the name Saint and that person finds life as a Saint who carries on Sainthood.' He explains:

> *'I take refuge in your Forgiveness from your Torment. I take refuge in your Consent from your Torment. I take refuge in You from You'* **Tefsiri Kebir Te'vilat / Muhyiddin Ibn 'Arabi**

I take refuge in the Forgiver from the Avenger. I take refuge in the Sustainer from the Subduer. I take refuge in Hayy from the Taker of Life.

Here, Ibn 'Arabi points out that all creation happens with a name and becomes a translator for the verse, 'The One is in a different creation in every MOMENT'. Whatever creation it is, He has wished mercy for that creation. In *Fusûs al-Hikam*, he specifically points out the Truth's Mercy is upon its own names. 'Truth's Mercy is found upon its own names'

> *'I climbed up the branch of the plum tree, I ate the grape in the Moment'* **Yunus Emre**

Both the plum and the grape are creations. In Truth their atoms are the same (ayn) however they are separate (gayr) from each other in creation in the way the atoms come together. This is the 'secret' knowledge transferred from generations ago, explained with the example of two types of fruit being different, meaning multiplicity, but being 'One' in essence. The meaning of the words cited by the wise have many meanings. Depending on which level the wise one attained, he speaks from that level. It is very difficult to grasp what they say when they are observing. The tree's essence is a MOMENT in some sense. From that essence hundreds of trees, and from those trees hundreds more trees, have a seed that goes back to the infinite. In the past, the seed of hundreds of trees have formed that essence. And its past and future are all contained in that essence. In other words, essence is the Son of Time, who is the owner of all times.

When the two times, past and future, decrease to one in the moment, depending on which creation the Truth is, the fruit of that creation is eaten. This is a blessing. This blessing of creation is given to humankind. Yet, the one who consciously receives it is the wise one. The wise one climbs up to the plum branch and if the fruit of the creation in that moment is a grape, he/she eats that. Each event that happens and is happening, creates a resonance and reveals the secret. Everyone will find his/her own pearl. If we could just comprehend the pearls of the wise, today humanity would be adorned with love. This knowledge is the molecular particle of the small amount of what needs to be known.

Humankind is living based on two times: on denial and appreciation, and on fear and hope. When will you live in the present moment so you shall be the wise? Humankind, lives in two times: one with divine names giving existence, based on hope and appreciation, and the other with the divine names that destroy, based on denial and fear, and is unaware of each one of them. One doesn't understand it and one is confused and ignorant. It is inside of one however it is always veiled so one cannot see or hear.

Knowledge is directed from one's internal world towards its apparent.

Sometimes one look is sufficient.

The heart of humankind is like one heart between Rahman's two fingers, which He turns as He wishes. And if Rahman wished, He would create all humankind equal and as believers. Divine names are infinite and each one of them continuously manifests as both creator and destroyer, punishing and rewarding, merciful and forgiving. Which is manifest at any moment cannot be known by humankind. This can only be known by the wise ones. Only the wise know which name is manifested in the universe at that moment or which divine name is revealed in which person. Because the wise know, in the present moment, with which name the Truth is manifest in each breath of the universe. Because the wise sits in the present moment, not between two times, and is *Qutb* and centered. The Truth is a Qutb in its own center. The wise one, whirls in his own center, yet humankind whirl around the center of the Truth. And all will return again back to the Essence.

Ibn 'Arabi explains this situation as following: 'There is neither an end to the Names of Truth to be revealed, nor an end to humankind's interpretation of this and their production of assumptions.' Humankind has a sickness, an inability to digest the water it is constantly drinking. It drinks and drinks water but because it cannot digest it, it dies of thirst. However, the sea of knowledge is eternal and right next to it.

All matter, material, existence that is seen as many and varied is made of the body of Truth. Everything that is secret and apparent is within the body of Truth. For this reason, everything that is seen as plural is temporary, a reflection, a virtual reality and a shadow. There is no world of many. All that is manifested is still within the body of the Truth's own names. If humankind recognizes in himself what is manifested, he has connected with his immortal part. This is the philosophy of 'Know thyself'. If you recognize and know what is manifested, you reach your immortal part, and from there you reach the holistic part, and thereby you reach your Rabb, the system that trains you and watches you. This moment of recognition connects you with your immortal part in Rabb – it is a reflection of Rabb on Earth. The apparent and the hidden find, recognize and fully see each other. From that instance, the physical human on Earth recognizes his immortal being from its Rabb; in other words, his hidden teacher. And, at this moment his Rabb sees its reflection on Earth. Two eyes meet and see each other and become mirrors of each other, hence the human reaches his own truth. At that precise moment, all his assumptions, interpretations, belief and faith systems collapse, just like the collapse of a computer system, just like the melting of ice under the sunlight. In that moment, the human finds his own shadow and knows where to turn his face. Humankind reaches his own Immortal Unity from his own nafs, his own entrusted soul that is his immortal part. From then on, he is only enlightened by the Truth, instead of belief, interpretation and assumptions. He reaches the Truth of everything that he sees. One reaches one's teacher, Rabb, by deepening in what is revealed and the apparent, reaching inside and sinking deeper into each 'state' and phase. In Sufism this is called dying before dying; dying within the body and being reborn in that body.

Ibn 'Arabi explains this as the following: 'The wise one who witnesses and approves what is manifested in him, and the Truth who manifests this in the wise and approves it.' When the Truth affirms what is manifest, and when the wise affirms what is manifested in him, if the two affirmations are in sync with each other, the wise one reaches the truth.

However, for the human who, limited by his own beliefs, knowledge and suppositions, interprets what is manifested in him and what is manifested and affirmed by the Truth, and who makes a causal guess, his understanding of the Truth will not go beyond an 'assumption' in line with his perspective.

Ibn 'Arabi gives a very good example of this. Water falls from the sky as 'rain' and reaches all molecular particles.

Water is water and it doesn't change. In Truth it is water, yet it manifests itself differently in every plant. It becomes a rose in a rose plant, it becomes a plane tree in a plane tree, a stone in a stone, and a human in humankind. In Truth it is water, yet it becomes that creation again in the creation that it manifests itself. The property of water doesn't change, its truth doesn't change, its atoms don't change, it is still constant as water in essence, yet it reflects in every molecule in a different way. Where it reflects, and what it becomes doesn't change the truth that it is water. It becomes water again when it evaporates to return to the sky through sweat, photosynthesis, saliva, etc.

According to Ibn 'Arabi; no creation, by the value that it attains, can find the complete and perfect unique unity of the Absolute through its own existence or can reach the One. This is not possible. If this wasn't the case, there would be no secret or unknown left for each conscious being either about himself (microcosmos) or the universe (macrocosmos). Only, for the Absolute, there is no secrecy or unknown. For the rest of the creation, there are levels of secrets and unknowns.

The name 'Allah' and 'Truth' are also included in these levels of secrecy and unknowns. Because the Absolute is the level of Blind (hiddenness) the hierarchy stemming from this contains levels of secrets and unknowns. The Absolute is the One that wants to be known. It is present in all molecules but is not apparent – it is covered and veiled. The first virtue is in the second virtue, the second virtue is in the third virtue and the third virtue forms all spirits and matter. But none of them has knowledge of the previous one because they are hidden, a secret and unknown. Only the Absolute has knowledge of everything.

What is indicated with the name 'Allah', is the most perfect form of the Absolute embodied. Allah is its embodied form, the Truth is the Universe. For this reason, in every section of his work Ibn 'Arabi says, 'the Universe is the shadow of Allah'. The complete man on the other hand, is the shadow of knowledge of 'Allah'. For this reason, everything visible around us, with borders, in truth does not exist. It is only shadow. It is shadow and not real. Only the wise ones can see their own truth. Only one who is at the center can reach the truth of matter and sees not shadow but its truth.

Just as a person's shadow is seen at the place where his shadow falls, the universe is also conceived or known through the matter on which Allah's shadow falls.

In the Qur'an, the verse, '*There is nothing that does not glorify Him with His praise (proclaiming that He alone is God, without peer or partner, and all praise belongs to Him exclusively), but you cannot comprehend their glorification.*' Qur'an / Al-Isra' / 44, points to this.

Allah's knowledge, is the divine 'command' that reaches all molecules, in terms of its ability to encompass the whole universe and its being separate from the whole universe. Ibn 'Arabi continues saying this is the most difficult to comprehend. Because, its encompassing of the whole universe, at the same time as being separated from it, its observation of the universe with the name of 'Truth' from the hearts of the wise, is a situation difficult to conceive and almost impossible to understand. Ibn 'Arabi says this can only be understood by the wise. Because, 'The heart of the wise is full of the Truth, and no place is left for anything else.'

Ibn 'Arabi, clearly answered the question, 'Where and how was Allah before creation?' and said, 'At the Blind Level, in silence, in deep peace'. It is this secret that, even those who are 'Close to Essence', will not understand. That unknown is the Absolute. Ibn 'Arabi says it is true 'Inexistence' and no mind can conceive this. We can only come a little close to its idea through this explanation. How baffled and insufficient would you feel when trying to explain 'color' to someone who has been blind since birth? This is similar to how we always feel 'incomplete' and 'deficient' in trying to understand or conceive the level of 'Blind'.

Divine Unity

No events that take place on the physical plane can deform unity, bring any fault to divinity or create any imperfection. The divine system is always whole and has no deterioration or imperfection. In the physical universe, worlds come into existence and worlds come to an end; stars die and new suns are born; people die and are born. None of these events damage or make the divine system imperfect. It is always

Whole, because it is not possible to disappear in the Divine Will. Since the Absolute (Absent) has created itself as the Truth (Present), there has not been any damage or deficiency. According to Ibn 'Arabi, we must separate the ideas of existence and disappearance and 'creation'. The creation is at every moment a new creation a different appearance and formation. In every single moment the universe is flirting with itself, in conversation, in flow, wearing one color or another, playing with differences and variety; the lovers are meeting, the spiritual hearts are flowing. One must separate 'existence and disappearance' that are created with the creation from 'Coming to existence from Absence'. Creation is temporary, a shadow. It is only a reflection of the name 'Truth' that is colored by the knowledge of 'Allah' in the form of universe.

In his work, *Fusûs al-Hikam*, the example of the 'mirror' has an important meaning. If the mirror in your heart is faulty, crooked or colored, the Truth sees itself in that mirror in that way and manifests itself as the image of that mirror. And hence, humankind knows the image in the mirror as its Rabb. This is an unreal 'divine' that is formed in line with ones own beliefs and knowledge. As many billions of people exist, there are as many 'divines' in line with the reflection of Truth in their hearts.

Ibn 'Arabi said the following for the Truth in his work *Futûhât al-Makkiyya*:

If you know yourself, He will also know Himself..

If you recognize your Nafs, He will also recognize His own Nafs...

Then you become the wise, reach the level of the Truth

The universe appears, become one and the Same (Ayn)

Becomes One Universe

You watch All the Universe from the eye of the Truth

When the wise live up to their own Truth, they possess the view of the Truth. The observation of creation for the wise, that possess the view of the Truth, is lived like a state. For the wise, no one remains other than himself/herself. In Ibn 'Arabi's philosophy, for the one who attains 'his own truth', there is not an 'other' anyway. If he says another, he hasn't lived up to his own truth.

Come life of my life

My supremacy

In those Moments longing for you

Your name echoed in my heart

Come and enter my heart my Supremacy

There shall not be anything other than you in that moment

I made it white, pure, I cleaned did you see?

Clear spring flows and gushes

Did you see? Did you know yourself?

I knew myself,

THE ENLIGHTENED ARE NOT BOUND BY RELIGION

In that moment, became apparent to my eyes, this 'beauty'

Made itself a visitor in my heart, this 'beauty'

The human worships his Rabb due to his witnessing and faith. The wise one, worships his own truth, his own reality, the Rabb of all Rabbs, in other words Allah. Here, there is no privilege or specialness. For the wise ones who discover their own shadow in the land of shadows, the Truth is wherever they turn their face. For this reason, they will not be bound by the obligations and teachings of any faith or belief system. The wise will only stick to their Own Truth.

'He whoever knows his nafs, will gain the wisdom of his Rabb, that moment Rabb knows itself and gains wisdom of the Haqq.' The wise, harbors in his heart the Haqq that is Rabb of Rabb, Rabb of the Universe, and then his faith becomes solely for 'Allah'.

> *Indeed, We have created above you seven heavens, one layer upon the other, and seven paths (for angels to move, God's commands to descend, and acts conscious beings to ascend along). Never are We unaware of creation and what We create (with all aspects of their lives).* **Qur'an / Al-Mu'minun / 17.**

The 'seven heavens' mentioned in the verse, refers to the 'structure of seven' in our universe, which has been stated here one more time in a different style. In other words, it refers to our seven dimensional universe. Quantum physicists have nowadays started talking about the seven fold physical structure of our universe, which is defined in esoteric knowledge in a more understandable way. The 'seven systems' mentioned in Ibn 'Arabi's works will be explained in detail in later sections of this book. But, firstly, let's try to understand what it is that they refer to as seven paths. Then we will look at it from the perspective of quantum physics.

In Arabic it is called 'Seb'a Taraika, meaning 'Seven Tariq'. Tariq means the star that pierces (the darkness with its light). Finding direction with the star is clearly stated in the Qur'an / An-Nahl / 16. It talks about the guidance of the stars and this star (Tariq) is even stronger than the strongest influence in the universe. Yet it's a star unlike any other light emitting star in the universe, because any other star may be destroyed by a black hole, but the star, Tariq, has great spirituality and is a light that will not be affected by even the strongest 'Black Hole'. A light that can pierce the darkness must not be of this physical universe. The word 'Tariq' has both Arabic and Ottoman roots and means 'the one that leaves'. Tariq's light is such a divine light that it has the power of making anything leave, and this power is stronger than all the powers in the universe.

According to esoteric knowledge, The Tariq star mentioned in the Qur'an corresponds with what we know as the Sirius Star.

Those who look with their spiritual hearts

Only those who know how to look with their hearts can see the Divine Light of Tariq. Those who see with the eye of their spiritual hearts and those who hear with the eye of their hearts are the wise ones. It is the 'divine surge' of Essence 'from self to self', it is the return of the Existing and Vanishing Divine Light, from the One to the One; in other words from the Essence to the Universe and from the Universe to the Essence, until another journey starts again. This is a continuous journey that is realized in the present moment.

And the human, becoming deeper in the visible physical universe, will return to his Rabb, and when all that is detected and all creation encounters the End, he will return to his Rabb with the light of the star of Tariq.

One of the pillars of Ibn 'Arabi's philosophy is, 'to see with the eye of the spiritual heart and to hear with the eye of the heart'. Only those who have faith can see with their whole hearts. Faith is a condition for the opening of the eye of the spiritual heart. In order to hear with the heart, to be able to hear the calling and invitation of the Truth, one's spiritual heart must be open. This is Tariq. And according to Ibn 'Arabi's philosophy, Tariq is the divine light of knowledge of 'Allah', which is the Greatest Authority of the place called '*Mekanen Alliya*'. Only the wise ones can see this divine light. For this, the spiritual heart's eye must be open and one must possess a very strong faith. This situation requires hearing with the heart. Arabi does not mention a situation to be heard by the ears. The heart, in other words the spiritual heart, must be awakened to be able to respond to the calling, because those who are 'dead in heart' cannot hear this calling. Being dead in heart is when the eye of spiritual heart is closed.

When the wise one reaches his/her truth, he has faith in his heart and is not bound by belief. And at that time, he will encounter the star of Tariq; the light of divine lights, the power beyond all powers in the universe will take away the wise ones who hear this invitation. They will reach the One by traversing seven roads. In other words, they will attain the knowledge of the Sirius culture.

Ibn 'Arabi's saying, 'The Truth is the Universe', is a thought that states the unity of everything. In physics, all matter takes its source from a power that results from the vibration of an atomic particle and that holds all particles together with a very strong power. All physical matter, everything around us, is a result of a vibrational frequency. This means the following: If you increase the frequency the structure of the matter will change. Right now, we are in a material universe whose frequency we refer to as 3 dimensional.

Our Earth is merely a small frequency pitch in our universe of unlimited energy and unlimited frequency pitches. The atomic particles turn with the speed of light in a vast empty space. And these particles are not material objects.

These particles are the waves of energy and knowledge in vast emptiness.

If you change the pitch, you also change the atoms within it. Using *zikr* (Islamic mantra citation), Sufi's change the pitch to create a center for spiritual and physical change, taking steps towards the road leading to Truth. Vibration changes the matter within the vibration and changes the body related to that matter. The only force that can change vibration is vibration itself.

Since we are made of atoms, and since everything is interlinked, we are also changing our physical reality in its true meaning. In reality, it is consciousness that creates the fundamental structure that makes the universe. It is impossible for the universe to exist without us because our roles is not only to observe the world around us, while observing, we are shaping the universe that we live in and perceive. In every moment that we are alive, we are calling the universe into being. Consciousness is the language of programming for the universe. We are the orchestrator of the consciousness. We are whatever we do.

We are both parts of a whole and the consciousness that creates the whole. The physical formation of the universe continues with the consciousness within the universe. The energy produced by our consciousness affects and changes the material system we exist in because everything is a frequency. The frequency produced from our minds affects and changes the physical frequency of the system we are in.

This is the reason for the expectation of both spiritual and physical change during the Golden Age. When the spiritual influence changes, the physics also change.

The new age, the end of period, is the beginning of the age of the Wise.

One of the meanings of Israfil's blowing of the trumpet, which is referred to in various verses of the Qur'an, must be sought within these physical findings of quantum physics. According to quantum physics, we are calling the universe into being in each moment that we live. And in Ibn 'Arabi's philosophy, creation is recreated in every moment with a 'divine surge' of existence and disappearance. And soon, the above and below will recreate a brand new world 'with an coordinated awareness and open consciousness'. If there is Truth, there is no falsehood, if there is falsehood now there is no Truth. When the truth comes, falsehood will be convicted to vanish and be demolished.

Some of the realities found in the *Vahdet-i Vücud* (Oneness of Being) philosophy can be sought in this esoteric understanding. The new age is the age of 'kıyam' (rebellion, standing up). In his works, Ibn 'Arabi, hearkening from his own time, tried to explain 'Today's age of rebellion' using veiled symbolic statements. In his time, they could not be understood. Today, we are trying to use quantum physics' discoveries in attempt to understand the works that have recently been discovered and interpreted.

In *Fusûs al-Hikam*, Ibn 'Arabi talks about how judgment day is in a few different forms.

First kıyam (rebellion) is the 'divine surge' at each moment 'from Essence to the physical plan', 'from the physical plan to Essence' and the penetration of this surge to all seven layers of the universe. This points to the penetration, arrival and return to the origin of all the divine commands in the entire universe in one existing moment. Ibn 'Arabi stresses that all that is visible in the entire universe is included in this surge. This is the existence of a 'Divine Structure' that manifests with the divine name Hayy, through which everything is always alive and there is no sleeping or sleepiness.

According to him, the second kiyam happens as the human leaves his body.

The third kiyam is the life of the human being in the spiritual realm after his death. This is a mid-level of waiting. In this realm, the human finds himself in a situation to 'review' his life until the day he will become embodied again.

The fourth kiyam is, the wise one's knowing of his Rabb, by living the *Fana* (to die before one dies) and *Baqaa* (to live with and in God) levels as states, knowing his *nafs* (self) and becoming alive again in his own body with the Unity of Truth.

The fifth kiyam points to a time when those human beings' spirits are unable to reach the level of the wise ones when they are alive, are unable to live in the states of fana and baqaa, are unable to be reborn with the Unity of Truth, and, when their life as a human is over, leave their bodies and wait in the spiritual realm until they wake up together for the life to come.

Ibn 'Arabi thought the real awakening can happen this way: 'Everyone will wake up to being a real precious gem. The human is not separate from his Truth'. It is an awakening where we attain the Truth of 'what we are' by becoming free of the impositions of thousands of years, 'showing Truth as, what we are not.'

When everyone laughs, the wise one cries

When the wise one assumes the state of observing in observation by going deeper into his/her own world, then 'worlds' come to formation in his/her own internal, spiritual world. From then on the wise one sees the world and the universe with the eye of Truth. He is in a state of becoming one with the state that it is in. However, according to Ibn 'Arabi, 'the danger still has not departed' at this stage. When in observation of state and levels, there may be temporary situations similar to being drunken and being taken in by them. The road to Truth is thinner than a bristle and sharper than a sword and it is possible to be caught out. The wise one wishes in his/her heart to go even deeper, to drink when feeling thirsty, feeling thirsty when drinking and becoming one with all the states in the Moment.

In observation you become observation. The most dangerous thing is to enter the road of Truth and to be held up at one place. That means dying of thirst in water. According to the wise, this Road is such big sea, to drink as you feel thirsty and to feel thirstier as you drink. It is drunkenness of the Spiritual Heart.

What kind of drunkenness is this? When everyone cries the wise one laughs, when everyone laughs the wise one cries. Because the wise one's world is within himself and the wise one is in the visible world but existing in that world. He is in his own world. Even if Judgment Day comes, even if everything is razed to the ground, what difference does it make for the immortal wise? His inner world is always intact. He is not the one living in the world, he is the one where his/her own world lives. And there is no discrimination between 'them and you'; everything that is visible is incidental, temporary, a shadow and a game. It is a game within a game, and it is the shadow of a shadow. Ibn 'Arabi says that the Universe is the shadow of Allah; the Truth is the Universe. The Truth is Love and Love is the Truth. When the wise one reaches the level of Love, he is in his/her own world. Even if Judgment Day comes and everything is razed to ground, he sees something else, and there is so much beauty that cannot be demolished in his/her vision. The *Arif* (the wise one) has attained the truth of matter. So where is that beauty? The beauty is in the heart of the wise.

The Arif (the wise) is not the one living in the world, but the one who builds his/her world.

The wise one, having built his/her own world, raises this hue with the cry of heart:

'I was lost in the land of shadows, I took the wrong road. Now I Became Visible in Truth and came to understand what existed was only me.'

In Ibn 'Arabi's philosophy, in the idea of Oneness of Being/Unity of Existence (*Vahdet-i Vücud*), 'The Body is one but has many attributes', the body is one and there are no other bodies. Everything that is visible is the result of the divine attributes of the Truth that are manifested and have become visible. Ibn 'Arabi explains this visibility as, 'from Self of the One to Self of the One', meaning it is a journey 'from self to self'. The name Hayy, the source of life and the name in which all names unite when they are manifested one-by-one, is accepted as the prevailing attribute. Because, if an attribute, a name, when manifested does not gain life with Hayy, it only manifests as a name, becomes visible but does not realise existence. In other words, it doesn't gain mastery. In order for it to gain mastery, the manifested divine name, attribute, must gain movement and this comes from the name Hayy. In the divine order, there is no 'stopping', there is continuous movement. Life is a divine name and attribute. For a name to become visible as a being, it must become active with Life, otherwise it is dead. In the absence of life, even if all the names are manifested, they will be of no use. All divine names and attributes, when they manifest, find vitality and gain movement with Life, in other words with the name Hayy.

Ibn 'Arabi counts the 'Attributes of Perfection (*Kemal*) as eight. If these Attributes of Perfection are not embodied in a being, that being is not perfect or 'complete'. The eight attributes are, 'Life (*Hayy*), Knowledge (*Alim*), Omnipotence, Will, Creator, Hearer, Teller and Seer. When these eight divine attributes manifest in a human being, that human being is Adam, in other words Perfect Man, the wise one. All eight attributes are in fact in unity within the name Hayy. To be perfect or complete is to be Hayy. Ibn 'Arabi says, 'One who is Hayy is Allah.' The last step of heaven is the closest place to Allah, in other words the 'Supreme Place' of 'those close to Allah', the immortals and the wise. In Arabi's philosophy, if 'time' that manifests with the name 'Saint' in the Moment, finds Hayy, it gains mastery, becomes whole, and then this period is called the Period of the Wise.

Seek and you shall find

In Ibn 'Arabi's philosophy, during the journey of observation, the divine names are manifested one by one in the human spirit. Ibn 'Arabi says that the one who asks, the one who hears, the one who delivers what is asked, and the one who manifests, are all 'one'.

Ibn 'Arabi says, 'Talent, on its own, is not useful'. This means, 'the capacity that solely 'exists' in you is not enough'. You become Whole if Mastery is manifested together with your potential. In other words, it is not enough for the name Wisdom to manifest on its own in one person. When that person becomes the owner of wisdom, the name 'Master' (*Hakim*) must also manifest for the whole to be formed.

"Our Lord is He Who creates everything and endows each thing with its particular character" **Qur'an / Ta-Ha / 50**

In his work, *Futûhât al-Makkiyya*, Ibn 'Arabi specifically emphasized, 'The one who gives what wisdom gives, is called Master'. The One knows what humankind asks and sends wisdom accordingly, yet the ability to master this wisdom lies with the human. When one is given the wisdom that one asks for, one must carry it, assume its responsibilities and gain mastery of it. For this reason, when one's heart's secret emerges out into the open, the power that one needs to carry it with will be under one's management. Whatever is in one's heart is given to one.

Jesus Christ also said, 'ask and it is given, seek and you shall find'. One must know who to give the '*necm*' (star) in one's heart. Because, one will carry the wisdom one is given and will assume its responsibility. If one ruins it in foreign lands, the wisdom will be taken away. Humankind is entrusted with everything for a period of time. If, during this time, humankind is unable to master it, it will be relinquished from them and this will be a cause of devastation. The responsibility of the wisdom one carries belongs to one and that is called '*Edep*'.

Suffering and pain are the result of people not understanding the secret of the divine name which the world is being influenced by. Ibn 'Arabi interprets this as being the manifestation of Haqq's name, 'Al Mudhill' (One who tricks away from the True Path), which is taking the world and people under its influence and which finds life through Hayy. For those who don't know the Truth, 'the world is a hell'. Yet, all works in the world are under the influence of the names of Truth. And the One encompasses and impacts all particles with His name Life. Humankind's pain and suffering is due to their inability to attain the secret of the name and attribute of 'Al Mudhill' that finds Life. At the moment Al Muddhil (one who leads astray) attains the secret of the attribute that leads to pain, the human being starts to awaken slowly and reaches awareness. Then the attribute 'Al Hadi' (the one who guides, opens the way, helps reach salvation) finds Life.

> *The one, who didn't know grief and the 'sheikh of good deeds' as one, suffered pain. The one, who becomes free from that pain and becomes sultan, understands us.* **Niyazi Mısri (Islamic Wise One)**

The name, Al Mudhill, indicates the pain that will be suffered in hell. If one resolves the secret of the name, Al Mudhill, and comprehends its meaning, one becomes free of the fire of hell. In other words, the world is a place of suffering and the name Al Mudhill commands with pain. If one realizes the secret of this name, one frees oneself from the suffering of the world.

Ibn 'Arabi says, 'The mercy of Haqq is greater than His wrath'. And continues, 'There is no fire in hell. Yet those who have not attained the secret of the name Al Mudhill burn there like fire. They are found in pain and suffering. Yet for this reason, they burn and burn but they don't become ash. Those who will stay there continuously, on the other hand, are those who have not yet reached the secret of the divine name. When they reach it, they become *Mansurs* (those who become conquerors with the help of God) with the Eight Flight levels, that have the unity of the name of Hayy, and they attain victory to become the wise.'

The Eight Flight levels are the eight divine names previously mentioned in this chapter. The eight divine names are the level of 'Perfection' or 'Completion'. The level of Perfection is referred to as 'Eight Flight levels' in Sufism.

Sometimes my soul, strolling in the deserts of the One like a female dervish, becomes water and flows, becomes a flower and blossoms, becomes an eagle and flies, and observes all concepts, all sayings, all meanings. There is neither a word nor a sentence there. You become both the word, and the sentence.

Only those who part the veils with their hearts are superior. Reason alone does not take the human being even one step further, it only makes worldly work easier. There are such events that reason accepts, but the heart doesn't; when you close your eyes to them, the tongue is in denial. They have forced the world into a pre-written destiny as a world of 'war and death'. Reason accepts this. Yet how shall the Heart accept it?

Far away, Truth is in its own presence. Knowing and recognizing are separate things, the heart knows, but isn't recognized. It shall be recognized so that it shall observe from Qutb what it witnesses. We are both in the world, have spread our reputation in its roots, and outside of the world, have become a moment. When we build our world of Truth, then good and evil will be One.

> *Secret, is secret for those who seek for the heart, and a glazer for those who attain it*
>
> *Secret, if it is a word, then the heart becomes a word, word recognizes word*
>
> *Secret, if it consists of a saying, then the heart becomes a saying, saying recognizes the saying*
>
> *Secret, if it is a look, then the heart becomes an eye, it is one that sees from everywhere*
>
> *Secret, if it is fire, then the heart becomes fire, fire recognizes fire*
>
> *And there is a lot fire would say to fire*

Fate and the Relationship of Cause and Effect

In terms of its absoluteness, *Ayan-ı Sabite* (Constant Forms - meaning the constant forms of matter in the Knowledge of the Divine before they are embodied) has a place between Haqq and the physical world. Haqq symbolizes Oneness, but when it manifests from invisible to visible it dissociates and appears as the divine names. In Ibn 'Arabi's philosophy, the One's emergence from invisible to visible is in the form of taking a breath. It is the exiting of the internal, the warm air of the invisible, to the cold air of the visible, the apparent. The great compression that forms in Haqq's body is like the inhalation and exhalation of a breath. The element that provides and triggers this compression is Işk, in other words Love. With the triggering force of Love, the Divine names dissociate by breath, and transition from invisible Oneness to visible Plurality. Each name constitutes a plan of Rabb. A plan of Rabb is a plan that observes, watches and develops. The Constant Forms that are found between Haqq and the physical world are the tablets outlining the organization and life platforms of Rabb's plans. Each human, each object, has a tablet in Constant Forms. Rabb's plan, and each divine visual drawn on this tablet, form the reflection of the shadow lives of the physical world. Each divine visual that is drawn on the tablet constitutes a cause. Cause is divine knowledge. The visual of the Truth formed on the tablet, reflects on the physical world with its reason. Everything that forms, every event that happens definitely has a Cause. In *Fusûs al-Hikam*, Ibn 'Arabi emphasizes 'the impossibility of the removal of Causes'. Everything that happens, happens upon a Cause on a divine tablet. Every situation that is created by Cause, is the Truth of the One. It is impossible to destroy the Truth. When we look around, every event that we face, every situation that forms, whatever we go through, comes into existence due to its Cause. It is impossible for the human being to stop or alter this creation.

Each divine truth that forms in Constant Forms is a word of Allah. The words of Allah, on the other hand, are nothing other than the constant forms of humankind and matter. For this reason, Ibn 'Arabi says, all visible matter and humankind, are nothing other than a reflection of the word of Allah that took form in Constant Forms. The objective of causes also only belongs to Allah, that which is the owner of life and creation. As an immortal, the human being cannot know the objective of the causes, they can only see the results. And since they only see and observe the results with a closed consciousness, they make interpretations through assumptions. The human, who is unable to master the causes of formation and creation, only feels happy when the results suit him; he feels unhappiness and pessimism if the results don't suit him.

The causes are the truths. Only the wise ones who reach their truth can attain the causes. Because they are able to observe the causes with the results, they don't interpret any formation but only observe. They are aware that everything comes from the Truth. This is a state of complete awakening and open consciousness. The unwise on the other hand only observe the results and interpret them according to their self-determined assumptions. They continue passing their lives by rebelling, feeling happy, feeling sad, feeling joyful, swearing, being content or discontent, loving or hating, by thinking life is not being fair to them, or by thinking how lucky they are.

For example, when a human closes his eyes and can't see anything, he cannot assume that nothing exists. When he says, "I cannot see anything now", it doesn't lead to a truth that everything has vanished. Or, when he purchases something, which then belongs to him, it doesn't mean it didn't exist before. In this way, looking at the results of something doesn't lead to the truth. Each human is included in the Rabb training system where one of the divine names of Truth is manifested. The human's life will reflect the shape drawn on the Constant Forms as part of the Rabb Plan, and he will live the results of the causes drawn on that tablet. Both the hand that draws and the human that lives are in truth ayn (same), but look gayr (separate) in the physical plan. This, in Ibn 'Arabi's words, is a formation of 'journey from self to self.' Every human, depending on whatever cause was formed on his/her own tablet before birth, will live the results in the physical world according to the Rabb Plan.

The human that succumbs to the influence of matter, partly through reason and partly through nafs, and through the pulling force of the body, forgets this complete Divine Truth. Due to this forgetfulness, he presumes that he is under duress to live this life and views those things that suit his reason and nafs as possibility and reward. He thinks of all his actions in terms of having reward or punishment, therefore he starts acting with measure. The thought that every step he takes will be recompensed spreads over his/her life. The wise one, on the other hand, realizes that everything that he lives is his/her own plan and completely submits to his life plan. Because, the causes either exist or don't exist, and the wise one knows very well that there is no middle way in this. He knows there will not be a third state, so the wise one is in a state of complete submission. The wise one knows that everything is realized within a life plan that reflects from a tablet that is drawn on with his/her own hands. For this reason, there is no fear or sorrow for the wise. For the one who knows the Truth, there will not be fear or sorrow. There will not be a punishment or reward. Because, in the journey from self to self, the only thing that will judge one person is the channel of compassion. Meaning, his/her inner voice. In other words, it is the Truth that he has drawn on the Constant Forms. And since he cannot escape this truth, he will live whatever is included in his/her life plan. He will not worry about feeling sad for more and feeling unhappy for less. The wise one knows that requests and desires are deterrents of the nafs and the mind. The wise one carries the consciousness that the act of asking for more can lead to changes that can change the direction of his/her life.

When emerging from idea (intention) to action, all creation is formed with a cause. This is what is possible. The possibility is entirely what the human determined as his life plan before his birth. And the Rabb plan provides the coordination of this life plan. Each human is under the watch of his own Rabb plan, and his life is carried out within the state of possibility.

Everyone personally determines his own faith. Whatever one lives one is included in the work that he formed in his Rabb plan. One plays the lead role in the painting that he drew and colored. Being lost in the painting and not knowing the outside is due to having a closed consciousness. If one had an open consciousness, one would be content within the picture, and would know what is outside the picture. One would witness a divine system that is operated by himself, instead of thinking of the existence of a creator that punishes or rewards. It is because everything operates within an order and in line with laws. Even the Truth itself and the divine names abide by this law and order. This is the will of the Truth. Will is the determining power and intention. The emergence and shape this intention takes is the recreation of the universe in each moment. It is a different creation and shape in each moment. Each creation emerges with a cause and the results manifest as events in the universe.

Accident and fate

Allah's judgment related to the creation is called *kaza* (administration of justice). The judgment is His knowledge. Knowledge also only belongs to the creator. In short, the knowledge of Creation is a knowledge that is fixed at the level of Allah and all knowledge about the creation is called kaza. Haqq also has limited possession of knowledge of the creation fixed at the level of Allah. The knowledge of creation is constant at the level of Allah and Haqq has limited possession of this knowledge. This is the kaza of all material and matter.

Each creation's constant knowledge in its nafs is its gem. While Haqq commands on creation, material and matter, it does so by staying loyal to their essence and without changing it. It realizes creation and formation by staying loyal to their Constant Forms. It cannot know their constant forms and cannot change their essence. And this is the fate of all constant formation that was formed in the first creation.

The kaza of one event doesn't contain time. It has a constancy that is created by cause. Time is determined by fate.

For example, the occurrence of an earthquake in an earthquake zone is a kaza. It is definitive and constant. The earthquake is inevitable due to the region's geology and settlement. This is the kaza of that region. In other words, it is a fixed truth. However, the timing of the earthquake is the fate of that region. Now, when humans escape the area due to a worry that an earthquake is imminent, this changes neither the fate nor the kaza. Their living with the constant worry of an earthquake does not change the fate. Only the judgment determines the timing of the earthquake and this authority belongs to Haqq and the divine names alone. Because everything happens in line with law and order; when the constant kaza state will transform into fate is determined by the energy of time.

Ibn 'Arabi says, 'Kaza is the Truth of each particle, each creation, at the level of Allah and even the being of Truth has limited knowledge of this.' The command of Truth, realizes creations by staying loyal to this secret Truth. Kaza is a cause that is previously fixed and the energy of time is included in this; fate is the result of command of Truth over the energy of time and creation.

In this section, Ibn 'Arabi divides the wise into two: those in the top rank and those in the bottom rank; also, those that understand fate in summary and those that understand fate in detail. He explains that those who know it in detail hold a higher rank. For, to know the details, one must attain knowledge of the constant forms. This information about the constant forms, that even Haqq only has in a limited way, is found at the level of Allah. Ibn 'Arabi indicated that only the wise that are closest to the level of Allah have this knowledge.

All creation from before time to eternity, each formation, has emerged and reflected from its own constant form. The constant form means plurality and is located between Haqq and humankind. The Constant Forms on the other hand are a secret at the level of Allah. When the wise one reaches his own truth, he only reaches his truth in constant forms. His reach of his truth in Constant Forms at the level of Allah indicates the wise one has attained a very high rank.

At this stage, let's touch upon Ibn 'Arabi's opinion of wishes to be granted. The immediate granting of wishes and desires, or their delay, is a result of fate. If the energy of time intersects with space it means its fate is realized and hence when a human being wishes something it immediately becomes real. However, if in his/her constant the kaza is formed yet the time for fate to be formed has not come, the wish is not granted immediately. One is kept waiting until its time comes. Ibn 'Arabi says when its time comes, the fate is realized in any way possible and it will definitely be realized even if one is in the physical plan or in the life to come.

Also, there are things granted to people without them having asked for them. Ibn 'Arabi explains this as follows: The demand of a human can be verbal or it can be determined in its private life plan. His verbal request can be realized, or it can be a realization of something in his life plan regardless of whether he asked for it or not.

Truth of unity in humankind

Ibn 'Arabi says there is a 'being related' human, who is a complete man, and there is a selfish human who is a mortal human. The human being is at a midpoint between Haqq and the universe. However, even though the human being is selfish, or mortal, he is positioned as the most honorable of all creation.

In truth, the symbol of humankind is complete man, in other words the 'being related' human. Yet, in terms of individuality not every human is complete. In the history of Earth, very few people have reached the position of Complete Man and become wise.

The state of '*cem*' which is defined as the state of being whole, is a kernel that is found in all humans, all mortals. Yet it only exists as an intention (latent power). Intention is the knowledge of truth. The knowledge of truth, wisdom, is granted equally to all humans at the moment of creation. However, intention transformed into action is known as '*Cem ül cem*' and this is becoming complete man.

Even though every person holds the kernel and essence of the Truth of Unity, not everyone is informed of this knowledge. Even though every one has the skill to manifest it, he doesn't have the skill to live in the state of Unity.

The highest consciousness of man is the consciousness of the First Divine name and Divine Forms, which are the main essence that man manifests from. The lowest consciousness of man on the other hand is his reason and intelligence that he possesses as a mortal. It is possible for the human being to reach the First Divine source by developing his spiritual skills and his worldly attributes of reason and intelligence. The state of one's becoming wise of his own truth corresponds to his reaching the first source. One needs to have a special skill to reach and reveal the intentions of the State of Unity there. For this reason, in the history of Earth only a minority among billions of people have been elevated to the rank of the wise and attained their own truth.

Individual people display differences in terms of their behaviors, colors, characters, lifestyles, likes, hates, desires and life plans, which all change. This difference and variety in the manifestation of each person is due to the compounded reflection of the various divine names in varied form. Otherwise, in Truth, everyone is a reflection of Haqq, which is the Unity of all divine names.

Ibn 'Arabi explains this using the following example: Water is water, yet the places that it flows and passes are different. Where it passes, depending on the condition of the soil, the water becomes sweet, its color changes, it becomes bitter, it becomes concentrated, it becomes dirty, it stays clear, it becomes still, it becomes fluid. Yet, none of these states changes the truth of water. Water only takes the form, color, odor and taste of the place it passes by.

Ibn 'Arabi says that individualistic people may possess various beliefs and thoughts and that this is a human state resulting from their needs, because their wishes are only related to the nafs (self) and their reason. All their wishes are at the level of nafs (self). He expresses that they constantly wish to have a lot and possess more.

Yet, the wise one who manifests the state of unity, wishes only for Haqq and cites only Haqq with all his existence. And Haqq grants this wish by enabling him to reach Himself.

The individualistic man possesses some ideas about faith and belief. However, these have taken form in his mind, and he thinks of Haqq in that form. He creates images such as a fearful, punishing being if he has fear, or a protective and guarding image like an angel, a granddad, a father if he thinks of the One in a good state.

However, there is a Haqq that is greater than and unbound by all such images. Haqq can never be perceived by the limited human mind. Haqq can never be limited by any religious belief. The One is beyond the form of all beliefs and thought systems. He has nothing to do with the shapes created by human minds.

The wise experience and witness Haqq's knowledge that is indicated by the Prophets, by attaining it through their spiritual hearts.

Individualistic men, on the other hand, create a form in line with the image they have drawn in their minds, by copying the knowledge of truth indicated by the Prophets. And they never go beyond this image again. They always wish and pray and cite with that image in mind. Yet, what they pray to is not Haqq but a shadow that has superficially formed in their mind. For this reason, they do not know that even if they pray and wish for hundreds of years it will not come true. Ibn 'Arabi calls these people imitators. Those who try to reach Haqq through imitation cannot reach anywhere and get lost in the darkness of their nafs (self) and within the reason that follows measures and calculations.

Ibn 'Arabi points to the verse, '*Surely, over their hearts We have laid veils (made up of their ill-intention, wrongdoing, and arrogance, which caused them to lose the ability to believe,) so that they do not grasp (the Qur'an with faith and understanding), and in their ears, a heaviness (so they do not hear the Qur'an)*'. (Qur'an / Al-Kahf / 57). It refers to those who listen, not to those who imitate.

The wise, the complete men, have power over matter. For many centuries, due to this power, they were accused of being cheats, wizards and deceitful, moreover many of the wise have been killed on this route. Ibn 'Arabi called this spiritual energy of intention that results from the concentration of the power of the wise 'himmet'. The wise one that has 'himmet' has faith and his faith is greater than all individualistic people. He has reached the truth and knowledge of matter. For this reason, he can walk on water, he doesn't burn in fire, he can reach from one place to another in a short period of time, and he can make astral journeys. In literature, there are many tales, stories and examples pertaining to the power of the wise.

Ibn 'Arabi explains how this is realized: The individualistic human being creates his own thoughts in his own mind, in his imagined shadow world. The realization and enactment of thoughts created in a world that doesn't exist is impossible. What is created in shadow is also shadow. What is casual or temporary will be a result of the temporary.

However, with the help of his spiritual strength and power, the wise one creates his thoughts outside of his mind and outside of earthly time and space. If the wise one can reach and shape the image in his thought on the tablet that holds the truth of the matter, he realizes a true creation. Then, this creation takes shape through reflection in the physical world. Rumi's entrance from seven doors, Hallaj's opening of the locks in the prison with the click of a hand, Haji Bektash Veli's change of physical space, are small examples of this. All the wise ones had a thousand and one skills and para-psychic capabilities and experiences, and these were recorded in history by those who witnessed them.

III

The World and the Universe

'Haqq, in terms of meaning, is the spirit of the visible. Haqq is internal, and spirit of the world'. **Fusûs al-Hikam / Muhyiddin Ibn 'Arabi**

Muhyiddin Ibn 'Arabi tried to communicate the worlds using his own language and an understandable style. However, he points out in his works that: This is a state, it cannot be told, it can only be lived. By assuming this difficult role, he tried to tell, transfer and, in a way, be a translator for what he had lived. Surely, it is important to be at a certain level to understand the things that he is telling. Because, we will try to read, describe in our minds and understand an invisible, unknown subject. Firstly, let's try to define the hierarchical ranking using examples from esoteric explanations and holy books:

'The Almighty Absolute Creator', is the power that commanded 'BE' and created the first creation. The One is the owner of 'Creation from nothingness' that we will never understand in any way. This creation from nothingness is not related to 'inexistence and existence'; that will be explained later. This creation from nothing is the manifestation and embodiment of the Oneness of Existence (*Vahdet-i Vücud*). It is Him that is called the One and Absolute, who gives this command, is unknown, the unfound Blind (A'ma) spot and Placeless. We can explain the Blind spot like this: It is the point of Sole Reality, nothingness, void, where the essence of all existence, creation and beings are found as a Whole and where their complete Truth is known. Ibn 'Arabi interprets the transition from Inexistence to Existence as Haqq's Breath. Haqq emerges from the internal to the visible, from bottomless darkness to light by Breath. The Blind spot is the point of eternity, the point before time when this Breath didn't exist.

Nothing can be known about the Almighty Absolute Creator, and no mortal can form a thought, a mental image or an assumption related to Him. It is not the first step of the hierarchy. Because, He, in the darkness of His own Divine Light, is at a Point that no creation can view, in other words, according to Ibn 'Arabi, can be 'Ayn' or can see.

The First Emergence, is Essence, Self, and is the top level of the hierarchy. It is the Body in which all the divine names and attributes are One and Whole, are not separate or detached. The Rabb of the Universe: They have tried to explain the One to people in different religions and in different names. Lastly, when the Qur'an was talking about the One, it cited Him with the name 'Allah'. Allah is the highest level in the Universal Operating Mechanism. Allah is defined as the 'Rabb of the Universe' in the Qur'an. In other words, He is the observer and watcher of the universe. Also He is the manager. He is Single, One, Pure, Unborn and is Not Given Birth to. The Elif (first letter in the Arabic alphabet) that enables one to gain voice through Bismillah is 'Allah'.

The Second Emergence, is the embodiment, the systemization of Essence, the Power that is indicated by the name, 'Allah'. And His becoming 'Ayn', in other words, taking the form of 'Eye'. Haqq provides unity to all divine names and all names; it is the emergence and manifestation of all names and attributes. However, there has been no separation yet, all names are apparent as Truth yet in unity they are named Haqq. This is the emergence of the Rabb System. In the holy verses, it is what is referred to as 'Rabb' or '*Cenab-ı Haqq*'. Haqq's dimension has something to do with the hierarchy that descends from its own divine dimension to the smallest particle down to the mortal human being. The condition of being 'closer' than the jugular vein and of 'come closer' emerges between Haqq and His servant. Haqq is the eye that sees and the ear that hears for humankind and the universe. At the same time the letter 'B' of Bismillah is Haqq.

In the Arabic alphabet, Elif is the first letter, and the letter Ba is the second. However, Ibn 'Arabi stresses that Ba is the first letter and Elif is the second. It is because the 'eye' of all visible and invisible worlds is B, in the secret of B and is named 'Haqq'. For this reason, all the chapters start with Bismillah, which is the secret of 'B'. The only one that doesn't start with Bismillah is the Tevbe chapter and its first letter is still 'B'. It starts with the word 'Beraetun' meaning 'this is a warning'. It doesn't start with Bismillah, but with the purpose of pointing to the letter 'B' it starts with letter 'B'. Bismillah is the 'single' and very important code that transfers by gathering within all the divine steps from the top levels of the hierarchy to the physical world. Ibn 'Arabi says, 'What 'Be' means for Allah, is Bismillah for the servant.'

After the Truth of 'Absolute, Allah and Haqq', which are the first three 'virtues' of the hierarchy, the fourth step is where the divine names and attributes separate. In truth they are 'eye', in other words 'Ayn', for each other, however when they are visible they are 'Gayr', meaning separate from each other, in terms of their meaning and roles. Each divine name and attribute becomes visible in 'Forms of Knowledge' and the 'World of Spirits'. In esoteric knowledge, this is the dimension known as Spirit.

The fifth dimension is, the Spirit Realm or World of Illustration where each divine form manifests, and becomes visible. This is the world of dreams or in esoteric knowledge it is known as *spatyom*. It is the world that all hierarchy reflects from space to the Earth as plurality. Each divine form carries a divine name and attribute. It first takes shape here and then becomes visible in the physical world.

The sixth dimension is the visible world, the world of matter, the material and physical world where the world of illustration manifests and becomes visible. The world that is the whole of all beings is called the quantum universe or our universe. It is the first physical 'Unity' encompassing all differences and variety within itself, yet it is the world that is 'Whole'. It is the name 'Adam'. Adam is the wholeness of the physical world, and the wholeness of the physical world is referred to as Adam.

In the seventh dimension is the Complete Human Being, the Great Human Being who is trained and skilled to carry the Divine Trust. He is referred to as the Great Human Being because he is not dry and of matter, he is an immortal dimension of 'humankind' which 'Allah' blew from His own spirit, power, and who carries eternity within him. In one aspect, the internal, he is Elif, in another aspect, the visible, he is a representative of the letter Ba. However, by saying 'humankind', Ibn 'Arabi didn't mean us mortals. The rank of 'humankind' is the holistic and divine humankind that comprises all rankings within. Sole Creation, Sole Nafs is the 'Divine Humankind'. Divine Humankind is the Nafs of Haqq and the Nafs of Allah.

The 'human being' in other words the Holy Being, is transformed later on, and its opposite is created from its own nafs and is named as its 'wife'. And it is sent to the lowest of the low, in other words to planets like Earth, as a 'mortal or human'. It's the spreading of the One Nafs, from the marriage of Rahman to its Wife Rahim; in other words it is the reproduction, breeding of Rahman and Rahim as 'woman and man' on worldly planets.

These successive seven steps are symbolized in esoteric knowledge as a descent. In Arabic, it is the letter 'V' which is the symbol of number seven.

Ibn 'Arabi stresses that this sequence is one step, but each step is the emergence of the previous step, its apparent, and the internal (spiritual) of the subsequent step. In fact, there is no beginning or end. Each one is within the other and each one has become 'Ayn', in other words, eye for the other. None is detached from the other, in Truth they are all one, but they show difference and variety in their emergence.

This comprehension is beyond our understanding as mortals. It is because in the Moment, when in observation in the infinity of the Divine Point, it creates existence in the same Moment. This can best be completed by the following sentence:

Secret is the point within the World of Body, in the same Moment, the World of Body is within that secret point.

This sequence is not a descent from top to bottom, it is an expansion to outside from within. It is emergence from a point to Whole, a manifestation, a signal and an appearance. By Ibn 'Arabi's definition, it is called 'manifestation'. Each one is not separate, on the contrary it is One Body that is also called the divine body or oneness of being (Vahdet-i Vücud). Each one is the same, similar, one and whole in its own truth, but when they occur, manifest, emerge and appear with a duty, they are 'gayr', separate.

There aren't two bodies in the universe. There is only Haqq's body. It is impossible for the beings to become embodied in the visible world. In the spiritual world, the world of similitude and the world of beings, embodiment is only realized by Haqq's Truth, meaning when Haqq's Truth has spread, mixed up and reached all the worlds. As we previously indicated, there is an important relationship and communication between Haqq and even the smallest particle. Haqq has reached everywhere, every particle and has lefts its 'signature' with the Rabb training system.

No particle can emerge without its Truth that belongs to Haqq. In the visible world too, even though everything appears to be plural and different, there is in fact no detachment or separation. It is only manifestation, the appearance of each divine name. It is the seer in everyone that sees, it is the hearer in everyone that hears, it is the spreading of Haqq's Truth in everything that is apparent and manifest. The one who sees is the One, the one who shows is the One. The universe is both the image and the manifestation of Haqq. Haqq is the spirit, internal secret and truth of the universe. In another meaning, the universe is a living, seeing, hearing 'Grand Human Being' with a soul and is surrounded by Haqq's Truth. If Haqq is the soul of the universe, it is also the soul of the Human Being. If Haqq is the internal secret of the universe, it is also the internal secret of the Grand Human Being.

'The divine name Al Zahir (Apparent), is the Universe in relation to Haqq, matter in relation to the spirit.' **Futûhât al-Makkiyya / Muhyiddin Ibn 'Arabi**

Al Zahir, is one of the divine names. Because the universe is apparent, the Universe is the zahir name of Haqq. Haqq, that is the meaning and truth of all 'things' that manifest from all forms of matter, mental and emotional, is the spirit of the universe. The universe is apparent. In appearance it is the Universe, in its internal secret it is Haqq.

If the apparent universe and the internal Haqq is the Grand Human Being, then the human being is the image of Haqq and Haqq is the spirit of the human being. The spirit is what controls, commands, and manages the human being. It has surrounded the human being's physical and internal worlds. The Grand Human Being is surrounded by Haqq's Truth, internally and externally, from the inner world and the apparent world.

'The Visible World is Haqq's Eye.' **Futûhât al-Makkiyya / Muhyiddin Ibn 'Arabi**

Up until here, I have tried to explain the sentences that have been taken from two of Arabi's works. In order to make it more understandable, let's elaborate on this subject a little more.

The divine words *Batin* (internal/secret) and *Zahir* (Apparent) indicate the visible world and the invisible world. That is secret and apparent. What is referred to as the One is Haqq's Self, in other words its Essence. Haqq is the gatherer of all divine names within itself. Haqq is the manifestation of the name Allah and is a divine name that is only secret to the visible world. As we explained before, each apparent world is a secret and shadow to the other world. The matter that starts to vibrate more forcefully and possesses an even stronger vibration when it reaches the visible world emerges as plural. In the entire hierarchy, from a single point to plurality, each 'manifestation, appearance' is a shadow of the other.

From bottom to top, each world is the manifestation, in other words the visible form, of the previous and is the internal secret of the subsequent world. And each one is the shadow of the other. The Divine Light of the A'ma (Blind) Position that is seen first, lights up the whole universe, each turns its face to the One and the other world becomes manifest in the shadow that is left behind it. The world that is left in the shadow of divine light is apparent, and the part that looks at the divine light is the internal.

I would like to explain the meaning of this difficult to understand hierarchy using one example.

Each world is *Elif* (the first letter of Arabic alphabet) in its own position, and *Ba* (the Second letter of the Arabic alphabet) in terms of its subsequent position that becomes apparent. The world that is Ba in the previous position is still Elif in its own position, yet it is still Ba according to the subsequent manifested world. Elif and Ba are in truth ayn (same) to each other. Even if they are ayn to each other for the purpose of Truth, they are gayr (separate) from each other in terms of appearance, meaning manifestation. However, the symbolic dot under Ba is the starting point of Elif. In other words, the letter Ba contains the letter Elif in itself. Elif also contains in itself the starting point and the letter Ba.

Elif is what appears, finds signal, emerges in its own position but it is internal for Ba, in other words it is invisible and unable to be found.

For example, the spiritual world is both apparent and Elif in its own state. However, it is a secret in relation to the world of illustration. If the spiritual world is Elif, the world of illustration is Ba. This example shows they are in each other's position. The world of illustration is Elif and apparent in its own position but it is Ba in relation to the spiritual world. The visible world of witnessing (our universe) is Ba in relation to the world of illustration. The world of illustration is internal and Elif in its own state, and the visible world is Ba in relation to the world of illustration.

Each world is Elif in its own state but Ba in relation to the state of the previous world. Each one of them becomes Elif and Ba in each other's positions. For this reason, the Ba universe that is manifest, is defined as 'The Divine with the name Ba' with Bismillah. Elif is internal (secret) and not visible. Without Elif, Bismillah cannot be voiced. Elif is the internal and Ba is in the visible world. It means, 'That which is voiced by Elif' and finds Life.

That which finds voice and Life with Elif is the Divine that is indicated with the name B. The deeper meaning here is this: In the whole hierarchy from the position of La to the universe, in other words, from the point of the unknown, untraceable to the visible world, that which is Elif based on its state, is internal in the visible world.

Elif (the Qur'an's word) is internal and it becomes a sound, life and spirit in the invisible, in the secret domain.

The universe spreads, expands and reproduces with Rahman and Rahim and with the 'divine' power that is indicated by Ba (the Qur'an's word).

Lastly, I can express this: Everything from Earth to infinite space, from the secret of the secret to the world of witnessing, the visible world, is ordered in a hierarchy. The first three levels are not rational or with time. The three levels are only one Truth. For it to be understandable, the three levels are ranked rationally but not with time. They lay completely outside the meaning of time and space. These three levels that are above time and space are Truth. All other levels that come after this are with time and rationale. The world of spirits, the world of illustration, the visible world, and levels of complete human being on the other hand are all levels with time and rationale. Time and space are relative to each world and dimension. The time and space in the world of spirits cannot be compared to the time and space at the level of the complete human being. They are ayn (same) with each other in terms of Truth, but they are gayr (separate) from each other in terms of being and appearance. They show difference and variety yet their Truth is ayn (same).

Each particle becomes apparent and a divine form through love and also through the interrelationship of the divine names and attributes of Haqq. Divine forms become apparent and models in the world of dreams. And from the world of dreams, meaning the world of illustration, they manifest in the world of matter and become apparent. They spread in plurality as beings. Yet, in the entire hierarchy from (the blind) point to plurality, the 'power' of point expresses itself in every particle. This expression happens through Haqq. In other words, Haqq is the soul of each particle, yet the soul is not Haqq. Haqq is the unity of all the divine names and attributes. In other words, Haqq becomes a body for the universe as a whole, and at the same time reflects as plurality what emerges and manifests in each particle. The soul is the looker from each particle, and the seer from each particle is Haqq.

The level of the Complete Human Being is the final appearance of the Absolute Body. It is like the cover of the Absolute Body. The level of the Complete Human Being is the cover of the Absolute Body that can gather all the worlds, divine names, attributes and forms in the entire hierarchy and is surrounded by the power that can carry the Divine Trust. Each world is an appearance and a reflection of the other, and in order for the Complete Human Being to emerge and become apparent and to be seen by the universe openly and explicitly, according to Ibn 'Arabi, it must be 'Painted with the paint of Allah'. To be painted with the paint of Allah means to be in resonance with divine influence and to attain understanding of the grand unity.

The complete human being who is eligible to carry the Divine Trust and who is wise and possesses wisdom, manifests the power and action of the command of divine names and attributes in himself. In its simplest explanation, the complete human being is all the divine names and attributes in action. He is a Living being that is a divine name and attribute internally, who walks with the sound of 'dabbe', who hears, sees and is in the state of 'being the hands and feet of the above' by displaying all its physical properties.

Haqq witnesses its own image, its name and attributes in Adam, the Complete Human Being. However, it must not be imagined that it is looking from the top level down onto the human being. Haqq is the 'seeing' and 'knowing' soul in each particle of the complete human being. The One is the one that looks from each particle, sees from each eye. He is not watching from afar. He sees, hears and knows every atom of the human being and of material creation through observing their state.

The human being is a reflection of each divine name and attribute. The immortal being, meaning the human being, can never know which divine name and attribute it corresponds to. This is only known by Haqq and is the meaning for which it possesses its objective.

The complete human being is the true shadow of the Grand and Visible World. Mortal human beings on the other hand are metaphorical shadows that stay in the shadow of this true shadow. The complete human being, as a true shadow, is 'Allah's shadow'. However, the existence of mortal is metaphorical, it is the shadow of the shadow. In other words the mortal's shadow is metaphorical since it stays in the shadow of the complete human being. Allah's true divine light has lit the complete human being and the shadows of the mortals that are shaded by the complete human being are formed by the reflected metaphorical shadow. The mortal human being is not Allah's shadow but the shadow of the complete human being.

Ayn and Gayr

Haqq is free of matter in terms of Self, but not free of it in terms of apparent. Haqq is the same as matter in terms of its self, yet it is separate in terms of what is apparent. Oh, the one that creates matter in its own nafs (self)! You are the gatherer of what you create. You create in your body that which has an infinite body. **Fusûs al-Hikam / Muhyiddin Ibn 'Arabi**

Ayn means the same and one in truth. It is said that this is an ayn of 'One'ness and 'Wholeness' that is related to each other, that is the 'eye' and look of each other.

Gayr, on the other hand, means different and varied in appearance and emergence. Gayr doesn't have to be split, cut, detached from the whole. If it is ayn in Truth, it is gayr in its embodiment. If its ayn internally, it is gayr in appearance. It can be said that the soul is ayn and the body is gayr.

The world of plurality is connected to unity. Being is Oneness. Plurality doesn't have a being. Plurality is temporary. Evil is in plurality, and since plurality is temporary, evil is a temporary situation. What is True is peacefulness and essence. In that case we say this: Ayn is truth, one and real, gayr on the other hand is temporary, plurality and variety.

The divine names and attributes are ayn to the Absolute and emerge from Haqq. Haqq is a gathering place for all the divine names and attributes, in other words it gathers all the divine names and attributes within its essence. It is richer than the absolute worlds, it doesn't need worlds. They only emerge with Haqq. The divine names and attributes that are gathered in Haqq again manifest from Haqq. Yet this manifestation cannot be perceived by the visible world. It is internal in relation to the visible world.

Haqq created all beings in its own nafs (self). We can say it like this: What emerges at all levels is Haqq. In *Fusûs al-Hikam*, Ibn 'Arabi says, 'Oh, That which creates the matter in its own nafs!'; Haqq has created in its own nafs, meaning created in its own nafs and separated. And at the same time what it created completed what it separated. It means that it gathered all the divine names and attributes in its own self. What is one and whole in truth in terms of duty are what is various and different in terms of meaning.

Let's explain the meaning of 'in Haqq's own nafs', with examples from the Qur'an:

And I have attached you to Myself (and so trained you to My Service) **Qur'an / Ta-Ha / 41**

"You know all that is within my self, whereas I do not know what is within Your Self." **Qur'an / Al-Ma'idah / 116**

There is only one body, and that is Haqq, there is no other body. Haqq creates all beings that are an 'entity', in its own body. When beings appear plural, they become apparent in Haqq's body. There is no other body other than Haqq's body. All created beings, all visible beings, emerge and manifest, at all levels, degree by degree, starting from the divine names and attributes found in Haqq, until the visible world.

The body that is at the Level of *La-Taayyün* (No Emergence), that is at the Level of Ama (Blind), which is a hidden point, unknown and that is only expressed as the One or the Absolute, belongs to Allah. What emerges and manifests from Allah's body at each level is again Haqq's body. Haqq is the ayn of all existence and gayr to the previous one in each degree. Because in each level and layer starting from delicate, subtle, more graceful levels descending down to the more forceful vibrational material dimensions, the previous level is the internal for the subsequent one. The subsequent one is a manifestation of the previous one. What is internal is ayn for manifested, however what is manifested is gayr to the internal; because the vibration level and combination changes, what is visible is gayr to what is invisible. We can express this simply like this: The internal identity of our beings is Haqq, what is manifested in our material beings is ourselves. Internally our truth is Haqq, in appearance it is ourselves. For this reason, in holy texts 'We, You (plural)' concepts have been openly expressed and stressed. The divine names and attributes that say 'We' are Haqq, the ones addressed as 'You' on the other hand, are us who are gayr and the manifestation of a more forceful vibration. Our truth is ayn to Haqq, our apparent being is ourself. For this reason everyone is responsible for his own self.

The verse from the Qur'an, '*And so, whoever does an atom's weight of good will see it; And whoever does an atom's weight of evil will see it.*' (Qur'an / Az-Zalzalah / 7-8) expresses this. It means that you are responsible for what you do in the material world with your own conscience and reason, and you will see the result of this.

As expressed in the verse, 'We turned, threw you to the lowest of the low', the meaning of 'turned' is the transition from internal to manifested. The lowest of the low means, on the other hand, the descent in level degree by degree, and the process of the vibrational level becoming more forceful. The plural is all the divine names and attributes that become a whole in Haqq's Self.

The subject of Adam, on the other hand, Allah's creation of Adam, means the transition from relative nonexistence to relative existence rather than absolute nonexistence. However, this transition to relative existence, the manifested, the visible, is internal according to us. The teaching of all names to Adam is the state of Haqq's gathering all the divine names and attributes in itself. Haqq gives presence to all the divine names and attributes in its own essence. And Haqq manifests beings through creation from these divine names and attributes in its own body. Adam is in inexistence according to the material universe and is one with all the divine names and attributes.

The divine forms that exist in Haqq's knowledge are not and cannot be manifested in the material world. This is not a situation that can be witnessed. Accordingly, the invisibility of the divine forms, their internal aspect, inexistence, is a 'relative' inexistence in relation to the visible world. If we say they don't exist because we cannot see them, it is a relative inexistence. It means 'inexistence' is relative to the degree of obscurity. The truth of all visible beings being Haqq's body is not true but is relative and metaphorical. There aren't two bodies, there is one body and that is Haqq's body. Since each visible thing manifests from Haqq's body, everything that is visible is metaphorical, or misleading and deceptive. One's manifestation of plurality is completely a deception. For this reason, matter, material and the body are called 'false'. The 'Masiva', which has an internal truth that is ayn with Haqq but expands as plural in manifestation, is in truth a deception and not real. In each moment it returns back to its essence. The visible universe is not real since it returns to its essence, its truth, in 'moment' time but we are unable to conceive this 'moment' time. It only emerges and returns back to its essence. Internal Truth becomes false the moment it manifests in appearance; it is only visual. And because our consciousness cannot conceive this, we perceive everything as constant, visible and always staying the same. According to Ibn 'Arabi; 'The Divine names and attributes that are ayn to Haqq in terms of wisdom related truths, are gayr to Haqq by their forms and bodies in the visible world.'

The wise ones that are experts in discovery, see that Allah manifests in each breath. **Fusûs al-Hikam / Muhyiddin Ibn 'Arabi**

The subject of the Wise will be explained in more detail in the coming section yet, in order to understand the meaning of wise, we must elaborate on the meaning of emerging and manifesting in each breath.

What does it mean to manifest in each breath? The Qur'an contains verses relating to this:

> ... *Every (moment of every) day, He is in a new manifestation (with all His Attributes and names as the Divine Being).*
> **Qur'an / Ar-Rahman / 29**

> *These people of ours have adopted deities other than Him, although they cannot bring any clear authority for them.*
> **Qur'an / Al-Kahf / 15**

The most important word in the first verse is 'manifestation'. To make it more understandable, we can also refer to it as 'appearance, emergence and existence'. We can explain 'being in a different manifestation in each moment' as follows: Ninety-nine divine names have been revealed to humankind. We cannot know the others. The names that we have learned emerge in time and manifest according to their truths. The names become visible in time. The time is in fact a 'moment' and that is now. There is no linear time other than this. What we see as a length of time, on the other hand, is a temporary perceptional situation. Depending on which name is manifested in that moment, that century takes shape with the truth of that name. Humankind cannot deny or dislike time. For this reason, *hayr* (good deed) and *küfr* (denial) are together. In other words what you deny or get cross with is in fact for your own good. What you are in denial about will still be one of the divine names of Haqq.

In each century, because Haqq's eye, in other words, ayn, continues you can find beauty in distress. It is said that convenience comes together with difficulty. Like the front and back of a piece of fabric.

It is not possible for us to perceive 'moment' time, however it is possible to witness it with a heart-related faculty called discovery, in other words *Şübut*. Ibn 'Arabi says this can only be done by the wise.

The meanings of each breath, each moment, each creation have similarities with each other. The creation in the moment is continuous and doesn't have any similarity. No one visual, carries sameness or similarity with each other. Divine names, attributes and forms are infinite. We only know those that belong to our universe, there are also those that we don't know. However, these divine name and forms are in a state of creation in Moment time in relation to each other. Moment contains coming into existence and inexistence. In other words, both existence and inexistence belong to the Moment. The moment we pronounce Moment, both existence and inexistence are realized.

The universe expands, contracts, expands, contracts and this continues infinitely. And each event that has happened and that is happening is repeated every time.

Even though each being seems to be the same, in truth the same thing is not repeated and nothing is repeated in the universe twice. Life continues by being rejuvenated each time. Each time the knowledge flows from our essence and transmits to our essence. Life energy always renews itself. All change is in this rejuvenated Life energy.

In *Fusûs al-Hikam*, Ibn 'Arabi explains existence and inexistence in this way: The divine names are divided into two. They have given presence to the meaning of existence and inexistence within themselves. The divine names such as, Al-Muhyi, Al-Mubdi, Ar-Rahman, Al-Musawwir, Al-Khaliq and Al-Qayyum require beings to Exist, in other words to become embodied, emerge and manifest. The divine names such as Mümit, Darr, Kahhar and Kabız require Nonexistence, in other words internalization, withdrawal to secrecy. The entire universe that is now visible creates an existence and a nonexistence between the two groups of divine names. This is a continuation, variety, difference and rejuvenation.

We can explain the verse that tells us there is a new creation at every moment like this: The divine names and attributes that are one and single, meaning gathered, in the Moment become dual with two meanings - existence and nonexistence. All visible things, that are the appearance and creation of the divine names, exist in the moment and become inexistent with the internal names again in the moment. This existence and inexistence are relative. They are not an absolute existence or inexistence. Existing doesn't mean remaining until infinity, or to be completely nonexistent, disappearing until infinity. A relative existence and inexistence takes place. Because existence and inexistence happen in the moment, like a breath or a heartbeat. Our conceptions can never perceive this, because there is a continuous and fast creation; each moment there is rejuvenation.

However, a manifested eye watches the universe, perceives everything as the same and continuous. In the verse, 'Their eyes and ears are shielded', the word shield refers to the limit of our perceptions. We perceive everything we see as being always the same and continuous. However this is relative. It is because everything is continuously given a new existence in every moment. The human being happens to be right in the middle of a heartbeat that constantly becomes existent and nonexistent. However, he sees everything he observes as constant and continuous.

Moment time is only in the power of the One. All other time periods after that are for beings. The relativity of time is stressed with importance in the verse:

> *a day the measure of which is fifty thousand years (of your normal worldly years)* **Qur'an / Al-Ma'arij / 4**

In other words, when fifty thousand years of earth time passes, only one day passes in the internal world of divine names and attributes. And, at Allah's level, the only time period that exists is momentary time. Time perception is different and varied in each particle of the universe. We are mortals who have been fixed in the time period that corresponds to our own world, Earth. We are shielded in the dimension of the immortal and cannot perceive the change, the creation realized in moment time. Only the wise ones can observe this 'breath' of existence and inexistence.

In philosophy, they refer to the saying, 'you can wash in a river many times however the water will not be the same although the rivers is'. In recent studies, and the latest discoveries of quantum physics, scientists have observed that sub-atomic particles come into existence and disappear indeterminately. In reality sub-atomic particles cannot be observed, their location is undetermined and they come to existence and reemerge in a moment. Scientists conduct experiments on these particles to verify what they see, however, when they don't see them they slide to another dimension and they have no idea where they are. The saints and the wise ones, on the other hand, related this information hundreds of years ago. The Qur'an also transferred this knowledge through verses that explain the momentary nature of creation.

Everything that is visible becomes apparent in existence and internal in inexistence. However in each existence, it is no longer like the previous. Creation that is similar doesn't mean it is the same or it is exactly that.

You cannot be mortal, neither stay Infinite. **Fusûs al-Hikam / Muhyiddin Ibn 'Arabi**

In the internal world you are not mortal since you are in Haqq. In becoming a creature in the manifest world, you do not remain infinite.

Surely we belong to God (as his creatures and servants), and surely to Him we are bound to return. **Qur'an / Al-Baqarah / 156**

All beings subject to the laws of existence and inexistence become apparent in existence by being gayr to Haqq. When mortal, in becoming inexistent, they are actually returning to the truth of Haqq, in other words their essence. Each being is Haqq and ayn of Haqq.

Each MOMENT,

What does a Being that returns to Essence need?

Only to latch on the peace, in the MOMENT it has reached

May your eyes that see that mine pit, that ore open!

When iron enters into resonance with fire it become extremely red and it says, 'I am fire'. However, it is never fire; it is seen as fire but this is superficial. In other words, iron becomes the ayn of fire. You cannot separate the fire and the iron from each other. When the iron is taken out of the fire, the separation becomes overt and distinctive. The fire-ness of iron is relative (the state in which it is not ayn, its visibility in the state of resonance, being different from its essence but not detached) and its iron-ness is its self (its essence, its own self).

If we come back to the subject of ayn and gayr, the names of Allah are both ayn and gayr. They are ayn in terms of their oneness and unity. Yet, because they contain unique meanings they are gayr from each other.

The human being and the universe are manifestations of divine names. Divine names on the other hand are the internal world of the human being and the universe. If both sameness and separation exist between the divine names and the Essence (Self), they are ayn and one in terms of Essence. They are gayr in terms of name because each name has a unique meaning.

The first emergence - transitioning from the state of obscurity to the state of distinctiveness, becoming explicit, is also referred to as the first emergence, The One, in other words Essence, knows itself only by its own Essence. All names are gathered there. It is One and Whole. It doesn't need anything and it is not needy.

The road of Haqq opens as it is walked on,

It is the road of changeability that is seen as it is conquered.

Because the One is created differently in each MOMENT.

At His Level, fire balls determined for each 'one' wait for their time, for their targets.

Surely God is Self-Sufficient, in absolute independence of all the worlds. **Qur'an / Al-Ankabut / 6**

Names and attributes are entirely ayn (same) to Self, meaning the One, Essence. There is no gayr (separation).

Here I would like to start a new paragraph to humbly share my own opinions. The holy book says, Single creation and Single Nafs. The one that creates from 'Single Nafs', is the one that creates its partner from that and reproduces them as men and women in the physical world. The world, the universe is the ledger of the human being. It is the unity of all the divine names. We, material beings, are the ones that reproduce and seem plural. We may not be able to understand the meanings of the verses, or solve them in our thoughts, but it may be possible for us to reach and understand them with our spiritual hearts and our emotions. However, this is also not definite and constant. It is possible to reach different understandings and conceptions in each state and situation, yet this is not what breaks UNITY but it is one that supports it. The meanings of verses can be interpreted by the servants based on which 'state' and 'level' they have reached at that moment, which is dependent on their own authorization for witnessing. Nevertheless, the internal meanings of the Arabic words are much deeper than our knowledge of them and witnessing at each level reflects as translation. Everyone can make an interpretation based on his own state.

> 'The One sees with each seer and is seen in each visible being. The Universe is the image of the One. He is the soul of the universe. In this way the Universe is the ledger of the Human Being.' **Fusûs al-Hikam / Muhyiddin Ibn 'Arabi**

If we return to our subject: the second emergence, referred to as the second appearance, is the separate emergence as divine names and attributes. This is called *a'yanı sabite* (Constant Forms). In *Fusûs al-Hikam*, all beings in the visible universe, the world of witnessing, are ayn of the divine names. In other words, they don't have a separate body or form. They are all ayn with the divine names. There is difference and variety in the visible world because each of the divine names is different in terms of meaning, so each being is different and gayr (separate) from the other. In the world of witnessing, the visible world, the manifested divine forms are the reflection and shadows of the meanings and definitions of each divine name. These reflections and shadows are the internal truths of each being in the physical world, and their Rabb-i Has that trains them. The meaning of Rabb-i Has is the emergence of each divine name in humankind and that name being that person's Rabb (teacher). Rabb's training system is a system that sees and watches and dispatches tests. Each divine name is a human being's Rabb.

There is sameness between the divine forms and Haqq. These divine forms have meanings that are different from each other, hence there is separation between them.

The divine forms that are at the second level, the Spiritual Level, are manifested as essences. However, this manifestation is the internal of the visible world.

Each soul conceives itself, its similar, its own Rabb. This moment is the first manifestation of the first separation. As soon as it realizes its own Rabb, it becomes gayr (separate).

Am I not your Lord? Qur'an / Al-A'raf / 172

Here the concepts of I and you (plural) have divided and this separation is manifested as being its own trainer and teacher. This first separation, although it shows separation in terms of meaning, emerges more explicitly at lower levels.

This calling of 'I' is the emergence of a piece of knowledge in the souls with one cry. This is a reminder. The 'I, You' separation does not in fact mean that there are two bodies and two separate beings; it is in fact a calling from the self to the self, and results from the internal not seeing the manifest and the manifest not seeing the internal; the I being internal and the You (plural) being apparent. If each emergence is apparent, it is internal for the subsequent level. Hence, this is the reason for calling 'I' to the internal and calling 'You' to the manifested souls who are also Himself. This is the meaning of a call from the self to the self; a waking up, a reminder and a conquering of the internal. This is a call from its inside to its inside, its essence to its essence, from its self to its self, and it can only be expressed symbolically, indirectly, as 'I and You'.

Come closer and closer!

That moment it says,

I came and could not find anything other than myself

I shall come and not find anything other than myself.

Prepare your hearts, when I come I shall not find anything,

Other than myself.

I, is One, but 'You' is a reminder to that emerging, plural manifestation. In fact, there is no plural I and You. In fact, it is the emergence of One as I and You. It is a reminder of the 'I' that is internal, to the apparent own self that is 'You'. The souls that manifest, emerge as 'You' cannot see the internal 'I'. Because in terms of grading, it is possible for the internal to see the apparent, but it is impossible for the apparent to see the internal. It is a call in the form of a reminder. There is no question to be answered. There is no such question as, 'Am I not?' The answer is *Kalu Bela, Şehidna* (Yes! We are witnesses),' not yes meaning yes. It is the conviction, faith and acceptance of the souls Manifested in the position of 'Yours' there, of their own oneness that is 'I' in the internal. In other words, it means even though as plurality you are my manifestation, in terms of oneness you are 'Me'. The meaning of your plurality in my manifestation is the creation of your internal 'I'. It is the reminder of that. There is no call, no question or answer. It is the catching fire, burning and turning fiery red of the knowledge of Oneness that is awakened in the essence, in the Self of the Souls. Even though the souls are plural, in their invisible internal worlds they keep the knowledge of 'I' that belongs to the One.

Read in and with the Name of your Lord, Who has created
Qur'an / Al-'Alaq / 1

This is a 'reminder' that enables a journey to the Truth. In the divine command 'Read', the whole hierarchy from earth to space is traversed in the Moment and you come to know where you belong, you know your Essence! Read and am I not? This is a divine 'command'.

Allah's Command is always stronger than its Essence, which is its Self. The creation of everything with a measure and balance is an indication that everything is created according to 'Divine Laws'. The 'divine command' here is the measure and balance. Its Own Nafs is also subject to these commands, and is always under the power of its Self and Essence.

We are reflections of the 'divine forms', that reflect in the world of illustration, in the physical plan.

The world of illustration explained in *Fusûs al-Hikam*, is the emergence of the One outside, in elegant forms and shapes. In this world the individual images, similar to the image of every individual that are manifested in the visible world, are created. It is also called the world of dreams. There is no division or separation here. It has a stronger vibration than the world of spirits, but compared to the visible world, it is subtler and more delicate. This world is more explicitly and distinctively separated than the level of spirits.

The level of witnessing defined in *Fusûs al-Hikam* is its material emergence in the visible world. One that cannot be separated and is whole in the world of illustration, is separated, divided and united at the level of witnessing. Because the eye can see, it is called the world of senses and the world of witnessing. Everything in this world possesses a soul. Each being is a form of one of the divine names of Haqq and the divine name is the soul of this image.

All divine names unite and gather in Allah's self. This is called *ayn-i vahide* (meaning the same as unique). Each divine name has a relationship with this ayn-i vahide. Yet, they may not have any relationship with each other. Each divine name is given a portion, a share. Each divine name feeds from Allah's Self and is attached to the One in terms of wholeness. Yet in relation to each other their shares may be different. For example, the share and properties that are given to the divine name Al-Muhyi may not be similar to the share and properties of Al-Mumit. And the emergence of the name Hayy may show degrees of difference and variety in the beings. For this reason, in some beings life is hidden and in some it is apparent.

This way of rating beings is gayr (separate) from Haqq. Since each being related to a name of Haqq, they are not only gayr from each other but also gayr from Haqq. For this reason, names such as *masivallah*, *gayrullah*, *siva* are given to the world of matter; the visible world. Each being in the visible world is ayn to Haqq's truth and gayr to the image of its emergence in manifestation. According to Muhyiddin Ibn 'Arabi, similar to the mutual opinions of all saints and the enlightened, *Mawla* (God) is Mawla, the servant is servant, and creation is creation.

Again, as written in *Fusûs al-Hikam*, complete man and the visible world of witnessing are suitable for the emergence of all the divine names and attributes, commands and works. And with its completion, all has been formed, gathered in human beings. The objective of the presence of the human being is to be a polished mirror for all the divine names and attributes of Haqq. There is separation between Haqq and human beings. The complete human being is the one who consciously witnesses existence and regeneration in inexistence. However, the immortal is the one who cannot conceive of this. He assumes that everything is the same and constant.

We said that the complete human being is suitable for the manifestation of all divine names and attributes. How is this realized? If we can understand this, we can understand 'the wise' slightly better.

At each moment, existence and inexistence are realized. This realization, happening, is not within the power of any being, and is a law that all beings are obliged to abide by. Unconsciously and without conception all beings abide by this law. The One who owns the moment, realizes existence and inexistence and with His own power renews creation each moment. The conscious being, Complete Man, is in a state of knowing all the divine names and attributes in His own Self, meaning Essence. And none other than the complete man knows this.

Haqq, the complete man, is conscious and has power. The momentary existence and inexistence includes all unconscious beings as well as conscious complete man. The human being is superior to all other created and visible beings in terms of his honorability and his state of Knowing. It is said, 'We made humankind superior, honorable'. The human being referred to here is the unification of all the divine names. For this reason, the human being is conscious. Because he is conscious, he is in the state of knowing. In the verse that says, 'Nafs that is the only creation', the nafs that is the only creation is Adam; in other words the manifestation of Allah from internal to visible as Haqq, and the embodiment of all the divine names and attributes.

Adam, the complete man, is conscious. He is the one in the state of knowing. And the names that are existence and those that are inexistence appear as two. This is the meaning of, 'One nafs is created and its female partner is created with a piece taken from that nafs' in the holy books. This is what happens in the internal world. And its manifestation in the visible world is 'reproduced as woman and man and spread out'. In other words, one nafs, Adam, is created, it is internal; it is the symbol of the formation that will give rise to all beings. Then, from that single nafs, its female partner, its opposite is created, and this 'partner' is the wholeness of all the divine names, which provide the inexistence of all beings. The reproduction and spread to the visible world as men and women is the world of plurality.

It is the realization of existence and nonexistence in Momentary time, from internal (*rahman*), to apparent (*rahim*), and from apparent (rahim) back to internal (rahman).

We said that complete man is conscious, and when existence and inexistence are happening, complete man is consciously involved in this law that he is subject to. Because in inexistence he becomes ayn in Haqq's body in the internal, wakes up, but becomes gayr to the world that was visible in his own previous existence. In existence he dies in Haqq's body and becomes gayr (separate). However, existence and inexistence that manifest in each moment are relative and not absolute.

In short, as explained in *Fusûs al-Hikam*, all beings are subject to the law of existence and inexistence: in the moment of existence they become manifested meaning visible as the gayr of Haqq, and in the state of inexistence and death they returns to the truth of Haqq, withdraws to their essence, and become ayn (same) with Haqq. In state of Withdrawal and Death (Inexistence), the beings that return to Haqq, meaning their essence, become ayn with Haqq. In state of Beka (existence) on the other hand they become gayr from Haqq.

In *Fusûs al-Hikam*, Ibn 'Arabi uses the term salik for the person who attains wisdom and intuitively perceives the internal world beyond all visible 'things'. First, he realizes that each visible being is a manifestation of a divine name. Furthermore, *Fusûs al-Hikam* explains: Every 'thing' is a manifestation of a divine name. In an effort of elevation and conception from the heart, he witnesses Haqq's names, attributes and Self with the eye of the 'heart and insight'. From then on, the merited person, reaches the degree of seeing each thing he looks at, in addition to what he sees with his immortal eyes, as the manifestation of Haqq's Self meaning Essence, attributes and names.

As opposed to what is viewed with the worldly eye, the merited person, who possesses a 'seeing' eye, witnesses that there is a greater divine creation behind what he physically sees. It is because his heart's eye has been opened as a result of knowledge and wisdom. In Sufism, this route is called

Marifat. The person that knows and senses the invisible internal dimension behind each visible thing also knows that each particle and each part of creation belongs to a divine name and attribute. And from this token, each being one-by-one, makes a journey from the heart to a divine name, and from there to a divine attribute and finally towards its Essence.

This journey is the journey of 'meaning' in terms of spirituality. The merited person has now reached the reality, the truth behind 'things'. He will understand and conceive of everything he sees. Other than this, the one who reaches Essence reaches Haqq and starts to see with Haqq's eye. The level after seeing with Haqq's eye is to see from Haqq's eye and from then on that merited person is a marifat expert. After this, one becomes one of the wise that looks with immortal eyes yet watches the universe with internal eyes. One becomes an arriver, an enlightened one who seems just like everyone, but who is not like anyone.

The entire universe, planets and stars always rotate with longing and are always on fire with their limitless energy. Spirit and matter find life with love in the universe.

Regret and vanity, either kill a human being or make life miserable for him/her! Look forward and walk! This is a REMEMBERing that doesn't regret because it has forgotten and doesn't become arrogant because it remembers.

The road to Haqq is to wear a shirt of fire and to walk on a sword thinner than a hair. It is not sighing, 'Ah', even though you suffer a thousand cruelties.

In that darkness, the ones that are enlightened with light greet each other with 'Salam'. It is because they are the 'owners'. The road is long but it is relative. Because the One manifests in a different way in each moment. Because the One is a different manifestation in each moment. It is said Whose Estate is it? Distance is a word that the Estate owner does not know. Reaching the truth behind the visible, seeing the visible with the internal eye, and attaining the chance to be able to see with Haqq's eye, the Khadir look, is something even a prophet loses from time to time. However, the Khadir or the Ayn look always exists. It is the look of the immortal. It is the look of the one who is the recipient of immortality and who is helped by God. It is to look with Haqq's Look, whose past and infinity, whose beginning and end is ONE.

Since we will explore the subject of the Arif (the Wise) in a separate section, let's return now to the definitions of the divine names and attributes.

All names and attributes that are one in essence and truth, display differences in terms of their meanings and definition, and hence they increase in number. The example given in *Fusûs al-Hikam* is this: The divine names including Al Alim, Al-Sami and Al-Basir are one in Essence and are gathered and unified in Haqq. However, their definitions reflect different meanings such as 'Knower, Hearer, Seer', creating separation from each other. Nevertheless, in Self or Essence, they are ayn to each other. The divine names that are gayr in meaning are ayn in Essence. On the other hand, the universe and the complete human being, which are the manifestation of each divine name, are gayr to the divine name in the internal world. They are ayn to each other in their essence in appearance, and gayr in meaning and action, emergence and objective.

To give a very simple example; the atom of a stone and the atom of a human being are equal to each other; the atom is one. In essence, the human being and a stone are ayn, but gayr in meaning, form and objective. As manifestations of the divine names and attributes that are one in Haqq, all human beings are ayn in terms of essence, but gayr in terms of form, objective and meaning. Everyone is gayr from each other in terms of appearance, meaning and objective. However in Essence they are ayn. The human being and the universe are also ayn to each other in essence, but gayr in form and objective.

Fusûs al-Hikam explains the subject of ayn and gayr in detail with examples so that we can understand it better.

One of these is the example of water vapour-ice: Water vapour is subtle and cannot be seen with the eyes. Depending on its level, due to the resonance it forms with changing weather conditions, it becomes a cloud that is visible to the eye, and later becomes water that can be touched with the hands and finally it freezes to become ice. Water vapour is subject to certain degrees and conditions until it becomes ice. It changes form and transforms degree by degree. Yet it doesn't lose anything of its essential knowledge. And its change and transformation doesn't alter its knowledge. Water vapour and ice are ayn in terms of their essence, and gayr in form and their conditional state. This is a very simple example yet it is different in terms of this: when water vapour becomes ice, degree by degree, there is no vapour left, it becomes ice, in other words, it goes through a complete transformation. Nevertheless, the Absolute, meaning the One at the La level, Who is larger than Before time and Infinity and the Universe, is in its own state. He becomes visible through the divine forms. And the divine forms become visible through Haqq that is One in essence and meaning with the divine names and attributes. Each divine name and attribute becomes manifested in the visible world. This transformation and ranking to the lowest of the low, the layers, a decrease and a vanishing, is not a complete transformation. In other words, it is not that there is no vapour left when the vapour turns into ice. In the manifestation that descends down to the universe, there is no decrease or division of the One which is the Absolute, or in any other appearance.

I would like to reiterate these words of Ibn 'Arabi, which he emphasised many times: 'Haqq is Haqq, Creation is Creation.'

In *Fusûs al-Hikam*, he gave the example of a seed and a tree. When the seed is thrown in the darkest parts of earth, it gradually grows over time to become a young tree with a trunk, branches, leaves and fruit. When that seed is still as small as a particle, all this potential existed in the seed as a 'power'. However, this was its internal state because it had not yet emerged. In time, in line with the law of gradualness, it developed, blossomed and gave fruit by becoming a tree. And when the seed in the fruit, which again carries a 'power', is buried in the earth, it will again gradually develop and will enter into a line of descent that will become a tree and give fruit. In other words, in each seed there is a fruit producing tree and the seed that is in the seed of the fruit of that tree is the power of each one of them.

Hence, between the seed and the tree there is a sameness due to truth. Yet, even though the tree emerges from a seed, even if there is also a seed in the fruit of the tree, they are separate from each other in terms of element, form and objective.

Fusûs al-Hikam uses the symbol of the mirror as one of the most inspirational examples. Lets imagine that there is a person in the middle of a room and surrounding this person there are various types of mirror. Let's assume these mirrors are concave, convex, of different colors and different sizes. Let's assume the person in the middle is Haqq and the reflection in each mirror corresponds to a different divine name and attribute. Each mirror reflects the same person, however, the visual reflections are different in meaning, form and objective, creating separation. Even until infinity, there will be no difference between the reflections in the few mirrors; they will only show a difference in the form and visual; however, the person in the middle remains the same. The person standing in the middle is single and one, and even though his reflection goes on to infinity there is no decrease or increase, nor any damage or benefit to him. However, he sees and knows himself as different in each mirror. This is what's important. He knows himself and practices his knowledge in each reflection. Even if you break the mirrors, color them, make them smaller or larger, or bend them nothing happens to the person in the middle, he always remains the same.

The sameness and separateness between Rabb and His Servant, Haqq and the Universe, Names and the Creation are like the example. There is sameness in essence and separateness in meaning and objective. This not only brings no harm to the relationship between them but it also doesn't create any diminishment or proliferation. Again Rabb is Rabb, the Servant is the Servant, Haqq is Haqq, the Universe is the Universe, the Names are Names and the Creation is Creation.

Another example given in *Fusûs al-Hikam* is that of a shadow. In order to understand a shadow better, we must also understand the hierarchy. As I mentioned before, there is a hierarchy in Fusûs al-Hikam. The visible universe and all beings are shadows of the world of illustration. The world of illustration (divine forms) is the shadow of the world of spirits. The world of spirits is the shadow of the Constant Forms (Divine names and attributes). The Constant Forms are the shadows of the First Appearance (Self, Essence, wholeness and oneness of all names). The First Appearance is the shadow of No Appearance (the unknown, a point unable to be found, the level of A'ma (Blind).

Consequently, our universe is the shadows of the Truth of the Truth. These shadows do not create any diminishment or proliferation in Essence; the True Body and its shadows, and finally the visible universe that we are in. In Fusûs al-Hikam, a large section is devoted to this example of the shadow.

Between a person and his shadow, there is sameness in the meaning that carries its attributes. However, whatever happens to the shadow, the person is not affected. For example, if the shadow becomes wet, the person is not wet. If the shadow increases or decreases in length due to changes in light, the person doesn't suffer any harm. He stays the same. For this reason, there is separation between the shadow and the person.

Have you considered your Lord – how He spreads the shade?
Qur'an / Al-Furqan / 45

The shadow is the visible world. The visible world lengthens and shortens yet this does not affect Rabb. Even though the shadow lengthens and shortens, or goes through changes, there is no change to the original.

In *Fusûs al-Hikam*, this is stressed with importance: Regardless of how much effort we put into defining with examples, it will not be possible for us to attain the truth of sameness and separateness between Haqq and the visible world. Examples only add a little to our understanding yet they do not enable us to reach the truth.

Divine dimensions

When Ibn 'Arabi talks about the divine dimensions, he uses the term *Hazarat-ı Hamse-i İlahiye*. There are very deep and internal meanings hidden in this word, which we till try to explain as much as possible. The aim of repeating topics is purely to make them more comprehensible. The topic that I especially want to explain is this: as Ibn 'Arabi clearly states in his teaching, philosophy and his works, the places called 'universe' are those places which manifest Haqq's divine names and attributes. In other words, the infinite divine name and attribute manifests itself as the universe, appears and finds sign. Haqq's Self is infinite, the divine names and attributes are also infinite. The visibility of the knowledge of the infinite is also infinite. For this reason, everything that is expressed numerically is merely to add meaning for our minds and thoughts. Otherwise, if the divine is infinite, its manifestation will also be infinite.

In *Fusûs al-Hikam*, Ibn 'Arabi stated, 'there is no body fragrance' in any molecular particle of the universe. Here, fragrance means 'invisible, unknown', so 'Oneness of Being' means there is only Haqq's body. There is no other body, neither a human body nor a material body. It has been said, 'no body fragrance is sensed' meaning 'there is no body'. Any being that has a body, is a manifestation of the 'Divine Forms' at the level of divine forms. This is the meaning of the words 'unborn and not given birth to' in the Qur'an's chapter, Ihlas. To be born and to be given birth to is the act of the body becoming two and infinite. There is no infinite body. There is only one body and all universes and visible things are the reflections of the divine image of that Self.

Each universe and the beings that manifest as plurality in those universes are the appearance of divine names and attributes. In other words, the beings appear in worlds of plurality with divine names. We are talking about an appearance that corresponds to each name. The divine names show themselves in two ways: the divine names that enable existence and the divine names that enable non-existence (that destroy). Beings come to existence in the universes through the divine names that enable existence, and they become non-existent through the names whose meaning enables non-existence, or destroying. This existence and non-existence happens in MOMENT time. Each existence and non-existence is continuously renewed. Each is different from the others. Each moment gives rise to a new existence and non-existence. Creation is constantly renewed in moment time. It appears and comes into existence with new forms and visuals in moment time. There is not the same manifestation of two beings and there will not be two similar manifestations of one being.

In his works, Ibn 'Arabi stressed with importance that there is no 'end'. As for the universes, he talked about eighteen thousand universes with the universe of Earth being only one of them.

These eighteen thousand universes, among the infinite universes, are all gathered under '*Hazaratul Hamse-i*' meaning 'Five Divine Levels', 'Five Divine Dimensions'.

Before talking about the dimensions, let's have a small reminder. *Hamse-i* is an Arabic word. It means 'Five'. It doesn't have a meaning by itself, but when used with other letters, it adds meaning to them. For example, when used with the letter 'Alif', if it is placed above Alif it makes the letter 'E' and if it is placed below it makes the letter 'I'. The fact that it doesn't have any meaning on its own, its placement in relation to other letters and it's being a symbol of number five better explain why it is Five Divine Dimensions.

- **Five divine dimensions / Five divine universes**

The First Universe: Gayb (The unknown world)

In *Fusûs al-Hikam*, Ibn 'Arabi talks about the level of A'ma (Blind), *La Mekan* (No Place), as the level about which we have no idea – the level of the One and the Absolute. He also referred to it as the Absolute Body (*Vücud-u Mutlak*) and No Appearance (*La-taayyün*). It is also called the Absolute Unknown (*Gayb-ı Mutlak*), the Divine World (*Alem-i Lahut*), the World of Spreading (*Sirayet Alemi*), the World of Letting Go (*Itlak Alemi*), the Absolute Blind (*Mutlak A'ma*), the Pure Body, the Absolute Body, the Essential Book (*Ümmül Kitab*) and the Unknown world of Unknown worlds.

With Him are the keys to the Unseen; none knows them but He. **Qur'an / Al-An'am / 59**

This is the point of the Truth of Truth, the point that cannot be Found or Known. There is neither a post nor a rank, neither a name nor a picture, neither a form nor an attribute. The One is larger than the universes; there has not yet been an appearance or a manifestation. It is the world of the Unknown, about which we do not know and cannot know anything and which no created being can approach. It is the world of the unknown where the Absolute is the Secret Treasure and where there was only the One but nothing else. Haydar 'Kerar Ali's interpretation for the Unknown World is as follows:

'EACH MOMENT like the old! This MOMENT is that MOMENT.' **Haydar 'Kerar Ali (Caliph)**

The One is the owner of the Moment, only the One is present in the Moment and nothing else. It is like this MOMENT and THAT MOMENT. The time concept that forms in all universes and dimensions becomes non-existent in the concept of MOMENT. The Moment exists and nothing else.

The Second Universe: Ceberrut

The First Appearance, First Emergence, is the level of Self. This is the level at which all names and attributes are one with the name Allah. Ibn 'Arabi used the meaning 'First Shadow' for this level. The meanings of Unity, early manifestation (*zuhur-ı evvel*), resting place after death (*berzah-ı evvel*) are used when appropriate.

This is known as the Ceberrut World. The names the First Manifestation, the First Emergence, the First Sign, the First Reason, the First Ore, the Whole Soul, the Book of Universal Laws (*Kitab-ül Müb*) are also used for this level. Everything that is gathered in the Divine Book (*Ümmül Kitab*) starts separating at this level. It is also known as The World of Names, Constant Forms, the World of Properties and the World of Resting After Death. It is the level in which everything is 'küll', meaning whole.

The Third Universe: Melekut (Angels World)

This is the level called the Second Appearance, the second emergence, the level of oneness and divine forms. In *Fusûs al-Hikam*, Ibn 'Arabi describes this as the level where the truths of all beings become visible as forms. The divine forms here emerge for the first time as plural. Each divine form emerges as its Rabb that is the truth of beings and its trainer. It is vital to reiterate this subject that is stated with importance by Ibn 'Arabi: All beings that emerge in the visible world, in this level – the Constant Forms – are their reflections and shadows. This means that all beings in the visible world are shadows of the divine forms. There is no body in the visible world, everything that is seen as a body is a shadow of a divine form. In Sufism this is also referred to as the breath of Rahman.

The world of illustration is also known as the world of dreams. Each being in the witnessing world meaning the visible world, first takes shape in this world. These shapes are reflected in the visible world, meaning that each being in the physical worlds are the shadows of the forms in world of illustration.

> *Merit of Three, Three Merits*
> *Alif, Lam, Mim*
> *The First Merit, is within the Second Merit, the Second is within the Last Merit.*
>
> *The Last, cannot reach the second, the second cannot reach the First.*
>
> *The First Merit is in both but also nowhere.*
>
> *The Second and Third, are Ayn (same) of The One.*

The Fourth Universe: Mülk (Witnessing)

This world is also known as the World of Estate, the public world, the world of emotions, the world of fates and the world of witnessing.

It incorporates all wishes and desires, all essences, plants and animals.

This world is everything that is visible, in truer words everything that we are witness to. The world of plurality is the world that reflects as plurality, divides, spreads and derives. The four worlds before it are the unknown, internal aspects of this world.

Mülk, Melekut, Cebberut and Lahut, these four worlds, four selves, four seas, don't have a beginning or an end. They are infinite and divine.

Those is the absolute Sovereignty on that Day? It is God's, the One, the All-Overwhelming (with absolute sway over all that exists). **Qur'an / Al-Mumin / 16**

These are the universes that form in the blink of an eye. These universes did not emerge from nothing, but from the manifestation of Self, its reflection. When it was hidden and unknown in *Lahut*, the level of A'ma (blind), Self-Essence-Allah emerged and became embodied as Haqq. Ibn 'Arabi says about the universes: 'Haqq is the Universe. All universes are a sea of Divine Light, manifesting with joyful surge.'

The surge comes from the Self and again returns to the Self. There is no diminishment, detachment, stagnation or separation. It surges as one whole. This is a divine surge from the Self again to back to the Self. The Divine Light lights up the Self and reflects on the face of all universes, and its shadow that is left behind manifests the other universe. Each manifestation turns its face toward the divine light and the other universe becomes manifested from the shadow it leaves behind. Each universe is apparent and the internal of the other.

The Divine Surge, the surge that emerges from the Unfound Point, continues until matter, and then returns to the Point with another divine surge. In each surge there is no detachment, neither a decrease nor a diminishment. Each surge is from the Essence to the Essence.

As the surge swells with divine love, each molecular particle emerges from the Point and burns up with longing for the MOMENT of reunion.

It becomes the word of the plural systems and the intelligence that says 'I am Haqq' ('*Ene'l Haqq*'). The tongue says it but what about the comprehension? When it is said with its true nature, mountains and rocks tremble, all universes vibrate. To proclaim a word without this conception or understanding is mere imitation. Because we cannot understand what kind of creation and what kind of state there is.

Mansur Al Hallaj says, 'The moment you define the One means you don't yet know Him. Because the One has nothing to do with shape or form, the One always manifests in the human being, but He is not a human being. A human being cannot be the One either.

To God belongs (absolute dominion and full knowledge of) the unseen of the heavens and the earth, and the Him alone is the whole matter referred (for final judgment). So worship Him, and put your trust in Him. **Qur'an / Hud / 123**

God is He Who has created seven heavens and of the earth the like of them; His commands (concerning the creation and its operation, and the life of the inhabitants of the heavens and earth) descend through them, so that you may know for certain that surely God has full power over everything, and that God indeed encompasses all things in (His) Knowledge. **Qur'an / At-Talaaq / 12**

These are verses that support Ibn 'Arabi's qualification of Self's journey to Self as a divine surge.

The Fifth Universe: Adam (The Complete Human Being)

God taught Adam the names, all of them. Then (in order to clarify the supremacy of humankind and the wisdom in their being created and made vicegerent on the earth), He presented them (the things and beings whose names had been taught to Adam, with their names) to the angels, and said, "Now tell Me the names of These, if you are truthful (in your praising, worshipping, and sanctifying Me as My being God and Lord deserves)." **Qur'an / Al-Baqarah / 31**

The Qur'an clearly states that before he was taught the names Adam was Adam, and after he was taught he became the Universe. Adam was created from dry mud and Spirit (*Ruh*), or infinite power, was blown into him.

The Complete Human Being (*Al-Insan Al-Kamil*) is the one who gathers all universes mentioned above in his identity, encompasses all universes and gathers all levels. '*Ism-i Azam*' is the name given to all the divine names of Haqq. The Complete Human Being on the other hand encompasses all universes including Mülk, Melekut, Ceberrut and Lahut.

The one who doesn't fit the space is the One.

But the one who sees from everywhere in the MOMENT is the One.

He is neither in us nor out of us but the one who encompasses from everywhere is the One.

The one who doesn't fit the skies and earths is the One.

But the one who is the sultan in the human's heart is the One.

In appearance and internally, there is no place that the complete man doesn't surround. The Complete Human Being is the commander and ayn of everything. *In Futûhât al-Makkiyya*, Ibn 'Arabi explained this with the following example:

The complete human being watches the eighteen thousand universes with eighteen thousand eyes by participating in those universes. He is the owner of all universes. He watches each universe with a different emotion and eye. He watches the world of senses with the eyes of manifestation, he watches creation with the eyes of reason, he watches meanings with the eye of his heart. Ibn 'Arabi specifically states: 'Those who assume they can observe the meanings with their eyes of manifestation are wrong.'

In Truth, the number of universes is not definite. The number eighteen thousand is only an assumption. When looking at other sources, Haji Bektash Veli talked about seventy-two thousand universes.

In *Futûhât al-Makkiyya*, Ibn 'Arabi explained the example of a universe as follows: 'Guiding angels. Since they became public, they have been fascinated and have admired Haqq's Beauty not averting their eyes for one moment. They are not aware of the existence of the universe, Adam, or Satan. They are not aware that they have been made public, their eyes only see and know Haqq's beautiful face.'

All universes dwell in the heart of the complete human being. Haqq who cannot fit in the earth or skies, fits into the heart of the complete human being, dwelling there as the sultan of sultans.

> *I drank divine love cup by cup, neither the wine was finished nor my thirst quenched.* **Beyazid Al Bistami (Islamic Wise One)**

In *Futûhât al-Makkiyya*, Ibn 'Arabi states that 'the Mumin (believer in Islam) is the mirror of Mumin'. One of the mumins here is the complete human being and the other is Haqq. The definition is as follows: 'The spiritual heart of the complete human being is Haqq's mirror'.

> *The One sees from every eye, looks from every molecular particle*
>
> *Yet, the key is to possess the eyes that can see the One*
>
> *To be able to see beyond the visible is not granted to all.*

The complete human being is the total of all ranks. As the mortal ascends through the ranks from the lowest of the low, he lives these ranks with joy and status. No rank lived is measureable or comparable because each rank is related to the 'heart'. In each rank, the level is lived with pleasure and status. That pleasure and status cannot be described. It can only take shape with a powerful word and transferred with a poetic expression. This transference is only for the ones who can comprehend it. For others it doesn't go beyond a poetic expression. The words of those who describe the ranks they live with pleasure and status can only be understood and comprehended by those who are close to that. What one person lives differs from what the other lives. For this reason, ranks and levels are lived in a state of 'pleasure'. While there are ones who live these ranks and levels in a state of pleasure, there are others who witness them and who transfer what they saw. Those are the ones who are travellers between the ranks, in observation, transferring what they witness and possessing wisdom. Those are the people who are not owners of any rank, but they are experts who witness all ranks.

> *We were High Letters some time ago, we became sentences after descending to 'lines of the universe'.* **Fusûs al-Hikam / Muhyiddin Ibn 'Arabi**

In *Futûhât al-Makkiyya*, Ibn 'Arabi says: 'The Universe is the spaces between the lines. When we were a letter in meaning, we descended to Those lines and became sentences, and came again to read ourselves and the book of the universe.'

Again in *Futûhât al-Makkiyya*, he mentions that the complete human being has a name mentioned in type in the Qur'an as ALIF, LAM, MIM.

> *Alif, Lam, Mim. This is the (most honored, matchless) Book: there is no doubt about it (its Divine authorship and that it is a collection of pure truths throughout).* **Qur'an / Al Baqarah / 1-2**

The three books that must be read are the book of the complete human being, the book of the universe and the Qur'an. Yet, what is also true is, the book that must be read before anything else is the human being, because the human being is the entire universe. The universe on the other hand expands in matter. The verse, Read, Ikra! means read your self. The human being exists before anything. No books were sent before the human being. The book will not be useful on its own. If there are no human beings to read it, nothing has any value. First there is the human being, then the universe, and then the book to be read. It is because each cell, each atom of the human being is also verse-by-verse embroidered and created. And the divine power is placed in his chest and his soul has been blown through his nose. Is there any creation more honorable than the human being? Yet, it is also true that when we remember the words, 'We sent them to the lowest of the low', we should not judge the human by his placement in the physical world saying 'where is his honour'. In other words, you can't assume a fish lacks skills by judging it in the pan or in the tree. If you judge a fish in the water, it's a living creature, a very successful swimmer and breather. Yet, it cannot display much skill on the land. To judge the fish in the tree is temporary. You will find its true skills by judging it in water. This judgment is related to the essence.

Self (Nafs)

In *Futûhât al-Makkiyya*, Ibn 'Arabi talks about self as True Self (*Hakikat-i Nefs*). The truth of all population is Haqq's self that is called One Self (*Nefs-i Vahide*). In other words, there is only one self and that is Haqq's self. Furthermore, this is Haqq's divine light including the images of human beings. The human being's self that is called Small Self (*Nefs-i Cuzi*), is one's own self and one image amongst the images of Whole Self (*Kulli Nefs*). The whole self is the self of the complete human being. The self of the complete human being is in its truth ayn to Haqq's self.

> ... *Him Who created you from a single human self, and from it created its mate, and from the pair of them, scattered abroad a multitude of men and women.* **Qur'an / An-Nisa / 1**

Self is two-sided with one side being Divine and the other side being collective. We can elaborate as follows: Self is two-sided with one side being Truth and other side being creation. Self is unique to us that are created. Meaning each person has a self of his own but this self emerged from the whole self. In Truth, in the internal, we are ayn to Haqq. However, in the physical worlds, we are the divine names made visible and embodied.

Adam was created and it was exclaimed to him, 'Come and enter my paradise and live an eternal life'

Adam was living a decent life in heaven. But he couldn't see himself, and was trying to define himself by touching with his hands.

In that moment, it was exclaimed to him, 'A partner will be created for you, from your own kind and in whom you can see yourself'

With a piece from the level of his heart, his wife became Ayn with him.

Each being in the created universe appears in each breath with a divine name. Haqq is in continuous manifestation from the eternal, becoming a sign and then emerging. The world of creation emerges from every breath and is realized in a very short time. This emergence happens at a rate beyond our comprehension; while one is in being, the other is in the internal with its dream. When the dream emerges in manifestation, another comes to existence in the internal as a dream. This is not something the general population can ever notice or comprehend. No mortal can understand this. One who looks at a rock sees a rock there for hundreds of years, yet the creation of that rock is renewed in every moment with every divine breath. In every moment, that rock changes and a new one is created. The creation started with Be and continues infinitely. This is the interpretation of the verse, 'We came from the One and we will return to the One'.

Everything is a moment. There is both death and birth in that moment. The one who is born in the apparent world dies in the internal world, the one who is born in the internal world dies in the apparent world. Hence, the One that is closer to the human being than the jugular vein is as close to the human being as death. The One who says, 'I am close', is as close as death to the human being. For each one that comes into existence in the internal world, death occurs in the apparent world, but the Moment that death occurs in the internal world, emergence and manifestation occurs in the apparent world. And the one that is closer to the human being than its jugular vein, is as close as death. The one who dies in Moment time in the apparent world returns to the One in its internal world; it reunites with its essence. Again, when the one who dies in the Moment in the internal world, emerges in the apparent world and becomes existent in world of being, it is separated from the One; it has come from the One. What comes from the One returns to the One and this happens in Moment time. Coming into existence and disappearing into non-existence happens in the Moment.

Everything emerges from Internal towards Apparent,

The warm air of the Internal, warms up the cold air of the Apparent

Then,

It pulls the cold air of the Apparent into the Internal.

What we call evil is dependent on plurality. Plurality is reflection, temporary; and because it is not real, evil doesn't have an existential stance. Evil is not existential. The only thing that exists is 'Hayy'. It is 'Good Deed', meaning it is Haqq. The temporary situation that emerges, in the moment with the absence of the One, is called evil. The expression 'both good and evil are from Allah' refers to this.

The only thing that exists is the One. In the heart beating or in breathing when 'One' becomes existent in the Internal for one moment, it becomes Haqq, and the 'false' surrounds everywhere in the remaining time period. In other words the air becomes cold. The temporary and cold air then becomes warm again by warm air being blown with mercy from the internal. Haqq has manifested again.

In *Futûhât al-Makkiyya*, Ibn 'Arabi says, 'Each being is deprived of its own truth. And not in command of its own self'. He continues, 'If they were in command of their own self, they would not be deprived of their Truths'. At that moment, the truth of the human being will be clearly discovered. The objective of the creation of matter is to serve as a tool for the human being to attain the truth of its self. The human being that can see itself through matter will only be able to know its self in this way and will be able to discover the truth of its self.

Ibn 'Arabi said, 'Essence is what is one with its own self'. The only way to reach the essence, meaning the Truth is by 'rising up' (*kıyam*). The human being has to rise up, it is the uprising of the human being. It's uprising means reaching the Truth of essence.

When they descended to Earth, Adam and his wife took shelter in a tree canopy and fell into a deep but sweet sleep.

The birds that perched on the door of the tree canopy were told:

'As long as my lovers don't want (wish), do not wake Them up from their sleep.'

When describing the human being, we sometimes refer to it as the 'Thinking animal'.

Thinking is temporary. Temporary means; transient, reflection, existing after, not original. We say that the human being owns matter. Yet, 'owner' is a relative concept and is transient. We say that the human being is body. Body is transient. We say that the human being is an emotional being. Emotions are also temporary. We say that the human being is cognitive. Cognition is also temporary. We say that the human being is what makes 'dabbe' in the world, meaning movement and what makes sound as it moves. Movement is also temporary. We say that the human being has will power. Will power is also temporary. To define something requires specifying its borders and giving it a shape. For this reason, the human being is temporary because it can be described and its borders become clear. The human being with clear borders is temporary. The Absolute Body is essence. The world of appearance is temporary. The Truth of this temporary state is where essence emerges and becomes apparent. For this reason, the universe is also temporary. Essence on the other hand is Truth. Yet in the internal world, essence is also temporary in relation to Haqq and Truth.

The person that reaches and knows his self will have reached the Truth of his essence. Yet again, for the Self, even essence is temporary.

There is Essence and everything other than that is temporary. In other words, except for Essence everything is in need of Essence. Without Essence no 'thing' can exist. By itself or individually, no 'thing' can have any value or carry any Life. It takes Life from Essence and finds life. The human being is temporary. Without Essence there is no human being, it is nothing and it never existed. All 'things' are created from Self, that is Essence, and everything other than Self is temporary. It needs Essence to be able to show its existence and to become apparent. Everything from the self of the human being in the physical world, to the world of illustration, to the world of spirits and to Essence is temporary.

If light doesn't exist, nothing can be seen with the eyes. Light is needed for the eyes to see. If light is Essence, everything visible is temporary. Light, meaning Essence, must exist for every visible thing to become visible. Wherever light is reflected becomes lit up and can be seen by the eye. Light is divine light. The divine light that emerges from Essence and penetrates the whole universe spreads, gives color and light, and enables 'things' to be seen. Each universe becomes embodied one by one and appears. In the shadow of what appears, a new world manifests. In the shadow of the manifested world, another new world manifests. Each one of them is a manifestation of the other and is also internal for the following one. And all is temporary. In others words, it doesn't exist in reality. Through divine light, they become embodied and apparent. Yet nothing exists except for Essence. Just like in the expression, 'There was Allah and nothing else'.

There is no shape or limitation. Whatever accepts shape and limitation is temporary. As soon as it is accepted, it takes shape in the mind and this is temporary. It is only a dream. Anything that is not one with its own self is temporary. The one who is one with his own self, also becomes one with Rabb's self, and the one who knows his self also knows Rabb's self. In other words, his transience disappears. It means that his self, within himself, becomes connected to the true self. The one who knows his self is again temporary when he knows his Rabb's self because this is also not truth. Truth is to know the self of Essence. In that moment, one reaches the Truth of the Truth and this is the level of complete human being (*Al-Insan Al-Kamil*).

And Adam is taught the names of all KNOW'n and, Existence and Beings.

Except for the knowledge of death.

He was in the infinity in the presence of Three Merits.

He asked Gabriel who informed him that he would die on Earth. 'Dying?

What does dying mean?'

On Earth, the Human Being became those that tasted death.

In *Futûhât al-Makkiyya*, the definition of object is: 'Object is an essence that takes space (*Cevher-i mütehayyiz*) and accepts the three dimensions (*Eb'ad-ı Selase*).' In other words, the visible form of Essence in three-dimensional form is called object.

If we elaborate further; *Selase* means 'three' in Arabic. *Eb-ad* means distance in Arabic. Science describes these three measurements as width-length-height, in other words our universe as a three dimensional system. Yet its internal meaning is as follows: It is pointed with the sign Gayn, which has a dot on it and defines the distance of two arches. The dot is the unknown Absolute One. The distance of the first arch is Self meaning Allah and the distance of the second arch is Haqq. Hence, what accepts this distance of three and reflects from its essence is called object.

About the Mi'raj journey, (Prophet Mohammed's ascent to heaven), the comment, 'It is the distance of two arches, maybe even closer.' is related to this. In other words, it is the distance of ayn. To approach in the distance of two arches is the 'Mi'raj' example of Prophet Mohammed, who, as an apparent being, reached a place even angels cannot reach.

In the Qur'an, the phrase, '*kabe kavseyni*' (Necm / 9) in other words, 'as close as the distance of two arches, maybe even closer'; the state of passing the physical world, the world of illustration, the world of divine names, the world of divine forms and reaching the Rabb of Rabb, meaning meeting Haqq, and being close to Allah, is explained as the distance between two arches and maybe even closer. 'Object' on the other hand, refers to all visible beings including the human being as man and woman, and means the reflections of their essences that 'accepted' the three measurements.

The meaning of 'accepted' in the sentence is a dream, not real. In other words, because there is no shape or image, it is acceptance but a discretionary acceptance and hence a dream. It is discretionary acceptance, because it doesn't become one with its self, meaning it has not reached its Truth; it is shadow, non-existent. Acceptance is the Limitation of Self of the essence - it is identifying the limitations of Truth. Because, 'Description means to draw the limit, the plane and border of something'. In that case acceptance is a nominal reality. In order for it to have a nominal reality it must be occupying a space, and occupying a space is identified according to what? There is no identification, border or limitation and hence it is not real. In other words it is again a dream and not reality. It is a discretionary occupation. For example, let's say a tree is occupying a space on earth. In other words, it has a width, length, height, weight, color and smell, but according to what does it occupy a space? In truth there is no tree. It appears as a tree because its borders have been drawn. That is not real. Because the tree has not reached its own self, its truth. If it had, it would not appear as a tree, it would appear in its own truth. In order to fit understanding, it appears as a tree. Because the brain behind the eye that sees is 'programmed' for this. It has been programmed to see it as a tree. In the truth of the tree there are no borders and it has no shape. But, because we cannot perceive this with our eyes, we need a virtual drawing. For this reason, in our brain-related programming, we need the technical drawing drawn as tree. And everything we see is in truth a divine technical drawing. We are in a universe created with 'measure and balance'. For this reason, everything, every object, is a divine technical drawing with a proper 'shape' and 'image' and this divine technical drawing has been coded in our brains so we can see it. In truth, we are beings that see a shapeless and imageless energy form as if it has a shape.

The Object that exists and doesn't exist is in relative creation, called 'in two times' in *Futûhât al-Makkiyya*, and is not permanent. Object is what is not permanent in both times. It is neither mortal nor permanent. Because object has not met its truth, it is not real but a dream. That which is a dream, is not true, does not stay permanent in two times. Essence on the other hand, stays permanent.

However, one who comes to know his own self, because he has reached his Truth, will have reached the essence that is permanent in both times. While he used to be a mortal who was not permanent in two times, he became a wise one that is permanent in two times because he knows his self, his Rabb and the Rabb of Rabb. He has reached his own truth.

These people of ours have adopted deities other than Him, although they cannot bring any clear authority for them.
Qur'an / Al-Kahf / 15

Here the ones referred to as 'these people' are the mortals. Meaning those who cannot reach their own truths and cannot be permanent in two times.

The Mortal, Loves with his Self, sees through the eyes of Self, lives with Self

The Wise, Loves with Haqq, sees through the eyes of Haqq, Lives with Haqq.

Dying before dying / knowing self

If the One didn't exist, 'I' would occupy everywhere. If Identity (being 'that') didn't exist, being 'I' would manifest.
Hiyet-ül Ebdal / Muhyiddin Ibn 'Arabi

Existence and non-existence is a continuous event of 'death'. This is the meaning of the sentence, 'self tastes death'. In non-existence it dies in the internal world and becomes existent in the apparent world. Then, it dies in appearance and becomes existent again in non-existence - the internal. This is a continuous death. This is the definition of 'I am close'. Being close means 'I am as close as death'. The self that continuously experiences 'deaths' in two times, dies before dying and 'doesn't die' again when he reaches his own truth. For him there are not two times but only a single time. These two times are transformed into Moment time. He stays infinite in Moment time - the unity of two times.

This is the journey to know the internal in the apparent and the apparent in the internal. Both are a longing. Both are the names of the One. What is closer to the human being than its jugular vein? The One is always in the heart. It is for this reason it is closer than the jugular vein. However, how does the One manifest and become 'close' in a way that we understand? How does the state of being 'close' find manifestation? This must be considered very carefully. In order to understand this topic, we must elaborate a little on the issue of 'being upon notions/assumptions'.

'I am upon the notion of my servant. I am how he thinks of me, I am how he conceives me.' Because 'I am what surrounds everything. I am the Internal, I am the Appearance, I am Before, I am After, I am Inside, I am Outside.' Even while an atheist says, 'There is no God', first he has to accept God before he can say it doesn't exist. In other words, even the non-believing person accepts the 'notion' of acceptance as well as the notion that 'there is no creator.'

The differences between understandings and conceptions do not change the unity of Truth. The saying, 'the Friend increases knowledge and the opposite increases duty' is a very old teaching. 'What is one in Truth is separate in appearance' is also an old teaching. Who is the friend? Adam. Who is the opposite? Satan. This is how it is named and transferred via symbols in the divine books. But we found it appropriate to call the one who increases duty and who is not a friend, the 'opposite'.

The promises of the opposite are vain.

But its seduction is lovely. It reaches from a forty-layered bundle.

It turns the selves and it confuses them.

Every time,

Don't you see that the Creator's tears are falling?

Those who don't know are blind in two lives like this,

Those who are prisoners of their dry bodies.

The friend increases our knowledge, the non-friend increases our duty and our precaution. In Truth, both the friend and non-friend are one. Yet, 'The Wise one knows how to separate the rose from its thorn'.

If the one that is 'One' in Truth is 'separate' in appearance, what is ideal is to be 'cautious'. And this state of being cautious or sober is the state of 'knowing self'. This is an effort of many life times and it requires work.

If the opposite were bad, it would be amongst those that had been destroyed and not one of those given a defined period of time. All saints and prophets have had discourse with Satan. What makes the mortal a 'human being' and complete is its opposite, its antithesis. Without opposition, one cannot progress in the journey of ascendance. If he had no opposite 'even Adam, could not be Adam at the rank of the wise'.

The human being with merit is half divine name (one who is helped by God, who has attained victory, who has come to know his truth, his self, who knows his self and his Rabb) and half human being. He is neither a divine name nor a human being; he is not either, yet he is superior to both because he has reached Haqq that is the closest.

At the level of the opposites there are saints of the opposites. It is difficult to discriminate them from Rahman.

Satan, who is known as the opposite, existed long before Adam and reached a state of obeisance to Allah. Yet, he cannot evolve and doesn't possess virtues; he cannot be wise or intelligent. Attaining wisdom is a rank given to the human being. Satan was jealous of the human's wisdom and became boastful and was banished. It is no doubt that this is a symbolic expression.

As long as we are not able to fully comprehend the concept of Haqq, we cannot understand the meaning of Rabb. Haqq is the unity of all the divine names and images and Rabb is the training system of the world of plurality, the physical world.

If Haqq is not conceived in a human's heart, his thoughts about divinity will not go beyond imposed ideas.

It is only possible for him to reach his own reality and Truth, the One, by freeing himself of all imposed ideas. For this reason, Haqq is upon one's notions. It surrounds everything. The One, is the face of the One wherever you look. We cannot say the One exists or does not exist when we are in a sphere that is from before time and infinite, and surrounds everything from inside and outside. We cannot say where is the One? Because the One says 'I am everywhere, I am what surrounds everything, I am the past and the future, I am Time, I am Space. However you think, however you imagine, however you describe, I AM like that. However you 'presume' me I am upon your presumption.'

When the divine piece is carried with trust in the soul it is seized by gravitational force. It sleeps and sleeps. The command, 'Do not wake up my lovers who sleep in the tree canopy until they wish to do so', indicates 'forgetting' - waiting until one wakes up on its own. Every person one-by-one, as an individual, will desire to wake on his/her own. Everyone seeks the light in the shadow-darkness of their own self. One can assume what one sees in that moment as true. What is real for one may be false for another. While one's discovery may elevate one, it may ruin the reputation of the other. Everyone will pick his own path through the stones.

When upon a sign in the meaning

I buried my soul in body with knowledge

And again a time will come that

I will dig it out from that grave with knowledge

The self of the human being is the visible state of Haqq's self. There is only one self. That is Haqq's Self. It is truth, it is in internal, inside. The human self that spreads and appears in the physical world, on the other hand, is Haqq's eye that looks with the objective of recognizing and knowing the material worlds that are described as the lowest of the low. In other words it is Its Ayn. Yet, the self of the human being that spreads in the physical world, has moved far from its true service, seduced by the material world, and has become temporary in terms of self.

The wise person knows Haqq's self through its own self. **Fusûs al-Hikam / Muhyiddin Ibn 'Arabi**

Haqq's Self in Truth, becomes temporary as the self of the mortal in the physical worlds. In his work *Makalat*, Haji Bektash Veli calls this, 'Seduction of Mud'. The real meaning of sleeping is this. This is sleeping by being captivated by the fascination of seduction. Upon the symbolic word of 'Don't wake my lover up until they wish so', the human being continues to sleep until he wishes to wake up. 'When you mention my name, I will mention you' means becoming wise to your own self; when you know your self, Rabb will also know you. Everything is reciprocal.

The human being belongs to *Mavera*, meaning 'the beyond of the beyond'. He belongs to the most glorious and is an ultimate being; he gains meaning within the whole. He is the honorable creation, the center of the universe, the creation. The human being has been appointed the highest rank.

Taking him from the noble of nobles, down to the lowest of the low doesn't harm his honorability. In truth he is ayn to Haqq. In other words, just as the world is Haqq's eye in Truth, the human being too is Haqq's eye; he walks with it, he speaks to it, he sees with it, he makes 'dabbe' (movement with sound) with it. The Qur'an says that the human is the being that makes 'dabbe'. Dabbe is an indication of Doomsday. Sur is the horn that will be blown to signal Doomsday. The pointed end of the horn emerges from the Divine Point, the wider side reaches the spiritual heart of the human being. It is continuously blown into that horn. The human being who is a tide between existence and non-existence, becomes existent in existence when he makes 'dabbe' (birth, the world of plurality) and is assumed dead in non-existence (In Adam-in Haqq), He becomes existent in Non-existence, but when he becomes non-existence in Existence he rises up (kiyam). The human being is in a tidal flow between Dabbe and Kıyam.

> *Life, is Divine Self. Life is sacred. When the divine, intends to will blessings, the whole universe is its food.* **Essence of Lokman, Fusûs al-Hikam / Muhyiddin Ibn 'Arabi**

How does a father or mother recognize their children from their smell? It is because this smell is a memory. It is very important. In the verses, the 'smell of the wind' and the 'Smell of Yusuf' have been widely used. Smell activates the 'divine' faculty in the nose. Hence, when the wise one smells his self, Rabb reunites with its lost child, it essence, its truth and its element.

> *There is no separation such as creator and creation. Human beings invent this separation. I am a servant of the One and the One of me.* **Futûhât al-Makkiyya/ Muhyiddin Ibn 'Arabi**

In other words, whoever understands (recognizes) that he is an element of Rabb, he also understands (recognizes) that he is Rabb. Because, there is no being other than Rabb. If what surrounds everything is the One, there is no being other than the One.

The human being is both *rahmani* (like Rahman) and *nefsani* (self-involved). One rahmani self is better then one thousand self-involved selves. Travelling a road that is thinner than a bristle and sharper than a sword, the human being who wears a shirt of fire will see an angelic divine light when he looks to the right and a shadow of self when he looks to the left. The one who is painted with the paint of the One knows both his desire and his goal.

Ayn-Bayn. Alif/Ba. Visible/invisible. Apparent/ Internal.

Existence/Non-existence. Goes to Infinity.

The states of pleasure. Cannot be told, their description are impossible, formless. Only

Sound, resonance, vibration, color, harmony, breath

'The One exists in its non-existence, non-existent in its existence. The One is where you suffer in longing when you become existent in its Non-existence and where you find your peace when you become non-existent in its Existence.

What an amazing contradiction it is to see All is happening in MOMENT time. It is an incredible 'measure-balance' that is 'renew'ed in each moment. The eyes are used to see what 'reflects' from glasses. The objective is to look at divine light without being dazzled. The wise one looks at the divine light with the eye of his heart and his eyes are not dazzled.

And then? What does looking mean for him? It is because he has become what 'Sparkles', the divine light.

Divine trust

We offered the Trust to the heavens, and the earth, and the mountains, but they shrank from bearing it, and were afraid of it (fearful of being unable to fulfill its responsibility), but man has undertaken it; he is indeed prone to doing great wrong and misjudging, and acting out of sheer ignorance.
Qur'an / Al-Ahzab / 72

The divine trust that was proposed to the mountains and rocks, yet wasn't accepted, is a subject studied by many wise people and saints.

The mountain symbolizes glory, height and power. The rock on the other hand is hard and strong. They didn't undertake the responsibility and were afraid. This is because they are not conscious. The human being undertook it because he is ignorant. What is undertaken? What is the trust?

In the *Kün* (Be) command of the entire creation, they are only given existence. Only the human being is 'blown' with the soul.

The trust is known as 'the soul (*Ruh*) that is loaded, transferred'. And secondly, it is the divine names that are loaded and injected. In every living being, every rock and earth, every plant and animal, you can see something of the divine names, yet the only being in which we see all the divine names together is the human being. The Qur'an says that the One taught all the names, even those that are not known by the angels. All the names that we cannot know as mortals were injected and loaded, in others words trusted, to Adam. We know only so much as we have been informed, yet if Non-existence is Adam then he knows all the divine names and attributes.

IV

Arabi's Understanding of Love

Until today the one who lives in the same house with me

I ignored that True friend

In the absence of my religion and I now abide by the religion of the One.

And now my heart came to accept all forms

The meadow of gazelles,

The abbey of priests,

The temple of the crosses,

The Kaaba of the hajis,

The sacred tablets of the Torah,

My heart turned into pages of the Sacred Qur'an,

Now I am following the religion of Love!

Wherever the Love Caravans head towards,

Love is my religion and faith.

I am practicing the religion of Love

It is my religion, it is my faith, I believe in LOVE.

Darü-l-Kütübi'l-İlmiyye / Muhyiddin Ibn 'Arabi

Love (*hubb*) is the principle that led to Haqq's creation of the universe. This principle is Divine Love (*Aşk*). Ibn 'Arabi is a symbol of Divine Affection (*Muhabbat*), Divine Love. Ibn 'Arabi is Divine Light, Love (Işk), Divine Affection (Muhabbat) and Divine Love. Hubb meaning Love, and Affection (Muhabbat), in other words Divine Love, are the principles of divine action. Every event and formation that happens in the universe is created with Divine Love. It is the work of Divine Affection's creative force.

There is only separation for the mortal. The mortal makes comments based on his presumptions. The words: bad, good, beautiful, ugly, terrible, disaster, fear, rage, animosity, jealousy, happiness and joy are duality for him. However, for the wise one, with Divine Love in his heart, any reason for his action is Love (Hubb). In other words, he interprets all that happens as Haqq's love and divine love, and from its divine love.

If there were no divine affection, there would be neither a living thing in the universe, nor liveliness or even life. The principle that triggers the emergence of each divine form and name is divine affection, or divine love.

The Divine Command is 'divine love'. Allah who gives the Kün (Be) command enabled movement in creation with divine love and planted the seeds of love in the dough of creation. Haqq's work is kneaded by the seeds of love, brought to life by the principle of divine love, takes shape and is lightened by divine light. Ibn 'Arabi says, 'Haqq's Self is Divine Affection.' If there were no Divine Affection everything would continue to exist in oneness and unity. Yet, because divine affection, divine love, is the principle of dynamics and movement, it would create a polarity. For this reason, the mobility of divine love, that Ibn 'Arabi calls 'Rahmani Self', which comes from the internal towards the apparent, from inside to outside, created the poles. The mobility of divine affection, divine love, led to One becoming polar, becoming variable and dividing into plurality. It appeared as a divine light that blew from oneness to plurality as a rahmani self.

> *Divine love, it neither stayed Infinite, nor did it become Mortal. It gave Life to dry bodies that breathe with its Existence and weaken with its Non-existence.*

It is the 'Rahmani Self of Divine Love' that blows from Oneness to plurality, from darkness to light, from the internal to the apparent, from inside to outside. Oneness and Unity reflect the variety within to the outside. From the inside to outside, Rahman's breath moves with divine love and is enlightened from 'blind darkness' with breath, and from this universes and beings are formed. Hence this divine affection, divine love, which is the foundation for creation, is the source of creation in Ibn 'Arabi.

Every human being has a divine form in Haqq's spiritual heart. This is the truth of each human being. On his descent, being reflects from that form, in his miraj, his ascent, he meets his divine form again. That form is the Rabb of that human being. It means to look at that image of truth without losing its look, without changing direction, without lying, without the eyes being dazzled, and reaching DIVINE LOVE without wings, without arms, without hands or feet. This is 'the enlightenment, arrival and miraj' of the human being. When he knows his Rabb, his Rabb, the divine form in the divine mirror, also knows about its reflection. And the inner journey of the human being that encounters his truth will again be towards the world. He travels towards the world, yet builds his own world. There is not one single world that he lives in, all worlds are within his spiritual heart. In that moment the Council of Divine Love, is at Haqq's level, in its own presence. What a boundless state of pleasure that is. There is no stop or stopping, there is no finish or end. What kind of word is 'beginning' in the dictionary of the wise one? Can one be satiated with infinite beauties? Surely the wise one will not become full, will continue to exist within divine love, with divine love.

When there is just moment time remaining to reach his Rabb, the human being meets the opposite at the last level. Without retracting its statement, the opposite that is burning with divine love of Allah, was banished from the level of divine love, because it said 'I in front of Haqq'. In the spiritual heart of the human being, the divine name that it is reflecting stands on one side and the opposite on the other side. They meet and talk there. The two sultans in the spiritual heart of the human being become united, become one. No one 'can become wise without beating his satan'. Then, the opposite, who is one of the two sultans in the spiritual heart of the saint, prostrates to the complete human being on the way to ascendance. The divine command is realized because the divine attribute also accepts the 'unity' in Haqq's spiritual heart.

Hence, the human being sees the truth. Haqq fills his thoroughly cleansed heart, which has become wide enough to encompass the universes and worlds. His entire spiritual heart, with the fire of divine love, in a way that leaves no space for anything else, like matter, false, shadow, dream, presumption. He salutes all religions and abides by his own religion that is divine love. Then the owner of divine love becomes wise. While the one who is in denial says 'I', the wise who speaks like Haqq that is Unity says 'We', by being a mirror to all divine names and attributes that he carries in his heart. In that moment, he becomes embodied with the divine light that he reflects from Haqq. However, the wise is not body, the one that tastes death. Haqq speaks, falsity keeps silent. Haqq comes, falsity collapses. The duty of the wise is to sense and transfer Haqq's magnificence, the particle of the particle of the particle and the beyond, and be an example. The human being fulfilled his statement, his promise, 'Yes, you are our Rabb' and became wise. He became alive and became one that gives Life and revives.

If you are in love, you are in Haqq's presence

Truth is Haqq, Universe is its shadow

The aim is not to be in the body that tastes death.

The skill is to be visible in body, when you reflect Haqq.

The Arif (the wise one) has become divine love, and is an immortal who journeys at the level of divine love. The one who has reached this supremacy and level is called wise, meaning 'one who knows the truth' and this knowledge is rightfully perceived as a state of true pleasure. This faith is the faith of the heart that unites with joy and happiness. This is the *hijab* (feeling of being ashamed), in other words the shield, between Haqq and its servant. There is no shape or doubt left in the wise one who has completed divine love in his heart. Haqq fills up the whole heart, the spiritual heart of the wise that it visits, and nothing else can find a place there.

Oh DIVINE LOVE!

Come some time! Enter my spiritual heart secretly!

No one shall see or even hear.

I called and no one heard my voice.

I shall clean make my house white clean!

It came and found a very clean spring.

While being lost in mortality,

You fall in divine love,

It recognizes you with the LOVE in your spiritual heart.

Then the smell of the rose surrounds each layer

Each name captivates you.

The joyous cries of all particles,

Becomes heard in the hearts with one cry.

The definition of divine love for Ibn 'Arabi is: 'Either you are straight like an arrow to be thrown to disregard, or you are curved like a bow that is withheld.' What is better is to travel towards far prosperous lands, planting seeds of divine love. You are both the bow and the arrow, you are both the earth and the seed. Each one of them has become divine love and the source of divine love.

The wise lived that love once and could anything extinguish that fire? Which measurable or valuable thing could take the place of love? A MOMENT passed in divine Time, equivalent to thousands and thousands of earth years, but even still that warmth, that DIVINE LOVE never diminished. Because Love was the image in Haqq's spiritual heart and couldn't be found anywhere else again. Nothing else could ever bring happiness. Which touch could make you happy, once you see the love at Haqq's level?

All expressions, meanings and measurable values fade in Love's illuminescence.

'Paradise and hell are not in different places. They are in the same place at the same time. To be in a deep passion, while at the same time your entire your soul and body is transformed into a fiery red fire, in the prison of hell, you find the Paradise of an ancient state of being lost in the Level of Divine Love.'

We Came gliding from the deep waters of darkness!

We brought true love.

We came with Rahman's breath.

Let the False that is hiding in the corners know!

We are in Victory with God's help!

We are where the humanity remembers itself to be

We will find life with Hayy! And be reborn again.

Love has no words, never speaks, it only looks. And from there starts a journey that is bound for infinity. An adventure that never ends. Love finds those who want to reach it even from distances as far as the stars, as long as it sees and notices that sparkle, love in those eyes. As long as it feels the *Nar-ı Aşk* (Fire of Divine Love) burning in the spiritual hearts.

'Do you feel those touches, the moments that the lover is flowing like a flood. The moments that you are arriving by momentarily leaving your body, touching infinity, becoming ONE with your own self, breathlessly covering distance like tearing curtains and coming back again. That is a moment and it has no return. Wake up and Notice it!'

The human being is on the road to redemption. As redemption is realized moment by moment, Divine Love's light, source is reached. When the human being reunites with Divine Love he becomes immortal and then eternal. Love swaddles, it heals all creation and becomes a wellspring flowing to the entire universe. The part of Creator Truth, reaches his Essence. He becomes a road for those who say 'I am eternal as Divine Love', lovers who travel the road of divine love, flowing by finding a path from love to divine love, from divine love to love, those being the road. Those ones are the wise.

Divine love transforms, puts the human being into a kind of metamorphosis. From now one, he is no more the person that he was a second ago, or the human being of later Moments. The seeds of divine love burst into leaf in his spiritual heart. Each time in a different color, in a different musical note.

Before the glass of the body frees itself from self, it cannot be filled with the charms of love. In the universe, two 'things' cannot occupy the same space at the same time. If you are full of self you become self. One must open up a space for Love, must allow its flow, build the bridges that will connect with it.

The touch of (Absolute) Love is in Non-existence and Existence. In the universes of beings and its sons.

Love does not have time, it is timeless. Love does not have space, it is without space. It is not possible to possess it.

It burns the one who holds it in his hands with fiery fire, it chokes the one who hosts it in his heart, it manifests in the one who holds it in his spiritual heart and it transforms with its vibrations, feeds the whole earth and all living things.

> *Love, is creative on the journey from Nothingness to Being, for the Absolute. Love is the key for the awakening of the beings.*

In love there is no imposition, no doubt, no condition, no aim, no expectation. No merit is valuable in comparison to the perfection of love. All measurable merits lose meaning in front of love.

The vibrational image of love in the body is DIVINE LOVE. Knowing the DIVINE LOVE in that vibration and waking up is LOVE.

Adam is divine love and Haqq is love. All journeys are from divine love to love, from love to divine love. When divine love reaches its level, then 'hubb' (love) emerges.

> *It's not how many people, but how many worlds you host in your spiritual heart to be able to say my love is 'the One' in both worlds.*

Divine love is to continue, to become silent, to possess Merit, to respect, to love everything out of respect for the creator. And divine love, in universes, is an intense 'hubb'; love that is felt. Because love cannot descend, it can only be felt as divine love. Even this is a deep pain, it is burning.

You look in the eyes of the wise one but you cannot understand what state he is in. Yet, he is transported by the storms of DIVINE LOVE within himself, drifting without reason. He is travelling from land to land, walking in sands hotter than deserts and swimming in waters colder than the poles. Yet you would assume the wise one to be staying constantly in one place.

The only objective of the wise one is to reunite with the owner of divine love. To reunite with his real body, his spiritual dimensions, his divine image, his truth. Divine love is felt for every factor that helps to reach the One. Yet each one is only a step.

Love is continuous, DIVINE LOVE is immortal,

Love is in Nothingness, DIVINE LOVE is in being,

Love is Creative, DIVINE LOVE is transforming.

Love is the Owner of All Times,

DIVINE LOVE is a MOMENT in those times.

Love is the Objective of All Lives,

DIVINE LOVE is an indication in those objectives.

In every touch of love, there is only love, nothing beyond it. The ones who question its limits and interpret according to their presumptions are those who possess self. When two hearts beating with love come together there is an explosion of love that the whole universe witnesses. Each particle starts to dance with joy. Those dances accelerate the vibrations and attract what is mutual and better.

Love does not beg, it always flows. There are no beggars of love, there are only those who manifest love.

The One's love flows like waterfalls and is spread drop-by-drop through the heart, we transform it, evaporate it with divine love and return it to its owner. Love is the most powerful cycle of the universe.

Those in divine love are both pure and transformative. The force of their touch is traumatic, without giving distance any importance. After each trauma, what emerges is the awakened state of a mystic journey that has no return. The awakened from now on never falls asleep!

The fuel of the body is divine love. Divine love renews, transforms, purifies. It is the fuel of being; love is the reason of the cycle in never-ending infinity.

And the power of the One's love ceases, transforms with the fire of divine love in the spiritual hearts of the wise and spreads in silence.

What distance cannot be crossed in front of love?

Words lose their importance for those who are in love. Only the spiritual heart directs them. Love is the only thing protected from life's destruction; there is no other religion.

I love the 'friend' that is with me wherever I go. That is always with me, the one I carry with me. The one transforming my greatest joy into bitter sadness.

Thankfully I know! Whenever I look at the sky, in that huge universe, that there isn't only me. And someone 'from me' is very happy somewhere over there.

Love; is the first action in the belief of the infinite; it is the first and last flowing river; it is hotter than the fire of the sun. Love is a door. A 'door of secrets' that opens to the level of Divine Love. The wise one cannot find any door other than this on his journey of discovery.

The wise one is divine love, is in divine love. Those who reach the level of Mansur (*Mansur Al Hallaj*) will be those divine lovers, those who enter the road of divine love, those who have merit trying to reach divine love, those who unite with divine love and drink from the Kevser water (water found in heaven), those who fill their glass with 'Mansur wine'. There is life in the death and death in the lives of the Mansurs, the wise ones who reach their Truth.

In Ibn 'Arabi's opinion, prophet Moses was the person who was awakened yet was not aware of his awakening, and passed through the steps of awakening. Yet, '*Khadir*', the one who he walks with and the name that completes love, is a symbol of the state of the human being who lives in a complete state of awakening and is at the peak of awareness. The wise person that knows what he is doing, remembers, and is awakened. Khadir is the symbol of one of the highest levels that humanity can reach. It has no concept of time or space. It is one that does not belong to anywhere.

The wise one does not forget yet the mortal does. The wise one that unites reason and compassion and unifies love in his soul, spiritual heart and reason does not forget. The wise one is a complete human being (Al-Insan Al-Kamil) who is molded by power and given a soul. Hence the wise one first loves himself. The person who doesn't love himself, who is mean to himself, is not at peace with anything. The human being must know himself to remember. In order to know himself, he must gravitate towards 'hubb', love, divine love. Then he will become a wise one who is not bound by any belief, having only divine love as his belief, knowing his Rabb. This is of course not 'easy'. Yet, each difficulty comes with a benefit.

Ibn 'Arabi describes this as abandoning the world, letting go of masiva (everything related to the world), dying in one's own body and 'redemption'. He discusses this in *Futûhât al-Makkiyya* under the concept of '*mutekad*'. The state of 'mutekad', meaning abandonment of everything, giving up, is an attribute of the Expert of Araf (Araf is referred to as the place between hell and heaven).

'Redemption' and 'abandonment' create fear. 'Wondering' makes the decision phase difficult. It is only when everything has been turned upside down that it seems like it will end. Abandoning habits is very difficult. At this point, trust and surrender are very important; unconditional faith and unconditional love. The interpretation of this is again not to be bound by a belief system and to be 'mutekad'. The wise one's heart must be molded by 'courage', his reason must be molded by 'patience' and the road must be travelled.

Before realizing he is 'alone', a human being cannot sacrifice himself for another. The person who is lost in the physical world will first know and see himself. He must maintain the free will, must recognize, know himself, and must leave sacrificing for friends to the second phase. Those called friends are those human beings that are his own reflections.

> *'The one who doesn't complete himself, who doesn't surrender to love, who is dragged in the lightest wind, becomes wind with wind, becomes like the leaves. You will both sway in the wind, and know that you are a leaf.'*

The objective of love is to awaken those who are asleep. It is like the hand of the Supreme Soul over human beings. The human being becomes attached to names, forms and the material world and forgets that he is an illusion of the mind, generated in the mind, and makes mistakes.

Everything that is ours is first established in our thoughts, and formed in our thoughts. If one person speaks or acts with bad thoughts, suffering follows just like the wheel following the ox that is pulling the ox-cart.

Ibn 'Arabi says, 'Causalities, particles, the smallest things, material, physical things are in fact all things formed in the mind, by the mind. The wise ones' illuminations to our earth from their amazing sources in the unknown world, are a manifestation of love beyond our comprehensions.'

'In order for Haqq's merit and knowledge to descend to the earth, the light of compassion needs evolved spiritual hearts and reasons that burn wildly. Divine light and merit will flow to our universes from the spiritual hearts of human beings.'

And the human being is also lost, in the world of appearance

His state is understood with the DIVINE LOVE in his spiritual heart

Muhyiddin Ibn 'Arabi says, 'my religion is Divine Love. I am related to the religion of Divine Love, whichever direction the caravan of Divine Love takes me, my religion, my faith is there.'

The one who is created, the embodied one who comes into being in the material universe and becomes nonexistent in the One, only feels divine love, sadness, suffers longing, because he has fallen apart, even if just for a moment in time. He has detached - this is a detachment and separation in appearance - but even for one moment he has lost it and stays in divine love. Yet again, when he existed in the internal in moment time, and came into being in Haqq in non-existence, he reached the lover. What comes from the lover is again for the lover. Everything is molded by Divine Love and becomes a being with divine love.

Yunus Emre said, 'The one who makes the world his problem, has a world of problems'

The problem of Honaz (devious) is with himself.

We have taken on a problem in our heads, the head has gone to the lover, become too large to fit in the universe.

The human being is a mortal and in fact how quickly he gets caught. When he becomes existent in appearance, when he falls down, it is spoken with divine love. Look at what he says and the judgements he makes, he continuously secretly exposes his character. He manifests what is in his spiritual heart. Yet in the internal, when one becomes non-existent in the One, he reunites with love. Love is the sharp look that aligns all details. There is divine love in the world of plurality, and love in world of Unity.

If one particle of love descended to the bodies, the whole visible world would become Non-existent. Love is a sultan in the spiritual heart. Only those who have the power to reach it are immortals.

Hence, the wise one that knows himself, is awakened and follows the Rabb that he sees in world of appearance and becomes the human being of divine love. His internal eye has been opened and he has realized that the one in appearance is temporary, and he has embarked on the journey of reaching the infinite Truth of this immortality, of uniting with Haqq. The entire manifest beauty is the image of the expression of God's divine love. He knows that all shortcomings, sufferings and losses, and everything that happens is in fact a reflection of a divine name. God says, 'That beauty that you see is my DIVINE LOVE'! It calls out to human beings. But human beings do not hear this and the one who has heard it has become wise.'

Truth, Reality cannot be captured by the body but by the immortal eye of the soul. That nearness or farness is defined in the Qur'an as: 'the distance of two arches' maybe shorter.

'Maybe' is used because it is relative. It is dependent on from where it is looked at, the distance of two arches or maybe even closer. Close. The nearnesses that are not far, the farnesses that are not near. Because it is you, in other words, when the wise one knows himself on the road to reach the Truth, the wise one knows that his Rabb is in fact himself. From then on, the wise one becomes free of all 'presumptions'. The one who is in divine love does not have 'presumptions'. The world of witnessing, the world of presumptions, the physical world, all have the same meaning. 'I am upon the presumption of my servant' means 'in the physical world, everyone has a Rabb in line with their beliefs, ideas and thoughts.' In the physical world, no one can reach Rabb's truth, other than by making a 'presumption'. The moment that he reaches it, he has become wise. The moment when one is free from all his presumptions he has reached the level of the wise. He that has freed himself from the presumptions of his self, has reached the truth of his self and has reached the comprehension of Rabb. Yet not everything finishes here. There is no end or point in the universe. The end and the beginning are only the One, the Absolute. No creation other than the One is the end or the beginning.

In that moment, the wise one understands, 'All the universe, planets and stars rotate with longing for divine love, and they are always like a furious fire with their never ending energy. Soul and matter find life with divine love in the universes. If that longing did not exist how would LIFE form?

Yet only a few of us recognize this. There is only one way to awaken it. It is the moment that life stops. It is hidden in the depths of reason and the voice of your heart. It is hidden in the secret of the existence and non-existence that happen in Moment time. The one who can recognize this has become wise.

Love is hidden from us, it is not obvious. Love is not a word, and it can't be seen, hence no eye can see love. Love cannot be proven. The physical world exists in the shadow of love. The divine light of love does not enlighten us we are enlightened indirectly. Our perspective is like the reflection of the sun on the window. Only the wise can look at the light of the Truth. The mortal assumes that the Sun's (the Divine Light of Truth's Love) reflection on the window is real.

Can you remember the times of love

But the human being cannot remember

He touched everything that doesn't belong to him.

And became Lost!

The only thing that remained was a little love left in the spiritual hearts

The soul that you carry in your body

Can you remember those that give you beauty?

And those who contracted in fields of Passion

And Oh you that Forgot.

Oppression is not in the sky but in you.

If you are in description, you are in a lie.

Because Meaning has no shape

The One, like a Huge Apparition manifests itself in every image

And said

'I AM that Meaning, such that no name or a doubt falls upon it.'

The dot is a secret within the Universal Body,

In the Same Moment, the Universal Body is in that secret dot.

The Physical World, is a World of Presumptions, it is Temporary,

Truth is only the 'Purpose of the heart'.

The One's hand that is continuously over the human being is love. Yet, the human being becomes attached to names, forms and the material world. He forgets that the entire creation is an illusion of the mind, and forms in the mind and he makes a mistake!

That hand is always love.

You are in divine love. Yet, if you cannot comprehend the DIVINE LOVE in your ESSENCE, this is what will burn you. The ones who are in divine love and Comprehension are Allah's friends and they are not afraid of anything!

Without exception, everyone came to existence with the Divine Love of the One.

Yet, the ones who comprehend with Divine Love are friends of the One.

And the one who becomes friends with the One, fears nothing.

Do they know that 'one who loves is the One and one who is loved is the One.'

Divine love is the 'triggering factor' that causes the entire universe to become embodied.

If Divine love didn't exist, we wouldn't exist.

Once divine love shines in your eyes you are left alone. That power is feared. It is for this reason you live love on your own. To be loved is a difficult task. If we could attain the delight and supremacy of being loved, we would have transformed earth into paradise a long time ago. For this reason, it is crucial to live divine love within the body.

The objective is not to give up on the Body, to destroy the Body, to leave the Body or to migrate to the world of angels.

What is demanded from us is, 'To die in the Body and become visible in the Body'. This is not destroying the body or leaving the body. It is one thing to do this with meaning and comprehension, it is another thing to leave it physically. The purpose is to attain meaning, reach comprehension and be filled with divine love within the body.

To cover distance over a large ocean we need a ship, if we leave the ship and jump into the sea we drown.

The body is molded by divine love, and love and divine power is blown into it. The body promised to carry this weight, this trust. The trust was offered to rocks and mountains, but they didn't accept it. Only the human being accepted this sacred trust. There is no doubt that the body is sacred, the body is divine love, the body is precious. Within the body, it is key to train, to remain modest, to journey, to journey across the ranks, to enjoy pleasure of states, and to comprehend with divine love. In their journeys inwards, Saints, Masters and Prophets reached within and melted in the knowledge of 'Allah', they became *Fena* (reached the secret of non-existence), yet they returned back to their bodies again and continued to serve the people of earth. 'It is easy to fly, what is difficult is to land'. The difficulty of the journey from the internal back to the apparent is as difficult as the journey from the apparent to the internal.

Without knowing himself, the human being cannot know anything. Knowing is to remember. Knowing is not about the flow of information to the mind. It is an expansion from within to outside; it is remembering. It is establishing contact. It is not possible to arrive anywhere without knowing oneself. Knowing oneself starts with loving oneself. We cannot love ourselves, hence all these rebellions, complaints, anger and hatred. First, the human being must love himself, must embrace himself, then everything will progress naturally. In that moment he will remember that trust is true love.

How nice it is to die, if the throat is from Me and the Sword is from You.

Kill me in my own body, I shall be Fena! (reach the secret of non-existence)

In that grave of a body, Hayy! I shall resurrect.

Your eye, is my eye, I shall look around to the full.

My body is your friend, I shall be a journey, I shall travel and roam

My soul is a part of You,

It waits with longing to reunite,

Say it, I shall be right with you.

V

Essences

'The Human being has no beginning, is Eternal and Continuous in its Hadith, Appearance and Emergence'
Fusûs al-Hikam / Muhyiddin Ibn 'Arabi

Ibn 'Arabi used the word Essence ('*Fass*') in the original texts when he was describing the names. Fass, is the essence, summary, main theme, of a word and a symbol of an attribute. Ibn 'Arabi explains this as following: If a ring is valuable, it is the stone that sits in it that makes it valuable. Hence this valuable stone is Essence (Fass) and the name of the ring is written on that stone.

Haqq gave meaning to the name of each prophet, wise one and saint and granted unique powers to each of them. Each one of them had a separate skill or power. Every name carries a meaning and transfers the essence of that meaning to the mind, thought and body. That body, before becoming embodied, is subject to the influence of the name. This is valid not only for prophets and the wise ones but also for every human being. Everyone chooses their name before they become embodied and sends it via some channels; such as feelings or dreams. On rare occasions he can change his name in the future when he reaches maturity. And each human being lives the attributes of his name throughout his life.

Now, let's look at the meanings of those names and what characteristics they bring unto the wise, and how they influence their life plans.

• The Divine meaning in the word 'Adam'

'If Adam didn't exist, the names and attributes, in which the Level of Divinity is a whole, would not appear.' **Fusûs al-Hikam / Muhyiddin Ibn 'Arabi**

In the Essence of Adam section, Ibn 'Arabi points to the meaning of the name Adam. He emphasizes the symbolic descriptions of Adam and Satan.

The state of prostration is the state of '*cem*' (unity). Ibn 'Arabi says cem is the realization of unity and oneness and the level of becoming one. Satan could not know the wholeness and oneness of Adam and could not understand that he lacked this conception. The word 'prostrate' means to accept and join this oneness and wholeness. Yet, Satan had a conception of a oneness that exists on its own. This manifested as 'Vanity'. And was left out of the circle. In symbolic expression, he became amongst those who align with him that were given time out of the circle. To be denied and thrown to the lowest of the low means to be thrown out of this circle of unity. For this reason, in the Essence of Adam section Ibn 'Arabi says, 'Because he is left out of Oneness, the Seer and Hearer are under continuous observation.' The One took those who reached for Himself, those who felt and heard, to His unity by including them within the circle. Throughout the entire history of humanity, there have been wise people and saints that returned to this circle one-by-one and shone light upon humanity.

Adam is the name of the rank in which all divine names emerge and gather. The divine names are found with their own attributes in Haqq. Whereas in Adam they are in a state where they have emerged, manifested and found symbol. In short, the divine names are found in Adam's existence with the symbols of Rabb's training system. Adam is a mirror of Haqq. The emergence one-by-one of Haqq's divine names, and their finding representation as a training system, occurs in the mirror of Adam. In short, Haqq sees itself in Adam.

Adam is the divine mirror, the first place Haqq drew its own names as images. And the reflections from that mirror are seen as objects in physical plans. Adam is a tablet. And every human being, every object, ever matter, every living being, every material has a truth in the mirror of Adam.

Adam's partner is Adam's wife and mirror. The entire physical plan is a mirror. It is a mirror of Adam. Hence, Adam is the mirror of Haqq and the Physical Universe is the mirror of Adam, his partner. Everything comes into existence from the reflections between Adam and his partner.

Adam was created as a dead body. It didn't carry life. The Divine Soul, his Sacred part, was blown into him. Then he became alive, found life. Adam's shape and body is the entire universe. Yet Adam is non-existence. Adam is the invisible one and the one that is in the internal, in other words, secret.

What is symbolically expressed by being banished from paradise with the forbidden apple is the knowledge of the universe. The symbol of being rejected is the explanation of the formation of the world of shadows. The human being who is thrown to the lowest of the low, every object in the 'physical world' in which the formations take place, have been symbolized as 'shadow.' Its being shadow is its rejection. This is what is explained in esoteric knowledge as descent from God. It is descending from the Truth of Adam to the physical plan. And the exit from the physical plan to the universe of Truth will again be realized with a jump.

The symbol of Adam is a name that is made secret. And this secret has been placed like a dot in each and every human being's body and spiritual heart. Every human being is created with the power to become aware of this reality and his own truth. Because this truth exists in Adam the human prototype. And the child is the secret of the father. And, as his sons, this secret exists in all us human beings.

- **The Divine meaning of 'Breath' in the Word 'Şit' (Gift of God)**

'Şit is Adam's secret in the internal and the apparent. It emerged from Adam in appearance and turned into Adam internally' **Fusûs al-Hikam / Muhyiddin Ibn 'Arabi**

In the Essence of Şit, Ibn 'Arabi explains that Şit is born pursuant to Habil's (Abel's) death after which Adam had become sad and wished for a child with merit. In terms of its dictionary meaning, the word Şit means '*Hibetullah*', in other words 'a gift'. It is a gift from Adam to Adam. It means, 'the child is the secret of the father'. The rank of Adam's wisdom is indicated by the name Şit. The symbolic story is that Adam and his wife had one boy and one girl each year with one birth. This is the main objective of the creation of the human species that explains the concept of duality; as feminine and masculine. There is masculine energy in the feminine, and feminine energy in the masculine. These energies exist within each other in sufficient amounts. If feminine energy is dominant a woman is formed, if masculine energy is dominant a man. Yet, at one time, in one birth only one being is born in the world. And after that they have no other children. The name Şit is given to him. The purpose of this being that is from Rahman's breath is to command self. Şit is the first embodied one to possess ability and to attain completeness. It is because in his body there are equal amounts of feminine and masculine attributes. He is wholeness and the first Wise one. Şit means Allah's gift.

The main objective of the Essence of Şit, is 'Wish'ing. Adam's wish was for 'A child with merits'. And this wish was reflected from Adam's Truth in Haqq's mirror. In this section, Ibn 'Arabi especially stresses that each person's wish reflects from his own Truth.

Ibn 'Arabi stresses that Rahman has two hands, one is a giving hand, other is a taking hand. Each wish and each realized situation comes from Itself and nothing other then Itself can become realized. In short, apart from the Truth in Haqq's Mirror nothing is given to or taken from human being. Its Truth in Haqq's Mirror is the self of each human being. And he is responsible only to the extent of his knowledge and his part or portion of his life plan there. He does not go beyond this piece or life plan. What is needed is a hand given by and a hand taken from Rahman. Even though the responsibility of all that happens is attributed to Allah, He is in fact outside of these things. Each human being is busy with the life plan that his own Truth grants him. He cannot go beyond this. For this reason, there is no punishment or a reward. Everything is as it is supposed to be.

Each person's self is his life plan. His life plan, on the other hand, is formed by the divine name that feeds itself upon his Truth that is his own tablet. Whatever happens is happening from himself to himself. This is the reason behind the non-realization of everything that he wishes. It is because True Self is the image drawn in the mirror. The little self that is owned by the human being is a piece of the self in that mirror and this piece is seduced by matter. He may wish for everything because he is deprived of his own life plan, he doesn't remember or know it. Because he doesn't know it, he expects everything he wishes to be realized. He becomes happy when his wishes are realized and rebels when they are not. Those who become wise to their own self, on the other hand, are far from this state of being happy or feeling rebellious, because they have witnessed their own life plans by reaching True Self. And they are the people that know what they will be given and will not be given.

• The Divine meaning of 'Subbuhiyye' in the word 'Noah'

'Those who wish to know the secret of Noah shall ascend in soul to Felek-i Shems (the sun).' **Fusûs al-Hikam / Muhyiddin Ibn 'Arabi**

He was the first Prophet and the first one who invited people to Haqq. In the Essence of Noah, Ibn 'Arabi talks about Noah being the symbol of Oneness who united the two sexes that were born after Şit's twin siblings and that there was no other birth after that. Noah also took the couples in his ark. He compares Şit, who was born as one from Rahim and who collected couples in his ark like a womb (also a meaning of the word Rahim), and the living that were born from his own ark with the symbol of the ark and spread and reproduced around the world.

• The Divine meaning of 'Kuddusiye' in the word 'Idris' (Şit's grandson)

'Supremacy is upon these: Supremacy of Space, Supremacy of Power. The Supremacy of Space is Felek-i Shems (the sun) and the rank of Idris. The Supremacy of Power on the other hand is of the Wise.' **Fusûs al-Hikam / Muhyiddin Ibn 'Arabi**

And we raised him to a high station. **Qur'an / Maryam / 57**

'The rank of 'Supreme'acy is one of the divine names of Haqq. And 'Mekanen Aliyya', the rank of supremacy (a high station) mentioned in the above verse, is granted only to Prophet Idris. It is the place of eternal silence and nearness. Nearness will be elaborated in the next section. This is the rank of Supremacy, the Rank of Aliyya that no mortal can reach. Idris is also known as Hermes. He is remembered as the saint of the saints. In some cultures, and unwritten knowledge, Idris and Khadir are accepted as being the same person.

In *Fusûs al-Hikam*, it is said that the spiritual rank of Idris is the Sun Universe. Because the Sun is the most supreme of all universes, it is a *kutb* (pole). In kutb only the immortals reside. They are not born and they do not die, they are above the times of existence and non-existence and they reside in the Moment. From there they watch all creation. It is the rank of the wise. And when they wish, or in any moment of need, they can beam from their rank and become visible in any body they want and at any place in the universe.

> *The most supreme of all spaces is the Rank of Empyrean. The All-Merciful, Who has established Himself on the Throne.*
> **Qur'an / Ta-Ha / 5**

The Rank of Idris, on the other hand, is the rank that is closest to the Empyrean. Supremacy, 'Aliyya', is the state of being closest. And no creation can reach a level of closeness beyond this, after reaching the Rank of Idris.

• The Divine meaning of 'Mühemmiye' in the word 'Abraham'

'Abraham, do you not see Haqq manifesting in your body? Haqq informed with its own self from Abraham. Abraham's body is Haqq's body.' **Fusûs al-Hikam / Muhyiddin Ibn 'Arabi**

The meaning of each divine name manifested itself in the name Abraham. He visited all the ranks indicated by the divine names. For this reason, Haqq's self became visible in Abraham. And the name, Halil, given to Abraham is due to Haqq having permeated the image of the One to his existence.

• The Divine meaning of 'Hakkiye' in the name 'Isaac'

'Abraham's knowledge was tested by sacrificing his son Isaac. He didn't interpret the dream, he acknowledged the dream and he implemented it.' **Fusûs al-Hikam / Muhyiddin Ibn 'Arabi**

Halil is the name of Abraham's son whom he devoted as a sacrifice to God. Yet, when he came to sacrifice him, the sword didn't cut and the sacrifice wasn't realized. In the Essence of Isaac, Ibn 'Arabi says that the son to be sacrificed was Isaac. Upon the Last Prophet's statement of 'I am the son of two sacrifices', and the Qur'an (Qur'an / Al-Baqara / 133) referring to Abraham's sons as Ismael and Isaac in the indicated order, led everyone to believe the first son Ismael was to be sacrificed. Yet, in the verse, the suffix 'eb' is used for Isaac. In the Essence of Isaac, Ibn-Arabi explains that because Isaac took the suffix 'eb', the generation of the Last Prophet comes from Isaac and his statement, 'I am the son of two sacrifices', indicates the real intended sacrifice was not Ismael, but Isaac.

Behold, all this was indeed a trial, clear. **Qur'an / As-Saffaat / 106**

Here Abraham tries to execute what he sees in his dream because he sacrificed his son in his dream. Yet, what he should sacrifice was not his son, it was the sacrifice of something he never owned and he most cherished. Hence, until the human being sacrifices everything it owns and doesn't own, in the cause of merit, he won't be able to reunite with his true soul. This is his test. Until this test is passed, the human being cannot be wise.

The human being creates imaginary delusions. The wise one, in his Truth, creates everything that manifests with the knowledge of Truth. Hence, when Halil Abraham sacrificed his son in his dream, what he in fact sacrificed was his own self. He killed his own self and became alive again in his body as a wise one.

• The Divine meaning of 'Aliyye' in the word 'Ismael'

'If you look at the One with the One, One knows his own self. When One knows his self, with his own self, there is no decline' **Fusûs al-Hikam / Muhyiddin Ibn 'Arabi**

Each divine name manifests in the human being. In *Rububiyet* (God's being omnipresent and training) there is a secret and this secret is 'You'. There are no two beings in the universe, Only the One. In that case, the secret of 'You' is in the human being. If the One did not exist then there would be no secret of You; if You didn't exist the One would not find existence. And the Rabb's plans are in acceptance of 'You' who is called the lover. The Human being is the lover and Rabb is also the lover. And the Supreme Lover Rabb, is in acceptance of the human being lover.

One of the prophets who was also accepted was Ismael. How does being accepted happen: 'You' is the person who has attained the ranking of Fana (coming to know non-existence), the secret of 'You'. 'You' is the person who has melted in his own Truth. When you look at your Rabb with the eye of Rabb, your Rabb also looks at his own self in other words the secret of 'you'. Hence, in that moment, the secret of 'you' disappears. It stops being two separate things - the Looker and the One Looked Upon - and duality disappears.

The secret of 'You' is the secret of the person who has not yet awakened, has not known his own self. When 'You' reaches fana, when he knows his Rabb, he becomes free of the 'You' designation. Rabb recognizes his own self. The duality disappears. This means that Rabb accepted the lover.

Hence, this is the meaning of, 'Rabb accepted you', one of the most important secrets of esoteric knowledge. The name Ismael also carries this secret. Ismael is the person who is accepted.

• The Divine meaning of 'Ruhiyye' in the word 'Jacob'

'The knowledge of Jacob is the fact that religion is a knowledge of surrender. It is a state of surrender to Haqq.' **Fusûs al-Hikam / Muhyiddin Ibn 'Arabi**

There are two types of religion, the first is the religion that Haqq transferred to the Prophet it selected at Allah's level and the religion the Prophet transferred to his followers. The second is the religion that the public knows and this is the one that is counted as valid.

The religion, defined above as the former, which is at Allah's level, is more supreme than the religion known by the public. Yet, what is in effect is the religion that is known among the public. The first definition of religion at Allah's level is complete surrender, the state of being closer, it is a religious understanding that the wise ones and the prophets abide by with a belief upon faith and that is not bound by the beliefs and convictions of the public. Although 'religion' has been chosen as a word, its true meaning is 'surrender'. The name 'Jacob' carries this meaning of surrender. Jacob means 'the person who is free from all beliefs in effect among public and has completely surrendered to the rank of Haqq'.

• The Divine meaning of 'Nuriyye' in the word 'Joseph'

'The meaning of Divine Light in the word Joseph is knowledge of interpretation. And whoever possesses the skill of knowing and interpreting takes that knowledge from the rank and

*spirituality of Joseph.' **Fusûs al-Hikam / Muhyiddin Ibn 'Arabi***

The meaning of the name 'Joseph' indicates the wisdom of Divine Light. It is the skill of knowing the truth of matter.

- **The Divine meaning of 'Ahadiyet' (the Oneness of Rabb) in the word 'Hud' (Magnitude)**

*'Each divine name is a Rabb. The definition of the word 'Hud' is the servant's relationship with matter and the test of the Rabb plan' **Fusûs al-Hikam / Muhyiddin Ibn 'Arabi***

In this Essence, Ibn 'Arabi says, every gravitation towards Haqq is a belief. There should be no measure between Haqq and the servant. Everything that is done with numbers and measures creates separation between the lover (loved one) and the lover. This essence describes the necessity of gravitation towards Haqq to be in complete surrender.

- **The Divine meaning of 'Fütuhhiye' (Victory) in the word 'Salah' (One who surrenders)**

*'Adam is hadith. Each hadith has a reason to exist' **Fusûs al-Hikam / Muhyiddin Ibn 'Arabi***

This essence talks about all events that appear as good and evil, and the divine name the human being is created with is the Rabb plan to train it. The ones it sees as Good are those that fit with its nature and demands, the Evil on the other hand are those things that are against its nature and demands. Yet the Truth that everything that happens is the test of Rabb's plan. In short, in this essence, Ibn 'Arabi explains that if a human being encounters an evil he must know that it is coming from his own self, from the expression, 'You did it yourself, you made it yourself'.

- **The Divine meaning of 'Kalbiyye' in the word 'Shuaib'**

*'The wise's heart is divine and fits in Haqq.' **Fusûs al-Hikam / Muhyiddin Ibn 'Arabi***

In this essence Ibn 'Arabi states that divine names are nothing other than Haqq. Shuaib means 'divine heart'. He talks about the divine heart's wideness to be able to fit the entire universe inside it.

- **The Divine meaning of 'Melkiyye' in the word 'Lut'**

*'Lut is an invitation from animalism to being human.' **Fusûs al-Hikam / Muhyiddin Ibn 'Arabi***

Lut means power. This essence explains how to attain power by reaching the rank of *baqabillah* from the ranking of *fana fillah*. At the rank of fana fillah, the human being is yet working on himself. He is defeated by his self and is about to know his self. Yet when he knows self and knows Rabb he reaches the rank of baqabillah and at this rank resurrection is realized. The resurrected person becomes strong, powerful, reaches maturity and is now an immortal.

- **The Divine meaning of 'Kaderiyye' in the word 'Uzair'**

'Only Allah knows fate. Uzair's question was of fate and he became among those who were scolded.' **Fusûs al-Hikam / Muhyiddin Ibn 'Arabi**

Where is supremacy? It is for sure in knowledge. Knowledge is power. Knowledge is transferred to each prophet. And the prophets transferred knowledge to their followers as necessary. What each prophet knew was not known by another prophet. Superiority of rank between them was formed amongst the prophets.

We have exalted some of the Prophets above others **Qur'an / Al-Isra' / 55**

Superiority was also created between the followers because of the differences in the degrees of knowledge transfer between them; just as in creation, there were differences between people due to their different knowledge.

And God has favored some of you above others in provision. **Qur'an / An-Nahl / 7**

Favors can mean both food and also the pleasure of harvesting spiritual states, attaining ranks. It can be thought of from both perspectives. These differences are a secret of creation and no embodied or mortal could know this secret, even prophets. The only one that knows is the owner of the purpose, the owner of time, the owner of life.

Among the prophets, there were those who fell into doubt. The state of doubt of Prophet Uzair is not indicated with the name in the verse but Ibn 'Arabi states in the Essence of Uzair in *Fusûs al-Hikam* that the one who asked questions was Uzair. Prophet Uzair asks in one verse: 'How will God restore life to this town that is now dead?' Qur'an / Al-Baqarah / 259.

Abraham also asked the same question: 'My Lord, show me how You will restore life to the dead!' Qur'an / Al-Baqarah / 260

Uzair was scolded upon asking because he wanted to learn the secret from the owner of Purpose. Yet, Abraham asked this in a different way and wanted to be a witness.

Here Ibn 'Arabi wants to bring our attention to this point: Each of our words is a *kalam* (the word of Allah) and good words full of surrender will help the human being to ascend spiritually, words of evil, fear, hatred and doubt will spiritually regress the human being, because every word will return to its owner.

Knowing to keep within limits and to have good manners are merits. This is true for all people including prophets, wise ones and mortals. Modesty always comes at the top of the list, even for prophets and the wise. The human being will first accept that he is nothing and then in that nothingness he will find existence.

• The Divine meaning of 'Nebevviye' in the word 'Jesus'

'Gabriel in the image of a handsome boy, by giving out a breath, became Murad from Ma-i (Water) Maryam (Mary)'
Fusûs al-Hikam / Muhyiddin Ibn 'Arabi

Each human being, even if he is a prophet, is born from a female womb. It is not possible to be born into this world in any other way. Even if male fertilization is not needed to be born to the world, a female womb will most certainly be needed. The name Rahim expresses fertility, reproduction and breeding and differentiation and individualization by being detached from unity. It is becoming you me, separating from Rahman. In the Holy book, Haqq revealed that a woman could give birth without needing a man by giving an example in the verse, Maryam.

Just as Maryam became pregnant without needing male fertilization, and gave birth to a child after it grew in her womb, another important example is her shaking dates from an infertile date tree. Hence, the name Rahim symbolizes the authority and power of creating a being on its own without needing masculine energy or fertilization.

"I am only a messenger of your Lord to be a means (for God's gift) to you of a pure son." **Qur'an / Maryam / 19**

The name Jesus indicates the divine Soul. It is the divine soul itself that resurrects a dead body.

*The Messiah, Jesus son of Mary, was but a Messenger of God, and Word of His (Power) which He conveyed to Mary, and a spirit from Him. **Qur'an / An-Nisa / 171***

Everything is the words of the One. They are the universes that are derived and expanded from the word Be. And each divine name is a high letter. And high letters become words by descending in between the lines of the universe. And Jesus is also a word that reached Maryam. He reached her differently compared to the rest of humanity. This is the symbol of the state of reaching by being blown from the breath of Rahman.

- **The Divine meaning of 'Rahmaniyye' in the word 'Solomon'**

*'The One is Rahman who creates and is Rahim who gives its creation Rahmet (Grace, mercy) unconditionally. The Human Being who is the Whole of all the names and deserves mercy, is before the names.' **Fusûs al-Hikam / Muhyiddin Ibn 'Arabi***

This is the symbol of power, omnipotence, authority and being in command. This essence explains that the servant is Haqq's self and Haqq obliges Mercy to its self. Its mercy is for its own names and hence for its servants.

- ## The Divine meaning of 'Vücudiyye' (Body) in the word 'David'

'David was given the power to melt iron. He made iron a shield for iron. This is the meaning of I Take Refuge in You from You. It is not difficult to melt iron, what's important is to soften the hearts.' **Fusûs al-Hikam / Muhyiddin Ibn 'Arabi**

Being a prophet is a divine gift, it is not a rank that could be reached through effort. Blessing or granting is upon the prophets of God. It is a gift of the One. In this Essence, the blessings given to the prophets are explained.

- ## The Divine meaning of 'Nefsiye' in the word 'Jonah' (Yunus)

'It became apparent with the apparent One and His body. The one who gravitates towards Yunus gravitates towards Haqq.' **Fusûs al-Hikam / Muhyiddin Ibn 'Arabi**

The human being is created in between the two hands of Rahman. With its knowledge and its names. He is created from its own image, he is blown from its own soul, he is given self from its own self. For this reason, no human being becomes non-existent through death. This essence explains that nothing comes to an end with death, everything returns to its essence. Death is not disappearance, diminishing or ending.

- ## The Divine meaning of 'Gaybiye' in the word 'Eyyub'

'The essence of everything is always ma-i (water)' **Fusûs al-Hikam / Muhyiddin Ibn 'Arabi**

When Eyyub became sick, water appeared next to him and healed him. The essence of everything is water. Life started in water. And water is what gives Vitality. This Essence explains: Water is life, Arsh (Throne) is the Alive one. Arsh is on top of water and is protected on water. The existence of the Alive one is protected only with Life.

- ## The Divine meaning of 'Celaliyye' in the word 'Yahya' (John)

'Yahya means living. The child is the secret of the father. Yahya is the one who is already Alive.' **Fusûs al-Hikam / Muhyiddin Ibn 'Arabi**

Yahya means the wisdom of the origin of all names. The name Yahya found indication with the word Hayy. The child is the secret of the father. The secret of the father is with the son. This was true for all prophets. He was mentioned by his son, Sam, he remained Noah and alive. He was mentioned by his son, Şit, he remained Adam and alive. Yet Zechariah was not mentioned by his son, Yahya (John the Baptist). The knowledge of the father's secret is the son, but this was not for Yahya. Yahya was among those given power when he was a child. The name Yahya was never assigned an attribute.

Yahya represented unity entirely on his own. He was the one visible in body with the divine name he carried. For this reason, he was Haqq's *Celal* (Supremacy). His father Zechariah prayed in the verse Maryam: 'Grant me a Saint, from the rank of *Ledun* (Rank of God)'. In that moment, Yahya was granted to his father, prophet Zechariah, and Haqq named Yahya with its own Hayy attribute.

- **The Divine meaning of 'Malikiyye' in the word 'Zechariah'**

Haqq's mercy encompasses everything. Yet Haqq's wrath is only towards those that do not gravitate towards the One. However, there is mercy even for those who don't gravitate towards Him, and this Essence explains how His Mercy surpassing His Wrath.

- **The Divine meaning of 'İnassiye' in the word 'Elijah' (Ilyas)**

Idris and Elias are the same prophet. Idris ascended to 'Mekan Aliyya', the supreme place. This ascent was not a spiritual ascendance through leaving the body, on the contrary, it was an ascendance with the human body. His body transformed into a big spectral figure. The crystalized body unified itself with its soul and took the soul body completely under its concentration and power. In the word '*inassiye*', Nassiye means being completely human, and also the drawing of the borders, planes. Yet the letter 'I' in front changes everything. Being the letter of having reached supremacy, the word Inassiye was assigned to Elias/Idris.

Elias/Idris was first embodied in the world and ascended to the sky with his body, and then descended back to Earth as a prophet.

In *Fusûs al-Hikam*, Ibn 'Arabi explains: The body is a delusion, in other words a shadow. Yet, the image that is Truth at Haqq's level, meaning the shadow of the true human being, is the image of the human being on Earth. If something happens to the shadow, if it dies, if it breaks into pieces, even if it is destroyed, the Truth does not change and remains original. For this reason, the shadow doesn't have any reality. Yet the shadow can lengthen and shorten. When it shortens, it is at the closest point to the Original Truth. The shadow of humanity is considerably far from its Truth and the shadow has lengthened because for humanity the sun is about to set. When the sun is about to set, shadows become elongated. When the sun is right at the top, the shadows become shortened and in fact have become one with the Truth.

When Elias/Idris was at the center of the Sun meaning the Supreme Place, his shadow was at the closest position to its truth. The shadow's becoming one with the Truth means its withdrawal to the sky. And its descent to the earth is its elongation. For the one who is Qutb and has ascended to the Sun's Supreme Place, it is not difficult to elongate his shadow and approach his Truth. For this reason, whenever Elias/Idris wishes, he can become visible as a body in the world (elongate his shadow) and then return again to the unknown world as invisible (shorten his shadow and make it non-existent).

- **The Divine meaning of 'Ihsaniyye' in the word 'Lokman'**

'If the One Wills for Blessings for itself, all Existence is Its Food' **Fusûs al-Hikam / Muhyiddin Ibn 'Arabi**

This Essence explains the abundance and equality of blessings upon all existence.

- **The Divine meaning of 'İmamiyye' in the word 'Aaron'**

Prophet Moses is told that his brother Aaron has been made a prophet. Aaron is older than Prophet Moses and his identity as a prophet has been granted to him based on a need.

- **The Divine meaning of 'Ulviye' in the word 'Moses'**

'Mu (Water), Sa (Tree). Musa (Moses) is remembered with Water and Chest.' **Fusûs al-Hikam / Muhyiddin Ibn 'Arabi**

In *Fusûs al-Hikam*, Ibn 'Arabi interprets the Essence of Moses in a different way. According to him, because Prophet Moses had to die, all male children that were born at the same time as him were also murdered. Yet, each male child that died had the same power as Prophet Moses. Each one gave Prophet Moses power. In each murdered male child, there was in fact Prophet Moses. Prophet Moses was born with a power equal to the sum of all the souls of the male children that died.

As it was revealed to her, Prophet Moses's mother put Prophet Moses in a basket and released him into the river. This revelation was an emotional revelation. And Ibn 'Arabi presents this as proof that every human being receives and has been receiving emotional revelations. Revelation of Words is only received by prophets. Prophecy in the world ended with Mohammed. And the Revelation of Words ended.

Yet revealed inspiration/divine inspiration comes to every human being. Divine inspiration never ended, it flowed to each created human being, each particle without exception. Divine inspiration flows to every human being; this is a power, the sound of divine inspiration, and Rabb's cry is always heard by those who can reach their spiritual hearts. Divine inspiration is known as the Voice of the Conscience in esoteric knowledge. And Prophet Moses' mother also received divine inspiration in this form.

Prophet Moses grew up next to Pharaoh. Pharaoh had a Moses. Both Pharaoh and Moses were given equal powers. Pharaoh used this towards the material as 'I' and enslaved humanity. Prophet Moses on the other hand used this power as 'You' and liberated humanity from slavery.

- **The Divine meaning of 'Samediyye' in the word 'Halid' (Unlimited)**

Halid is the symbol of gravitation towards Haqq with the objective of having the knowledge of creation manifest in him and also receiving the knowledge of *berzah* (the place where souls wait after death until judgment day).

• **The Divine meaning of 'Ferdiyye' in the word 'Mohammed'**

'The Truth of Mohammed, is before Appearance' **Fusûs al-Hikam / Muhyiddin Ibn 'Arabi**

His Wisdom is Oneness. When Adam was in between water and mud, He was a prophet. He was the last prophet as Mim. The attribute of his name is being the symbol of the Complete Human Being (Al-Insan Al-Kamil). It is the symbol in which all divine names integrate and appear individually.

Prophet Mohammed's thought is: 'a human being's knowing himself comes before him knowing his Rabb, and his knowing his Rabb is a result of him knowing himself.' He said, 'One who knows oneself will know one's Rabb'. If you wish, you could believe you can't have the power to know and reach, and you could be in a state of helplessness. To say this in relation to knowing the One is appropriate. Or, if you wish, you could say it is possible to know the One. According to the first idea, if you know that you don't know yourself (in terms of your truth in the unknown world), you don't in fact know your Rabb. And according to the second one, if you know yourself, in that case, you know your Rabb. Die before dying, because before Dying, not a single one of you can see your Rabb.

VI

The Wisdom of the Wise

'The states of the wise are beyond the comprehension of reason and, not only can they not be conceived through sight or comparison, these states are also not among those that can be defined scientifically or expressed with words.' ***Futûhât al-Makkiyya / Muhyiddin Ibn 'Arabi***

In *Futûhât al-Makkiyya*, Ibn 'Arabi devoted much space to the topic of the wise ones. He called to us from centuries ago, from his own time period, and through his works transmitted the information that 'the wise one is the person who has reached his own truth and knows himself' and is no longer bound by any belief system. He described with a perspective that views the century we live in from his own century. Hence, we found it appropriate to pass on to you his famous statement, 'The Wise one is not bound by religion' in the way it is translated in Arabic and Turkish:

The one who reaches from his own self to Rabb's self, recognizes Haqq's self and reaches his essence. The person who reached his essence is the wise. When the wise knows his self he transforms into a mirror, when he is in communication with his Rabb, Rabb sees its own reflection in the physical world via the wise. And the One also knows Himself before what He sees. When Rabb sees itself in the mirror of the wise within the physical world, he completes his education in the Rabb training system and graduates.

The wise one who has completed the Rabb training system is not bound by any faith or in other words a belief. He accepts all beliefs, sees everyone as they truly are, and his self on the other hand melts only in Haqq, his Essence. The wise one who reaches the essence that is the unity of all names and attributes, believes in Allah. This is called mutekadin (believing in something). This is beyond beliefs, it is a heartfelt faith, it is having faith in what he has personally seen, not what he has not. When the wise one recognizes Rabb by seeing its seal in every particle, his Rabb also knows itself in the physical world, they become mirrors for each other, and pursuant to this the heart of the wise one expands enough to encompass all universes within. His heart fills up and expands with the essence, Haqq, as well as all the divine names and attributes and the unity of all divine images, and no place is left for anything else. Then he starts to have faith in Allah.

The mortal one knows his Rabb by his own belief, faith. When he reaches his self and knows his self, then he becomes wise. Until then, he knows Allah, Haqq, Essence and his

Rabb only upon his assumptions. Depending on which belief he is subject to and whatever the requirements of that belief is, he knows it like that. Haqq reflects on each human being in line with his own belief and imposed knowledge. Because it has no other way.

What he saw in the contract in the beginning was not his Rabb. Rabb became visible to him and said 'Recognize me', the Soul also said 'yes'. Yet, when the names and attributes emerge in physical space, if what they reflect cannot find himself and is lost, his Rabb has also not found itself and has been lost. The training will take a long period of time and the training system will be cumbersome. The Rabb system that tries at every opportunity to introduce itself, finds the human being full of self, upon a presumption, and that presumption continues keep the human being in a state of sleep. When he wakes up from the suggestions of his own beliefs and from his state of sleep, he sees his true self, knows and recognizes it and then he wakes up. He understands that appearance is in fact a temporary situation and he gravitates towards what is true. He finds his course, in other words, his direction. He turns his face to the true sun of divine light not to the reflected light. And, wherever he turns, the sun of divine light shines on him. With the peacefulness of reaching his self, and his Rabb seeing Itself in his mirror, the wise one reaches his Essence with a breath that make the universes tremble, and develops faith in Allah, the Rabb of Universes. This is the meaning of '*mutekadin*'.

The wise one has faith, not in his own Rabb of which he is the subject of its training system, but in the Rabb of

Universes. When he knows Rabb, the owner of beliefs, and the Rabb system that is the owner of each belief, and when that Rabb system knows itself in the physical world, he no longer needs to be bound to any belief.

This faith is not a belief, it is surrendering completely, knowing what one is doing and wishing.

In that case, how can one human being become wise to his own self?

> *O you who believe! Keep from disobedience to God in reverence for Him and piety, and seek the means to come closer to Him, and strive in His cause, so that you may prosper (in both worlds)* **Qur'an / Al-Ma'idah / 35**

Here the one who speaks as 'I' is Haqq. To know Haqq is possible by becoming wise to your own self. Being wise to your own self means to become free from presumptions. The physical world, the world of witnessing, is a world of presumptions. With our frozen cells and our limited consciousness, our personal interpretations only constitute our assumptions. Hence, these presumptions are an impediment to knowing our selves. The first condition is to become free of presumptions before anything else.

Only the person who can become free from his presumptions, reaches his self and becomes among those that attain the rank of Adam, who was created as one self. The rank of Adam is the rank of the complete human being. He awakened in Rabb that is his own trainer, he knew and conceived his own self, he died before dying and became alive again in his own body and recognized himself in the mirror of the wise and reached an understanding of what he is. As a result of Rabb in the internal world and the wise in the apparent world seeing each other as mirrors, the wise one becomes *Arif-i B'illah*. He becomes wise with the secret of B, becomes immortal. He becomes a divine human being who transforms into every image, embraces all beliefs but, having no relation to them, by manifesting, becoming apparent, finding signs in every divine name and attribute, and becoming visible in 'body' in physical environments. The wise one is the representative and knower of the divine power on Earth. From then on, the Rabb system continues on Earth with the wise one, he holds with its hand, he sees with its eye, he hears with its ears. And, if the Rabb system is composed of the unity of all the divine names and attributes, each divine name and attribute, in moment time, exists in the wise one with a name, and in non-existence with a name. The wise one transforms into a divine human being who manifests, finds signs in divine names that become existent and non-existent in momentary time and becomes their ayn, in other words their eye. From then on he is wise, he is *Arifi B'illah*.

Since the wise one is created with a divine name in every moment, he displays variability and difference. With each name he transfers a new witnessing. For this reason, it is not possible to know what the wise one wants to tell. The wise one does not know himself as wise, yet others who witness him may understand. The wise one sees everyone as himself and becomes like everyone. Because everyone is in his spiritual heart, and there is nothing else beyond this. For the wise there are no others, everything is whole and one. He goes from whole to part. The mortal on the other hand travels from part towards the whole. That is the biggest difference between them. The mortal accepts only his own belief as a starting point and rejects everyone who is outside of this, and may in fact blame them. Yet, the wise one is not bound by any belief, he respects all beliefs, walks with all of them, yet is not bound by any. No worldly gravitational pull interests the wise. He set himself free from the seduction of the masiva, the gravitational pull of matter.

The wise who knows himself and sets himself free from the presumptions of selfhood, starts to travel among the ranks and witnesses the ranks one-by-one. While observing thousands of worlds, he starts to watch each with the eye that is suitable for the time and space conditions of that world. The wise one is not only a being sitting in the physical world, but has transformed into a divine power who can witness all the worlds at the same time, watching and seeing with Haqq's eye, covering the distance of ranks in Moment time. This is what is known as Heyula in Sufism. Heyula does not have a body, he uses every body. Heyula does not have an image because he commands all images. Heyula does not have a body, because he becomes existent with a power that is in every particle of Oneness of Existence and makes himself non-existent again with another divine name. He is not constant, he has become a True Being because he has reached the Truth, he is infinite and immortal because he knows his Essence.

The wise is the one who lives the 'state'. The state that the wise lives is a difference state. Only those who are in that state can conceive what the wise says. This STATE is not a continuous repetition in mind and tongue…. it is another state that cannot be explained and for which there is no definition. It can only be known by living it.

The wise one can reach the conviction, conception he wishes, his own Truth, not in light of existing knowledge, but he approaches his own truth in light of his own compassion and spiritual heart. He is in observation with his spiritual fire and compassion.

Only birth and death are true for the whole universe, every living being and everyone together. In fact, there is no truth other than being born from a mother and afterwards dying by surrendering the soul and mixing with soil. All other truths are nothing more than the 'states' predetermined for everyone.

Kün! BE! And everything became existent from inexistence. We don't know inexistence, and we presume existence to be the things we see with our eyes. We neither know existence, nor nothingness. BE is creation. It is one. Everything other than this is two. It is the spreading of Haqq and Haqq's divine names, its manifestations and its formations between two pillars, between the pillars of Rahman and Rahim. And it is always in formation in the MOMENT. The one that comprehends the meaning of two also has knowledge of the self. Because, Muhyiddin Ibn 'Arabi says, 'Knowing Rabb's Self is possible only by knowing one's Own self.' Self, meaning Essence, is covered with divine attributes, the attributes with verbs, the verbs with formations and works. Each one of them is a mystery, a veil, always in their border but in formation in their secret. The one who witnesses sees the formation of verbs with the removal of formations becomes wise. Ibn 'Arabi comments, 'When the verb's veil is removed, the one who witnesses the manifestation of the attributes accepts, surrenders and becomes wise.' The one who witnesses, sees the manifestation of Essence, its appearance, in creation at every moment, by the removal of the divine attribute's veils, reaches Oneness and becomes inexistent there. From then on, whatever he does, whatever he reads, he has become absolute *'muhavvit'* - the wise one that 'sees One, makes One'.

Muhyiddin Ibn 'Arabi collected the ranks of the wise in seven tours.

• First Tour: The Conception of the Immortal Part

An explorer who looks everywhere yet cannot see what is in himself, will only conquer Truth with a look that looks within himself.

A human being is included in the first tour when he conceives of the partial soul that exists in his own body of matter. Unity is Solitude and Oneness. Self, Heart, Soul, Mind are all one at Haqq's rank yet as the attributes change, all adopt an image and name and exist with that name and image on earth. Arabi calls this existence, *Nafs-i Natıka*. Natıka means faculty of speech. And Nefs-i Natıka secretly and openly conquers the body, it is found everywhere in the body but also nowhere in the body. It is a power that is unable to be broken. Even if a part of the body is cut or detached, there is no diminishment or detachment in this power. Moreover, even the entire body, or corpse, breaks, burns or becomes ash, this power stays the same and is always alive and immortal in its own center, in its own presence. In other words, the wise one has discovered the immortal part of his body. The wise that knows his self with this discovery, has covered ground towards the second tour.

• Second Tour: The Conception of the Holistic Self

And the power of the Love of the One, diminishes, transforms and spreads with the fire of Love in the spiritual hearts of the Wise.

The wise one who comprehends his own self in the first tour, comprehends the self of the world, the complete nafs, in the second tour. Then he views the visible world with a holistic 'look' and sees at the level of comprehension. What he sees is the single self, the holistic self. Muhyiddin Ibn 'Arabi calls this the 'Complete Nafs'. The wise one looks at the holistic self, witnesses the skies and earth becoming existent and inexistent like a heart beat. He witnesses them lit up by divine light. Because he is free from all presumptions and is not bound by any beliefs, his vision is broader and more divine. Just as the sun lights up the Earth, the wise also looks at the heart, the essence of the one who lights up, not the place that is lit. The soul is an immortal part and is Haqq's part. And the wise that realizes that part exists in himself passes on to the third tour.

• Third Tour: The Conception of the Divine Soul

When I was an indication in Meaning, I buried my Soul in the body with knowledge. Again a time will come, with knowledge, I will dig it out of the grave.

The third tour is one of the most important places for the wise one. Because the third tour is the rejoining of the trusted soul, his own divine part, with the grand soul; it is the rejoining of the trusted mind with the grand mind, the melting, the disappearance of his own soul and mind in the Divine Holistic Soul and Mind, in other words, it is the formation of the Fana 'fillah state. The wise one who attains fana and becomes inexistent there is 'closest to Haqq'. He has completely died in his body. The body is a corpse, or for a better definition, a grave. The state of the wise one in this third tour is of one who dies his own body, makes it a grave and attains fana - becomes inexistent in the Divine Soul and Mind.

Ibn 'Arabi relates seven meanings of the word fana, pertaining to its philosophical importance rather than its meaning in Sufism, and makes his analysis with this perspective. According to him, fana is what reunites the servant with Allah. It is surrendering to Allah's will.

By becoming inexistent in Haqq and reaching the state of fana, the wise one has reached the level of complete meaning. At this level, all symbols and signs materialized in human language are solved. Symbols, verses and figurative truths, are not necessary for prophets, saints and the wise. They are for those who cannot understand the Truth. For this reason, the symbolic words of essence, only point to the Truth. The wise and the prophets surely know their true meanings. Yes in their expressions they convey this by censoring it.

> *We have not taught him (the Messenger) poetry; further it is not seemly for him.* **Qur'an / Ya-Sin / 29**

The verses may be expressed in poetic language yet they are not poems. Poems with symbols and hidden expressions were not necessary for the prophet. The Qur'an indicated, 'That is a reminder and an open book' (Yasin / 69). It is a book of reminders that points to the Truth.

In *Futûhât al-Makkiyya*, Ibn 'Arabi said, 'The wise are above what they say'. He states that the wise live in their heart related senses and the knowledge of those ranks are open and apparent truths. There is neither symbol, nor sign, or language there. There is only Truth and its witnessing there. Yet in the state of fana, the wise chose poetic language to be able to express this. In *Futûhât al-Makkiyya*, Ibn 'Arabi said, 'Our knowledge is the knowledge of signs. If it transforms into words, it remains secret'.

- **Fourth Tour: The state of Fana 'The One exists, there is nothing else'**

Everything that comes from the lover, is again the lover and for the lover.

The wise one that melted, made fana of its insignificant soul and mind within the Divine Grand Soul and Mind, conceives unity. The wise one has now returned the trust and will revive again in the body with the grander Holistic Soul and Mind. He has reached consciousness and conception of the body - this state is the state of Baqaa. In other words, Ibn 'Arabi called this state '*Baqaa Billah*'. The wise one who has reached this tour says there is nothing in presence other than Haqq. Ibn 'Arabi says, '*la mevcuda illa hu*' for this state: 'There is no presence, there are no bodies, Only the One. Beyazid Al Bistami said, 'I consider myself free of all imperfections, how grand is my reputation', and Mansur Al Hallaj said, '*Ene'l-Haqq*: I am Haqq'. I would like to open a parenthesis here and say that there are those in our time who say, 'I am the One' yet this doesn't go beyond imitation. Be Mansur and say Ene'l Haqq. If you are not Mansur, you are an imitator. Being the One is something, Being From the One is something else. The One is the One. Adam is Adam. The human being of earth is mortal. If you are an imitator, you must also carry the weight of this, without complaining or rebelling. Being Mansur is not nothingness in everything, it is everything in nothingness. Those who say, I am 'the

One', only with their lips, cry as if they are making a small desperate attempt to save their own lives. Yet those who say, I am 'the One', with their hearts are cut in slices yet neither their voices are heard nor their breath is stopped. Is it in the corpse of Hayy!? Is it in the Divine Heart?

In the cloak of one body, the state of 'there is nothing else but the One' emerges. Here Ibn 'Arabi stresses the verse Mu'min / 40 that says, 'Whose is the Estate in the Moment? It belongs to the one who is Al-Qahhar and Al-Wahid.' And he explains: in Moment time the Estate only belongs to Allah that is the Whole. There is Allah and nothing else. There is no Estate, but Allah.

In the first tour, the wise one knows his internal world - 'self'. In the second tour, he sees and conceives his external world *afak*, meaning apparent. In the third tour, he conceives that the internal and external worlds, meaning the internal and the apparent, are one and unified. In the fourth tour, he reaches the conception that the internal and external worlds are his own world, and whatever belongs to himself melts and disappears in the whole.

It is easy to give up on what you own. It is the biggest torment to let go of what you never had for the cause of a virtue. It is not possible to see Shams before passing through hell. Plunge yourself into that torment. Plunge in, burn in the fiery red fire of hell, own the sacred loss of heaven in Shams' eyepiece and let it go. Reach inexistence, become nothingness.

• Fifth Tour: Conception of Time

Being inexistent in the MOMENT, becoming existent again from each particle of the One.

The wise one who has passed all tours, attains the conception of time in the fifth tour. From then on there is no more concept of internal time or external time or two times for the wise. Existence is external time, inexistence is internal time – two times become one. There is no existence and inexistence time; there is only one time - MOMENT time, that is center and qutb (pole). Hence when the wise one stops in moment time he becomes immortal. He has shed the temporary existence and disappeared into inexistence; he has become among those immortals who have reached infinity, rather than those who have die and don't revive, or are born and do not die. In every person's borrowed, temporary situation of existence and inexistence, there is an infinite and powerful divine soul. Yet what is important is to know the infinite and immortal part. Hence the wise one makes this definition in the fifth tour, and in MOMENT time becomes one with the owner of time. From then on he is not a time in those times, but has become a MOMENT in all times. Ibn 'Arabi gives this rank another name and calls it the 'Son of Time'.

- ## Sixth Tour: The State of Baqaa - 'I exist, there is nothing else!'

The wise is in his own presence.

The wise one who has become a mirror for everything, moves on to the sixth tour when he realizes that what he sees in the mirror is also himself. From then on, there is no separation such as others and himself. He sees all presence with one look, Haqq's look. There is no past, no future, only the Moment; since everything happens in the moment, it is found in the Moment qutb, the Moment center. And all matter and universes exist in himself. From then on he exists and becomes inexistent with every world. Only the wise one is immortal, close to Allah, in other words he is the expert of A'raf indicated in the sacred verses. The expert of A'raf is an expert of neither heaven nor hell. He is found in between the two, in other words he is qutb, center and found at the highest rank.

Hence in the previous ranks, the wise one who said there is no Presence but only Allah, in the sixth tour says:

'There is no existence, only I exist.'

Arabi calls this rank, 'Father of Time'. You don't exist, 'I' exist. It means there is nothing else, only 'I'. It is the highest rank and is indicated as 'Mekan' in the sacred verses.

The expert of the wise is neither body nor soul he is both body and soul. Yet he surpasses both of them.

• Seventh Tour: 'Mukarrebun' (Close to Allah) Immortal Human Being

Satan put himself out there, he was left out of knowledge when he was possessing knowledge.

Adam banished himself there, has become wise to his Truth with his knowledge.

The *mukarrebun* ones amongst those suitable ones that say 'there is no existence I exist', meaning the immortal wise with divine power, reach complete inexistence. In this place there is neither state, nor rank, neither matter, nor spirit. This is the state all saints refer to as 'night'. In fact, interpreting it as a state doesn't do it justice. It is a rank of Complete Inexistence, Nothingness. There is no description of this rank. No description will do it justice. At the rank of nothingness, there is neither explanation nor description; it is a state beyond all states that cannot even be called a rank. This is a holistic rank. It is the place where all ranks become complete, unified. It is here the wise knows his Rabb. From then on, no connection to any belief remains for him on Earth. All belief systems, Rabb's training systems, take place in the heart of the wise, yet he is not affiliated to any of them, he is above all of them. Because he has now known his Rabb, and his Rabb has known him. In that moment, he becomes one with Haqq, and has faith in Allah from there. He lives a life of surrender and inexistence beyond beliefs as well as the states of fana and baqaa.

When he looks around, he understands that he is the One which sees from every eye and he is the One which looks from every particle. The One is that which hears with every ear, looks from each particle, sees from every eye.

Only the Absolute is unbound from time and space. Other than this, every creation is subject to time. There is always distance between creation and the MOMENT. Except for only the wise because the wise exist in the 'moment' where two times are 'one'. For this reason, it was said: The spiritual hearts of the wise, the tongue of the helpless, the honesty of the Enlightened, Haqq's breath. The supporting verse in the Qur'an is also very striking:

> "He it is Who has brought you into being and endowed you with hearing, and eyes, and hearts." (sem'a vel ebsare vel ef'ideh) **Qur'an / Al-Mulk / 23**

The rank in the verse is noteworthy.

Sem'a: The hearing sense. The hearer.

Ebsare: Seer

It is among the divine names 'Al-Basir' which means 'Not every eye can see the One but the One sees from all eyes.'

And in the rest of the verse, it is indicated that each of these is in the human being, yet it will give account for each one of these separately. Each one is a tour, a reality, a step. When Rabb's cry touches your ear, you hear your inner voice, and you are directed inwards from the apparent by deepening. It is then that you become all ears from Earth to skies. This is a step, a tour. The first step is to deepen from the physical plan to reach the skies, meaning the internal.

El Basara (Al Basir), someone that sees Haqq from Haqq's eye, is a step. It means becoming inexistent in fana, becoming nothingness. From then on, there is no body or plurality, there is a 'look' that perceives the unity and wholeness. This is also a step, a tour.

Fuad, in other words, opening the eye of the spiritual heart, the skill of comprehension, is the last step, last tour. In that moment, you are wise: mukarrebun, an immortal human being.

In the tours, in evolution, in the spiritual evolution, there is no stop or stopping. The hierarchy is infinite; the phases, the ranks to be covered, the tours and steps are infinite. For this reason, what is described in a few points are in fact layers that are difficult, onerous and very important to conquer. Haqq's road is the road of variability that opens out as it is walked, seen as it is conquered. Because, the One is in a different manifestation, a different formation and creation in every MOMENT. The human being is recreated in every moment, it is the way port, the station of separate divine names. The human being is seen as constant in the body yet it changes every moment and is recreated. Haqq's breath is in a state of 'building' a new human being in each moment. At Haqq's rank, the divine light, that is fireballs which are determined for each divine creation, waits for the MOMENT for its target. The human being is recreated with a divine name and reaching inexistence with another in every moment. The wise one is a man of meaning and meaning does not have a shape. It is because the One reflects itself in every image like an apparition. It is like a seal in each particle. It is living and always alive.

> *The wise have opened the shop, they have whatever you need in it.* **Pir Sultan Abdal**

This is the description of the wise: The wise one is neither soul, nor body, he is both soul and body, he is neither of them, yet he is superior to both of them.

> *The sea is permanent, if you have been caught by the sickness of 'not being able to drink',*
>
> *what a big Misfortune,*
>
> *The sea is permanent, if you drink Water and cannot digest it, if you die of thirst, what a big loss.*
>
> *The sea is permanent, if You still stroll by the shore and seek for the Sea? What a big blindness.*
>
> *The sea is permanent, you become thirsty as you Drink, you drink as you become thirsty,*
>
> *Hence, neither the wise is satisfied with the water, nor runs out the flowing sea.*
>
> *The One sees from every eye, the One also looks from every particle.*

The mortal reaches the whole from the part, the wise one, from the whole to the part. So, as the wise one says, 'I climbed up the sky, I watched the earth, I descended to the earth and the universe watches me'. When one looks from the sky, everything is one and in fact is truth. Yet, when one descends to the earth, all divine names and images, all universes, watch the human being. Yet, let it be noted that, both the one who ascends to the sky and watches, and the one who descends to the earth and is watched by the universes, is Haqq. It is Haqq's eye. The One watches all universes every moment, in MOMENT time, in all times, in all universes in their own time and according to its comprehension.

> *They are like cattle (following only their instincts) – rather, even more astray (from the right way and in need of being led). Those are the unmindful and the heedless.* **Qur'an / Al-A'raf / 179**

Heedless! It is an attribute of one who is not a complete human being. It is also clearly indicated in the verse that they are like cattle. In other words, it is the description of the mortal who is heedless and is influenced by others, cannot control his own emotions and thoughts, is directed by 'influence' and takes action not with truths but by 'assumptions'.

Ibn 'Arabi particularly stressed this in *Futûhât al-Makkiyya*. Not everyone that wishes can be a complete human being. In other words, not everyone that wishes can be wise. Haqq, gave everyone this right equally, but the fault lies with the human being himself because he is heedless. With his own hands, the human being destroyed this grand skill, this skill which was given with his own hands.

In *Futûhât al-Makkiyya*, Ibn 'Arabi emphasized that one who surrenders to a *Murshid* (Mentor), becoming virtuous with his virtuousness, can become wise by reaching his own Truth. The Complete Human Being, the wise one, is not bound by a belief. Yet he should also neither be considered one without sect or belief. His sect and belief is the 'Divine wish' and 'Command of self'. His explanation is this, his belief and sect are not figurative. He is from the sect of Huda. His belief is Love.

When the wise one becomes wise to his own Truth, he doesn't remain bound to religion yet he walks with religion.

For the wise one who unites two opposites, punishment and trouble are blessings. He is one who does not turn his face once to the ground, even if punishment and trouble rain on him from the sky.

Ibn 'Arabi made two suggestions for the wise: The wise must talk to people within the limits of their reason.

The wise cannot be bound by any belief yet within the society he should seem like he is bound by a belief. Ibn 'Arabi specifically indicates that if the opposite happens, he is killed. He should not open his heart because it can lead to him being accused of hypocrisy, nonbelief, atheism. For this reason, the wise ones transferred the information of the states and pleasures of their ranks, only with a few sentences, with symbols, and by covering and dressing up. They transferred their knowledge in such a way that only those who witness such states and pleasures can understand it.

Being in a deep passion is,

When your soul and your body,

Has turned into red fiery fire,

In the captivity of hell,

In the same moment,

Finding Heaven,

In His eyes, a very sacred form of being lost.

The purpose is to see with Haqq's eyes not with the eyes of self. Yet, even better is to see from Haqq's eye. What kind of wisdom and power is this? If it could truly be comprehended, there would neither be a tongue to say a word, nor would a body be left. It would transform into an essence of immortality that would manifest, appear when its time comes, and then spread in the universe in particles in the MOMENT and would beat with the heart of the universe.

'I Am the person who is known in all parts of the Earth'

It is the One which creates with divine essence and surrounds its creation. It is the human being who squeezes himself in tight molds, and names with liberty. He cannot see behind the visible. He imprisons himself in his dry body. In the world of death and loneliness, whoever realizes he is not alone will become immortal.

'I Am that manifests in any way that I want'

The Earth's soil is attractive, seductive and provocative. One that dwells in that mud, wants to taste it thousand times.

Yet, there are such 'Ones who know what they want and wish, touch the space in the skies, and dive in the observation of the universes, and chime the sounds of dabbe in people's ears on earth'. Those ones are the wise and they need nothing. Life flows to them in a way.

From Heart to Heart Many Ways Are Granted

For those who know how to Conquer

For those who see with both eyes

That state is such a state. It dissipates one state and brings another state. That state manifests in each visible particle. 'The one who is blind in this world, is also blind in the after world'. The one who cannot see Rabb in this world will not be able to see it in the after world. One requires the merit of the eye to see those STATES.

'I AM the one who sees from every eye, who looks from each particle'

When I was upon an indication of Meaning,

I buried my Soul in the body with knowledge.

There will again come a time,

That I will dig it out from the grave with knowledge.

The ideal is to reach 'meaning' by deepening in manifestation. Otherwise, reading about all the wise, all the saints, reading the verses every morning and evening will address the ears and eyes. The comprehension of the heart starts horizontally and continues vertically. The stages are a journey between the horizontal and the vertical. What is horizontal is the 'B' Universe, it is in the form of mattress, yet its essence is the dot under it. There stands the dot that is the starting dot of Alif. In other worlds, the universes, including the physical universe, are bound by certain principles. In 'B', the horizontal plan, Haqq always exists because one of its names is Zahir (Manifested). Manifested is in fact Haqq. It is not separated, hence it can not be detached.

Three people came, whose eyes were visible.

Those were the ones who were about to enact

The agreement that was identified beforehand.

They loaded Him on the back of a camel.

'What have you done? The sultan of sultans is going'

Was said behind them.

Everyone turned and looked.

In the never ending desert,

There was neither a walker, nor a footprint,

Those were the ones who vanished into thin air.

They became a secret and finished.

The Heart

Haqq reflects only on the one who destroys all his lines, pictures, name and identity. **Hilyetu-l Ebdal / Muhyiddin Ibn 'Arabi**

It is necessary to understand the meaning of 'heart' in relation to the wise. The heart in question is not the piece of flesh that is found pumping blood in the chest. We can define it like this: 'If you know it as near, what they refer to as *cam-ı cem* (the glass of unity) is your heart. If you wish to see the universe, you can see the esoteric information of matter in that heart. The eye of the mind sees patterns and shapes, but only the eye of the heart can see what is secret, shielded from every one. If you can open your heart's eye, you can conceive of all matter internally and externally as a whole. What is referred to is the heart of the wise. It is the heart of the wise one who reaches his truth, knows and recognizes his self. Because the wise one sees the seal of Rabb in every particle that he looks at; he attains the nature of the matter, reaches the internal purpose; he has reached the conception of why he was formed and exists.

The heart is sacred because it is there that Haqq's mercy appears. Mercy is amongst the divine attributes and the complete human being is the whole of all the names, so Mercy is also within the heart of the wise. The wise is Haqq's self, so Haqq shows mercy to its own self. Haqq's compassion for its servants, is the One's mercy. Haqq is separate from the universes, meaning it doesn't exist in the universes, it only finds existence with the manifestation of the divine names. If each being is a manifestation of a divine name, Haqq shows mercy to its own divine names.

When Haqq fits into the heart of the wise one, there is no space left, and no particle related to matter can assume a place in that heart. Haqq is separate from the universes so It only fits in the heart of the wise: when it does, all of its divine names find various manifestations, and for this reason nothing else can fit, and nothing else can exist in that heart any longer. For example, the stars in the sky are alone and their lights shine separately. At night, thousands of them become visible in the sky in a moment, yet when the sun rises their light becomes invisible, because the sun's light penetrates everywhere. The sunlight appears as one light beam even though it contains an unlimited number of beams. And all other existing lights melt within the sunlight.

The heart that Ibn 'Arabi talks about in his works is beyond reason and logic. The heart is in a place that reason cannot conceive, that cannot be reached by reason. Reason is the whole of all propositions required for worldly matters. Reason is limited, and open to misconception. All knowledge attained through reason is a vicious circle and doesn't help one to reach anywhere.

The heart is work of intuition, of deep conception and comprehension. Reason is a bridge between the world and the human being. The heart, on the other hand, has a depth that helps one embark on journey to the secret worlds and reach the treasures there. Ibn 'Arabi qualifies the heart as a mirror. If a person that starts on this road polishes his heart like a mirror, he can watch all kinds of manifestations in that mirror. The one who cannot turn his heart into a mirror and stays at the level of reason, on the other hand, cannot have any knowledge of the secret worlds.

The place and rank of the heart that Ibn 'Arabi talks about is the secret internal world that is also known as the unknown world. Everything that is limited, that has a shape in the world of appearance, is unlimited and infinite in the unknown world. For this reason, the heart is in infinity and can expand to include eternity within itself.

Everything that is inclined towards the world obstructs the incline towards the heart. For this reason, when Sufis want to incline towards the heart, they isolate themselves from every worldly pleasure and every seduction of matter. They withdraw into a corner. Those who are purified from the effects of the world in the internal, try to reach the depths of the meaning of the heart. Every worldly affect leaves dirt on the heart. In esoteric knowledge, this is also referred to as a crust, cover, tarnish and contamination. These are obstacles to reaching the knowledge of the secret worlds. In order to overcome these obstacles, exercises for 'Knowing the self' are completed.

In the Qur'an, the 37th verse of Al-Kahf mentions, 'those with hearts'. There are many chapters with advice and proofs for those who possess reason, however, this verse refers to those who possess hearts. Everyone has a heart of flesh but not everyone possesses a *Rabbani* heart, a divine heart.

The heart is where the divine light of reason is found. Human beings' reason is a part of the divine light of reason. The small portion, meaning partial reason, misleads the human being. It cannot form a total wholeness. The divine light of reason is where the fire constantly burns. And a never-extinguishing fire burns in the heart of the Haqq lovers who are inclined towards the heart.

If you are warm within, even if you are at the coldest poles, it will warm up your skin. Do not be afraid, burn the Nar-ı Aşk (Fire of Love) within you; it will always keep you warm in both worlds. The human being should not be afraid of the fire of love and must keep the fire of *Tennur* (tender oven) burning fiercely.

The person who tries to reach his heart not only makes an effort for this, but also performs practices to completely polish the mirror of the heart having reached it. We cover these practices in detail in the following sections of the book.

The partial reason, limits, puts into form, measures and weighs, it is a binder and gives shape and makes the shape constant and records it. The heart changes from state to state. In each transition from state to state, what takes shape does not remain constant, it is variable, it doesn't ascribe limits, it observes an infinite transformation upon creation in every moment, and does not record it.

Divine formations, are never limited. If the sufi has reached his heart, he watches these divine formations and their creations in every moment. These observations are called states. A state, just like thunder strikes in the sky, flashes and disappears. States are signs for opening up the doors of the ranks. The state comes from Haqq, ranks, on the other hand, are realities in esoteric meaning that human beings reach through effort. Everything that is lived in ranks, or realities, is a state. States are lived in ranks, yet they don't remain constant. Each rank, reality, has a beginning and an end. Each rank has its knowledge, and every state has a sign. States leave the door of the rank ajar with signs and enable journey to the other.

The living of states in ranks is completely dependent on the personal effort of the sufi who is travelling the road of the heart. By freeing himself of worldly influences, he can be successful in covering ground. As long as he is not bound by any belief, he will achieve this. But, he will give up every time he submits to his reason or is seduced by worldly influences. However, this will not lead to regression; the journey can be restarted at any time. There is never an end or a beginning.

Whenever the wise one spends time on making an effort to save himself in this world, this is not through his own autonomous choice, but his surrender to the divine command and force. **Fusûs al-Hikam – Muhyiddin Ibn 'Arabi**

Assumptions

In the sacred book there is advice for the possessors of the heart, but not for the possessors of reason. Because reason is a bond, it is binding. The heart on the other hand is wide and divine. Reason can see only see what is worldly and apparent and makes comments based upon assumptions. The mortals' reason is full of 'assumptions' yet Haqq conquers the heart of the wise.

For those who wish to understand the physical world with their reason, the divine words, the words of essence of the saints and prophets, are not a measure or advice for them. They do not go beyond the states of pleasure that arise within due to memorizing, reading them. The reason misleads and confuses. In fact, for some it feels unnecessary and for some it feels marvelous. This situation of falling into these assumptions results from their conceiving of everything with their reason.

'They are blind' and are blind in both worlds. The blindness here is the blindness of the heart, they are the possessors of reason with blind hearts. Yet, those who have seeing hearts, who have the eye of their spiritual hearts open, are also helped by their reason.

Everyone has developed a 'divine' in line with the 'presumptions' that they create in their belief system, in other words, the 'Rabb' every person has created in its mind becomes its 'Divine'.

According to Ibn 'Arabi, 'What will remain after the end of belief, religions; when the apocalypse happens and all 'divines' become inexistent with the presumptions of human beings? Only Truth. Yet, if the human being could not know or discover the truth in the body, and assumed his non-existing divines real, then he will be left astray and become heedless. He will become heedless and will not know what to do. Hence what is important is to find the Truth when in your own body and to discover your real Truth by killing all divines, presumptions.'

Ibn 'Arabi says, 'Those who live bound to certain beliefs, impositions, teachings, do not like and love other systems.' In today's world, we experience situations where people are unable to love each other and they practice discrimination due to their intolerance of difference and variety, even within the same beliefs and teachings.

The 'divine' understanding that is based on the assumptions of each reason-possessing person, is as numerous as the breaths of human beings. For this reason, the 'divines' that form upon, develop, and are fed with presumptions do not like, approve of, or accept each other. For this reason, there are as many 'divines' formed by the 'presumptions' of human beings, as the number of human beings on Earth. The 'divines' formed upon presumptions are in fact temporary, like shadows; they have no origin, they are not truth. They only took shape in the minds of people based on their presumptions. These 'divines' that are invented upon presumptions are in a state of continuous conflict, or war.

The human being wastes his breath on presumptions. He produces a presumption in each breath. Maybe in that moment his reason cannot conceive of what is being repeated all the time, but a moment may come, so that during one of those repetitions, he may become free of the presumption in his breath and catch the Truth. As they say, enlightenment happens in one moment. He has changed within a moment. He sleeps with a thousand breaths, yet in just one of those breathes he becomes free of presumption and sees everything clearly in that moment; he witnesses, changes, all of a sudden. In scientific terms it is a quantum leap. The enlightenment of human beings happens in this way. From then on, even only for a moment, he goes beyond the reason-based conception, and becomes pleasure with heartfelt conception. In order to catch this state of being pleasure, he runs after this state and looks for what is similar. And when these heartfelt conceptions start to repeat frequently, a real awakening and quantum leap takes place. He is no longer the same old human being. He has lived this a thousand times yet he conceived it with reason and could not recognize it due to being drowned in presumptions.

Yet, with a momentary awareness, with a momentary opening of the heart's eye, he took in 'one single breath' equal to the breath he had taken thousand times and filled up with the light of the sun in all its particles.

The wise one doesn't reject any conviction, any belief, any opinion, philosophy, knowledge or learned truth. He enters there and accepts it there. Even though they seem separate and conflicting, in truth they are all connected to the same plan as a whole. Yet, the only problem is that they are formed upon presumptions. They are not real; they are temporary.

Journey

There is a journey within a journey. **Pir Sultan Abdal**

A journey within a journey, a trip, is a spiritual journey. It is a journey from the apparent to the internal; from the physical plan to spirituality. It is internalization. It is awareness. It is awakening. It is the journey of reaching the conception that the image in the mirror is not you, it is 'you' who looks at the mirror, and there is no 'you' in truth, there is nothing other than the One.

Step by steps are its marks
Inside this world
Eighteen thousand worlds I saw
Within one mountain

Yunus Emre

Each human being with a body has a Truth in Essence that is the Divine Self. The true human being is there. What becomes 'matter' in the physical plane is in fact the reflection of Truth as shadows. In his works, Ibn 'Arabi interpreted this as follows, 'in the shadow of the shadows of the shadows.' The being that becomes matter as a human being in the physical plan, is in fact the reflection of the Truth in the shadow of the shadows of the shadows. That shadow can only make the journey that will enable it to find its own shadow, through a flow towards the internal from the physical plan. This road is strenuous, arduous, a shirt of fire; it doesn't accept loss of power midway. The human being is alone on the road. For this reason, it is said that, 'Friendly conversation is beautiful, but the road of Divine Love, Haqq's road is the road of solitude. It is solitude in proximity. The wise are in solitude in proximity. They are in a solitude of proximity in which they find all existence within and surround the entire universe.'

Ibn 'Arabi described this journey as 'The Divine Surge, from Self to Self.'

- **The First Journey: The Journey from Essence to Matter**

The journey from the One

Every human being has a truth in Essence. In order for Truth to find life within the body on earth, he must go through various stages. Thus, Ibn 'Arabi defines these stages as a journey, a trip. This is a journey from the internal to the apparent, from invisible to visible, from the secret to the open.

The first form is determined in Holistic Reason. Ibn 'Arabi calls such an indication, 'divine knowledge' or 'divine mirror'. He stays there for a period of time, trains, and his life plan and conditions are determined. This is the divine mirror in which the journey of events and how they are going to happen initially take shape. In esoteric knowledge this is called the 'life plan'. After the life plan has been determined, he is moved on to the Holistic Self and there is given the self trusted to himself and is entrusted with his divine part, the soul. After this, he continues his journey to the highest rank in space (arş), kursiye, skies, 'Moon', and reaches the spheres of 'fire, air, water and earth'. When he reaches the earth, he finds his way through mineral, animal, plant and finds life as a human being via the 'Womb' (Rahim) and is transferred to Earth through birth.

The journey of the human being who has been created in His image, transported through layers and layers, and thrown to the lowest of the low, is shown by the 'Letter V, which is number seven in Arabic'. This is the 'descending' symbol of the Sacred Seven. And this is reported as the repeating seven.

This is the journey of the human being who is initially made 'public', given form, in the most beautiful way, and then 'Rejected' to the lowest of the low.

Ibn 'Arabi indicates that in his journey to earth and birth via the womb, the human being starts to view himself as 'only body', and forgets his truth. If he stays at that rank without making effort, if he doesn't awaken to his own self and truth, he will be heedless and ignorant and no different from a herd animal. The Qur'an describes such people as, 'they are like cattle, maybe even more heedless, or 'those dragged by their foreheads' 'the earth is a cradle for them'.

- ## The Second Journey: The Journey of Training and Seeing

Journey to the One

This is the journey of the human being who is born from a womb, takes form in the body, and becomes wise to his self and his Truth. It is his attainment of the Holistic, Whole Reason and Truth by deepening himself in the body while living; being within the body. In Ibn 'Arabi's philosophy, this can only be possible by being dependent on a 'murshid' (mentor).

Ibn 'Arabi explains for those who wish to reach their capacity and free themselves of the seductive power of earth, it is important for them to have a teacher to train them, and this is the rank of 'guardianship'. On this topic, the 'divine religions' are for teaching. The true purpose of religions is to provide 'teaching' and guidance for the human being to be able to reach his truth.

Ibn 'Arabi interprets the second journey as follows: This state of being dependent on a mentor, which is the second round of the journey, 'From Haqq to public, from public to Haqq', is the most dangerous one. On the internal journey, the human being who experiences 'ecstasy' in amazement may fall back to selfishness before training his 'self', by being captivated by the earth's seductive powers. The expression 'sharper than a sword' means this. Haqq's road is strenuous and difficult. The traveller who is in amazement and Divine Love, can become caught up in this cycle in that moment if he cannot find 'unity'; in other words if he cannot complete the circle. According to Ibn 'Arabi, 'his foot slips'. To remain in the seductive gravity of earth while in the body, and again to be lost in Haqq's beauty while in the body, are both dangerous. The one who dies while in the body must revive again in that body. Otherwise, the 'circle' will not be complete. He must complete this circle with the conception of unity with Love and Divine Love. He who dies within the body must revive again in that corpse and attain immortality, become wise. This can only be achieved by a few on Earth. On the second journey, the one who becomes lost in 'Haqq' must ensure his successful return and complete the circle.

The third journey starts for the one who can train his self while in the body, become free of selfishness, awaken from the gravitational field of Earth, reach his self and then the Whole, discover himself and his shadow, and reach his own truth. The journey from inexistence to existence will continue.

• The Third Journey: Revival

Journey of the One

The wise one who has completed his internal journey, returns from Haqq to public, wraps, covers himself with the body and under the cover of mortality, mixes with the public.

Following this journey, the wise one has become fair, just, insightful, informed of his direction, able to find his course, his route, able to see his Truth wherever he looks and has become wise with sustained peace and serenity. This is what Ibn 'Arabi interpreted as being in 'continuous salat'. He defines with great stress, 'Continuous Salat, with people in all appearances, with the Haqq in the heart'

For this reason, according to Ibn 'Arabi, it is difficult to understand the wise. Because 'one is assumed to be Enlightened if his worship is frequent' but 'True Enlightenment, is being with Haqq in the internal while being with people in appearance'. He continues his definition, 'The Enlightened person can only be understood by the enlightened person. It's difficult to describe the wise. Only the wise can understand the wise.'

The wise one is with people in appearance while being with Haqq in the internal. Being seen in the body, he has internally witnessed his truth, and is once again wrapped in the physical body to be seen in the 'physical body'. The wise one who is seen in body is together with Haqq. Being together with Haqq means he has reached and met his Truth, in other words, the reality of his real image at Haqq's rank. There is no belief system for the wise one who has attained this Truth. He is part of all the belief systems but not related to any of them.

In Ibn 'Arabi's philosophy, the verse, 'He has commanded that you worship none but Him alone.' (Qur'an / Yusuf / 40) is an important guide. It is for this reason, Ibn 'Arabi defines the wise only as 'He who worships Haqq.' Worshipping Haqq, on the other hand, means reaching one's truth and meeting one's own reality.

Anything other than his own truth is an idol, a form, transient, a deflection and directs him only towards the material, the form and the transient.

Ibn 'Arabi wanted to tell us that every event, becoming, existence in truth has been made real by the will of the Divine Will. Depending on which divine name becomes apparent in that moment, we cannot be free of wrong interpretations or 'assumptions', since we are asleep and we don't know the Truth; we concentrate only on what's happening, and we cannot be free of the dilemma of everything being a punishment or a reward. This is because it is our own beliefs, teachings, knowledge and judgments that constitute these assumptions.

Awakening is recognizing that all existence, in reality, comes into being through divine will. That moment, depending on which divine name influences us or which divine name is forming the event, may be rejected by us; seen by us as a 'curse' or 'punishment'. However, everything is under the control of divine will and happens with order, measure and balance.

Hence, if we cannot complete our journey from the apparent to the internal through internalization, we continue to see and interpret everything with our 'assumptions' and cannot be freed from our misconceptions. Ibn 'Arabi describes this as, 'those who will stay in hell eternally'.

Unable to become free of the Earth's pulling force, taking action based on assumptions underpinned by beliefs, if one is unable to wake up in the world of misconceptions created by assumptions, he will stay held up where he is and will be unable to complete the cycle.

Ibn 'Arabi uses the expression, 'Mirror-Self' – 'Human-Self', for the one who has completed the cycle. Hence, for those who reach their Truth and are awakened in the body; have become Complete, the wise become mirrors of the divine names.

Those who live in their own time are mortals, and those who abandon their time are the wise. The new age is the age of the wise men. Ibn 'Arabi pointed this out centuries ago. The new age, the age of awakening, the age called 'the age of Aquarius', is the age of the wise. The universe is a book and the biggest book is the human being. And those who read these books are the wise. Every molecule of the human being is a verse and is woven by the divine. The wise one falls into bewilderment with each reading and his journey within a journey never ends; because bewilderment never ends.

The wise one is always a 'state' in states. It is a state in which he realizes that there is no destination while he is on his journey within a journey.

The wise tells, but the human being doesn't understand, because the wise one conveys what he sees in existence at any moment with a cry of wonder. And everyone benefits from this, reads it and is flooded with joy. However, is it enough to open a road, to become a fellow traveller? Everyone opens his own road on his own, picks up the stones on that road one-by-one through his own efforts; the wise one merely sets an example. That state is personal to the wise one and is now his secret.

When in your Presence, where time almost stops flowing,

In the Moment, where space only consists of a meaning,

Who knows, how many times this moment is lived by your servants,

The things that are asked for have been listed one-by-one in the moment which time flows,

But they are forgotten in that Peace, that timelessness.

Find your own shadow in the land of shadows and know where to turn your face! The human being of soil knows what he wants, also what he wishes!

The wise one, specialist of the sky, is in his own presence anyway.

When the wise one is in his presence, he is the moment. What direction is his wish? How does he feel not to be able to wish for anything? When the tongue doesn't move, the reason doesn't work, and the heart only beats to the One. All that can be asked for loses meaning. What will be asked for other than reuniting with what is Real.

The One knows who to touch, from whom to talk, and who to talk to. Some come from beyond the far away lands and know, for some it happens with the turn of their heart between the two hands of Rahman. What about others?

Others are imitators. When the wise one who comprehends says 'I', each molecule of the universe trembles.

In 'fana', in other words, the journey of destruction, the wise one observes and witnesses Haqq's Unity and His Truth in himself and in the universes. The wise one becomes internalized inwardly to his own body. This state of destruction is an inward journey from the outside.

On the journey of Baqaa, the wise one has lifted the veils, and through attainment of his own Truth, lives the Absolute, with the occurrence of its attributes. The experts also refer to the journey of Baqaa as living with divine ethics and witnessing and observing the worlds of Baqaa. The journey of Baqaa is an outward journey from inside. It observes all attributes of the Absolute to find existence and occurrence in all molecules and gives meanings.

The Journey of Fana and the Journey of Baqaa are the 'Journey of Existence' for the wise. The secret the wise one attains from the Journey of Existence is the wisdom: 'the self is known by the self'. Once the knowledge of Haqq's existence has been reached, he will be called '*Ma'rifatullah*'. The wise knows his self from his self. In other words, he knows the Haqq's self from his own self.

In the ranks of witnessing and proximity, the completion of journeying in '*mahabbet*' means journeying in the ranks of fana.

Journeying in the ranks of finding existence with Haqq, on the other hand, means journeying in the ranks of baqaa. The wise that knows his self, his Rabb and his Truth, reaches the secret that he is Haqq and through expansion from the inside to the outside, witnesses how all formations and particles in the physical plan are created with Haqq.

The journey of existence that he witnesses is a 'manifestation'. It is a heartfelt faith. The wise one is in qutb, in his own center. From his own center, if he is in a state of wonder and heartfelt pleasure for creation, he is in a state of bewilderment and journey.

If we need to elaborate a little, the wise one, who sits at his Qutb (Center) in MOMENT time, has fused two times into one. Hence, when he sits at the center of Moment time, he is on a journey of Bewilderment with a heart full of Haqq's faith. With the drunkenness of Truth he is in the process of inexistence in the state of fana. In his internal world, his own truth and Haqq's truth have become one. At the same time, he observes all the formations of the physical worlds, he witnesses each particle being created and destroyed with the divine names and observes in bewilderment.

The journey between the states of Fana and Baqaa gives immortality to the wise one. From then on he is positioned close to Haqq.

Connoisseurs of A'raf (Inbetween)

Don't be afraid to become grand! This will not earn you vanity. Always hold the knowledge of the secret of unity and be in the service of Haqq.

'Araf', is the public version of the name '*Arif*' (wise). The expression, 'Connoisseurs of Araf' refers to the wise. The Qur'an refers to the connoisseurs of Araf as the highest rank, the honorary found between heaven and hell.

As we defined before, we talked about two times. The names that bring to existence and the names that destroy to inexistence are all Haqq's names. Humanity knows this as heaven and hell. Heaven means what brings to existence, giving beauties, and hell is what destroys and punishes. Hence, the wise are those immortals found between Existence and Inexistence.

> *If in Truth you are in love, your self body dies, you possess an immortal body with merits in which the Divine part exists.*

The immortals, *mukarrebun*, are closest to Allah. In the verses this is known as 'Mekan Aliyya'. In other words, the highest rank, the grandest place, the situation of being closest to Allah Self. The situation of being at a distance of two arches, maybe closer.

The word '*karibun*' used in the verse, 'I am closer than the jugular vein', means 'close'. In other words, the Divine Power is '*karib*' (close) to each of its creation. It is between the person and his heart. Yet, the person becomes wise only when he realizes this closeness, in other words when he is 'karib' between Haqq and the human being; he elevates to the rank of mukarrebun meaning 'closer than close' between the wise and Haqq.

The wise one who has met, known, the immortal piece, elevates to the rank 'Mekan Aliyya' and becomes a Connoisseur of Araf.

Close

Ibn Arabi sees the situation of 'Close' as a rank far from all kinds of doubt, fear, pain or worry. The one who is close is neither affected by sleep, nor hunger, neither hot nor cold. The rank of close is a complete state of peace.

According to Ibn Arabi, none of creation has ever attained this rank of closeness. Existence is recreated every moment in a new formation and goes through change and renewal. Because it is found in body, it is also in a situation to meet the needs of the body, and also has emotional delusions and attributes. The meaning of existence is to go through recreation and change in every moment. And it is impossible to come out of this creation and be in qutb.

The so mentioned rank of closeness doesn't truly mean close. Being close means being in deep peace. In all the other three ranks, the states of questioning, the questions and answers are experienced. Each created being that possesses a body, is not far from the creation that is being renewed and manifested in every moment. It will never attain true closeness while being within this creation. In the ranks of closeness, the witnessing continues. When it comes out of the state of witnessing, true closeness will be reached.

In *Futûhât al-Makkiyya*, Ibn 'Arabi gives the following example, 'Human beings know the Kaaba in Mecca, they are sure, they don't doubt its existence, yet they don't go and see it, hence this is the state of being Close through Knowledge. Later, they go in person and visit the Kaaba in Mecca, they see this place that they have no doubts about with their eyes, this is the state of being Close through Seeing. In that very moment, Haqq opens up their eye of insight and they witness the Truth of the Kaaba with the eye of their heart, they understand that it is different from all other buildings and understand that the real building is within their heart and Haqq makes them experience this state by striking their hearts like lightening, hence this is the state of being Close through Haqq.'

The true meaning of closeness, on the other hand, is to melt in Haqq itself and be seen in any body that you want, to appear in proportion to the needs and again unite with Haqq when there are none. Hence this can be resembled to a bodily beaming. It is a closeness that forms with the purpose of being beamed from the rank of Haqq at any moment one wishes and appears depending on the need of the person and goes back to its rank when the work is completed. This state of closeness is explained by Khadir (Green Man / Story of Moses / Khadir). Khadir seems like an apparition. Depending on the need of the person he can take any form he wishes, human or not, and can disappear again at will.

You are here, In the Time of Your Own Life,

I in the Time of All Lives,

And in the Moment, I travel the Universe

I come and stop right opposite you

You presume I am always there!

You may not know the Reason!

Ibn 'Arabi emphasized the understanding that says, 'until he comes close, the wise one is not secure'. The Qur'an explains coming close as follows, 'And (continue to) worship your Lord until what is certain (death) comes to you' (Qur'an / Al-Hijr / 99). In Ibn 'Arabi's philosophy this means, until you come close be dependent on Rabb, be in a belief system and walk in the command of religion.

Coming close on the other hand means to completely reach Self. The Self of the Human Being we tried to explain above is the Complete Human Being who has reached the essence and Whole. Being close is also qualified as 'Mekan Aliyya'. Hence in that rank the eye neither looks elsewhere nor confuses its route. It only sees its Truth. It has worn the dress of Truth. It moves not with the crosses or divines, or the presumptions of beliefs, but with the Reality of Truth. Hence there is no lie, confusion or surprise there, only the Light of Truth.

Being 'close' is to become wise to one's Self and Rabb.

Ibn 'Arabi examines the situation of being close as; being close through knowledge, being close through seeing, being close through Haqq.

• Reaching the Truth through Knowledge

The wise knows the One like seeing

I Know what I am doing, also what I will be doing…

Being lost is only coming back to the Body by leaving the One for one MOMENT.

Isn't our return again to the One?

It is the state of knowing all that is happening, being aware with knowledge, awakening and enlightenment. It is a state of 'Know'ing. The human being is aware of everything, knows what is what, knows the purpose. Yet he doesn't experience, feel or see.

• Reaching the Truth through Seeing

I Knew the One while He was watching the Earth through My eyes.

This is living the Truth by feeling. It is seeing and witnessing.

There are connoisseurs of rank and there are connoisseurs of witnessing.

One lives the ecstasy of each rank, and to some permission is given to witness each rank. To the connoisseur of witnessing, authority is given to see and understand each rank. Amongst the connoisseurs of witnessing, some witness, others translate and transfer. He tastes the 'ecstasy' of that rank yet he doesn't live it.

- **Reaching the Truth with Haqq**

Come closer! Come even closer!

This is a state of realization, conception, seeing from Haqq's eye, being Haqq's walking hands and feet on earth. Knowing Haqq through Haqq is the state of seeing all the universes from Haqq's eye, to understand, know and experience them in person. It is the highest rank. It is also called the rank of 'Mekan Aliyya'. It is the state of the immortals, the *karibun* ones, being mukarribe, closest, being the distance of two bows and even closer.

He is immortal. He lives beyond the states of knowing through knowledge, seeing with ayn. He enables realization. He possesses, commands, he is owner and he is loyal. From then on, he is neither with body nor without. He is covered in body but in fact he doesn't have a shape or material body. He joins, contributes to existence and inexistence as he wishes. He knows before time and infinity, he knows the purpose of things and he lives. The best example for this is the 'immortal' Khadir who doesn't have a material body but has the power to manifest in all material things and bodies.

Are many diverse lords more reasonable and better (to attribute creation to and believe in and obey), or God, the One, the All-Overwhelming (holding absolute sway over all that exists)? **Qur'an / Yusuf / 39**

Ibn 'Arabi said, 'The wise ones' faith is for the Rabb of the Rabbs. One who reaches Rabb, reaches the Rabb of Rabbs and from there reaches Allah, and only worships Allah'.

The wise one who reaches the state of 'Close' as a result of conception through knowledge, conception through witnessing, opinion, and finally conception through Haqq frees himself of the 'two times', the presumptions of hope and fear, the duality, and is united with the Whole. This is the 'the right way' indicated by the sacred verses. This is the state of awakening, enlightenment in esoteric knowledge. This is the state of 'reaching the Truth' in Sufism. The 'Righteous eye, Righteous ear, Righteous language' has manifested.

When the wise one who passes through all the phases, reaches the state of closeness through Knowledge, Seeing and being with Haqq, and on reaching the highest rank in terms of place, says 'HU' that is 'Breath of Rahman', 'the One Himself' appears in the moment. All the 'enlightened' ones that have expressed this have been assassinated.

When the wise that has reached the rank of Being Close to Haqq says 'Hu', he descends the breath of divinity on Earth as 'the One itself' in person.

As soon as the wise one who has passed all ranks, has reached the Truth and been revived again in his body comes close, he is elevated to the highest rank and in one breath the One itself finds a symbol with the attribute of creativity, shines on earth, and all his divine light flows to the Earth. The One only creates this through the breath of a wise one who has been elevated to the rank of closeness. Hence, this is the real rank of Adam, the rank of the Complete Human Being, the rank of the Grand Human Being.

The breath of the wise one is the appearance of the warm air of the secret world into the open and the return of the cold air of the open back to the warm air in the secret world. This is what founds the understanding of the ancestors' saying, 'The world turns for the sake of the enlightened'. The breath of the wise feeds the world, it transfers the warm, prosperous breath of the One to the world, retakes it and transforms in the secret world. The air that is transformed in the secret world and kneaded with prosperity again emerges from the secret world out into the open with the breath of the wise.

In Turkish 'Hu' means 'That person'. In Ibn 'Arabi's philosophy, 'Hu' means 'Self' meaning 'Essence'. It is That (the One) person who is referred to as 'I am' in the sacred verses.

Muhyiddin Ibn 'Arabi used this expression. 'By saying Hu, the wise didn't transfer the true meaning of this. Because this was necessary.'

While we are on this topic, let's specify a subject that Ibn 'Arabi stresses with importance and points to in his works. 'When the Divine Light, Haqq, comes to the spiritual heart of the human being and cannot find a faith beyond beliefs there, and comes across positive thought and humanistic thought, it transforms into an angelic shape and flies that person until 'Sidre', known as the world of *melekut* (the Realm of Angels) and leaves him there. In other words, angels cannot reach beyond the world of illustrations or the after world, its cycle is left half and it is not allowed to go beyond.'

'When the divine light, Haqq, comes to the spiritual heart of the human being and finds evil, commands, judgments and negative thoughts there, it is seen in the form of fire, takes shape as a black bird, and flies only to the level of the 'Moon' and stays there forever (until the day of apocalypse when mass awakening will be realized)'

When the divine light comes to the heart of the human being, it takes shape according whatever it finds there; to that belief, that conviction, those gods and idols.

When the Divine Light comes to the spiritual heart of the wise, who 'has reached his Truth and knows his Rabb, has reached Rabb of his Rabb, has reached a faith beyond Beliefs, it finds 'itself' there.' Because the wise one has become a mirror to his own Truth in that moment, has filled up his spiritual heart with Haqq's divine light. When the divine light comes to the spiritual heart of the wise and finds 'itself' there, it carries the wise one from below the level of the Moon which is hell, to beyond the world of illustrations, the world of melekut (Realm of Angels), to the after world, spatyom. Hence, the state of coming 'Close' is this. Every human being can only come as close as the distance of three arches but the wise one comes closer to the distance of two arches. For this reason, the heart of the wise is wide; it has been expanded. It fits the worlds, the universes in it, and holds only 'Truth' and nothing else.

Here, Ibn 'Arabi also gives away a very important secret: 'Haqq made itself Public.' This means 'Essence created itself, pointed to itself, indicated and generated itself in the physical plan.'

If we were to give a very simple example, a human being needs a mirror, a reflection to see himself. In order to hear his own voice, he needs matter for the sound to bounce off when he calls. Hence, Essence also needs the wise one who will be a mirror for it to see Itself. If he has reached his Truth through his own effort, if he has filled his heart and spiritual heart with Haqq and transformed it into a clear mirror, if 'Haqq sees Itself when it comes to that spiritual heart' then Ibn 'Arabi says, 'Haqq created itself in the spiritual heart of the wise' about this. This is known as the Complete Human Being.

Yet, in Ibn 'Arabi's philosophy, 'When Haqq comes to the spiritual heart of the human being and finds a god there based on the belief of that human being, a presumption, it takes form accordingly and does not go beyond that.' Because when Haqq comes to the spiritual heart, it will find a presumption, a god related to a belief as a result of one divine name's reflection. Hence that god will not like, will condescend the presumption formed in another person that is formed by another divine name.

The hundreds and thousands of beauties being reflected, are in fact none other than one truth's different and various manifestations. Hence, the mortal either likes or dislikes each reflection, believes or doesn't believe, sees it as beautiful or as ugly. Yet the wise one doesn't look at the variety or differences reflected in the mirrors but looks beyond them to the Truth that is real. He reaches the reality beyond the thousands of varieties. The mortal, on the other hand, generates 'presumptions' from the dualities reflected in the mirrors.

The wise notices one single white light, yet the mortal sees millions of colors separated in the crystal, he likes or dislikes and cannot be free of the world of duality with its presumptions.

Ibn 'Arabi stresses that, 'One who doesn't taste doesn't know this'. This is a divine wine, the one who doesn't drink does not know. This is a Mansur wine, Kevser wine, the one who doesn't drink doesn't know. This is a Truth candy, the one who doesn't taste doesn't know. Hence, for the human being who is the 'Taster of death', when he 'tastes' he becomes wise. Death is tasted. The one who dies in his body, meaning the one who tastes the Mansur, Kevser Wine, becomes immortal. The immortal person knows his Truth, Sees his Truth and becomes Truth.

I appeared to everyone in their own belief

Yet! Only to the wise, I appeared in my Truth.

VII

The Journey of Awakening To Wisdom

'The ending of the wise is to the Rabb of their Rabbs. The ones who become wise to the Rabb-ul erbab, worship Allah.'
Futûhât al-Makkiyya / Muhyiddin Ibn 'Arabi

Information, possessing information, and wisdom all have different meanings. Information is acquired through *marifaat*. The result obtained through research, chasing evidence, thinking and asking questions, is information. Information is not the truth yet it is closest to the truth. No information can be the truth. Because the truth is a result of each person's interpretations based on his existing presumptions. All interpretations a person attains on the way to reach his own truth are information, yet not the truth itself.

To possess knowledge is to reach the belief of the attained information, to adopt that information and to practice it in life. The person that feels its truthfulness and accepts it as a reality, starts to use that information in his life and sees the results of its practices. Where does this information take him, what will it help him gain, all this will constitute that person's life experience.

Possessing knowledge does not mean being equipped with certain and clear information. As we said, since knowledge is relative, the knowledge attained and used may lose its validity after a period of time. The different information attained according to need, in each stage of maturity, is called realities in metaphysics. The people who are open to change and who do not resist change also change their interpretation of the information as reality changes. Because their conception and understanding also changes.

The wise one on the other hand, attains information through maarifat, is open to change and goes through the periods of maturity; he knows what the information will help him gain and lose and he is sure. The wise person owns wisdom. Wisdom is to give command. In other words, the wise ones owning wisdom also have the authority to command, to decide.

Wisdom comes to the human being from Essence. The wise one is the person who owns the information coded in the soul and who controls it. Those who make decisions without understanding the consequences are those who possess information. The wise, on the other hand, are those who know and command the reason and consequence, the before and after of what they do.

Ibn 'Arabi explains this as follows, 'The commanders who are knowledgeable, possessing knowledge, are from letter Lam. The possessors of wisdom who are wise, meaning wise people, are from letter Ba'.

Possessing information is to know what one is doing yet not being certain of its consequences. It is not commanding your past or future. The ones who can control are only the wise who possess wisdom.

The command of one without wisdom is not valid. The command of one who could not attain wisdom is not valid because he doesn't know what the law of cause-effect will bring himself and, since he doesn't know it, he is not in command. The one who doesn't know the secret and the apparent, only knows information, possesses information. The wise one, on the other hand, is wise in control, he is in full command of the law of cause and effect, knowing the causes and consequences of one particle movement, in command of the secret and the apparent.

For this reason, the ones who reach information, possess information are from letter 'Lam'. They are on a journey on a road like the letter Lam. They witness, observe. There is no stopping for them, they will continue on their journey forever, until they reach their truth. Because they have not yet realised the secret of the dot.

The wise on the other hand are from letter Ba, because the wise have come to know the secret of the dot. The letter Ba has a meaning and conception that brings the secret and the apparent together. It is the letter for the rank of Haqq that is the rank of Divine Love. Ba is in the horizontal, the earth world, the physical universe. The dot below, on the other hand, is the dot of the letter Alif that is the symbol of Allah. The Secret and the Apparent are together, past time and infinity are together. For this reason, the wise are from the letter Ba.

Ibn 'Arabi says that, in their journey to their Truth, no one can describe the states that they go through or conclude a diagnosis for this. Because the wise is the only one who lives this journey of Truth, yet he cannot explain it.

The ones with conviction are not even aware of the states that they are experiencing, they cannot explain these but only live them. The ones with belief, trust the divine order and system for remuneration in all the states they experience. Because, in the afterlife they will receive the equivalent of all the worship they have performed. The person has attained the information yet he has interpreted this information according to his own assumptions. His Rabb will take him into his heaven according to his own interpretation, own conviction and belief in his mind. He trusts his Rabb in line with his belief.

The only objective of those who have a more conscious approach to belief, and reach certain understandings by conceiving outside of their beliefs, in other words, the owners of knowledge, is to know themselves by knowing their Rabb and by being closest to Haqq. Hence, all the states he lives on this journey of Divine Love will result in him seeing the ranks and experiencing the state of pleasure.

There are a series of practices that are performed on the road of initiation, awakening. The human being goes through a series of exercises that advance from a basic level proceeding to the subtle levels: fasting, zikr (invocation), mindfulness, and the development of parapsychological skills, etc. For thousands of years, the words of the prophets, masters, and murshids were spread from mouth to mouth, memorized and continuously repeated. Yet, as none of them could be conceived with their true and equivalent value, it was not possible to journey via the route they went. Because, certain rules, conditions, and the gradual process made the ones on the road of ascent very anxious, and resulted in their regression by giving up due to various reasons.

Those who chose the road of Haqq, the wise who reached their own Truth, chose this road through their own will and were trained. They too had teachers and masters. Any person can reach his own Truth by training on this path, by wishing and following certain rules.

However, there is a point not to be forgotten. Those enlightened souls who are referred to in the holy verses with importance as, 'Those given wisdom from our level, those given power from our level, those whom we elevate their space, those who are from our 'salah' servants.' are different from those humankind who wish to 'Reach Haqq'. How are they different?

In relation to this, Ibn 'Arabi says: 'Those Seen in Body, Those Are in Body'.

The expression, 'Seen in Body', refers to those who are born with Infinity; those who are born from their own sources with a duty. Those who are only seen in body and seen in the form of a mortal on Earth, who present a living example to the human being of Earth, the mortal. They eat, drink, breathe, live and die like humankind. The essence they presented and conveyed was the knowledge of Haqq and the wisdom of their own infinity. Ibn 'Arabi was a wise man such as this. He was known as 'the wise of the wise' and conveyed his infinite essence and was seen in body like us.

Their journey within a journey wasn't like the journey of a mortal. It was being born with this duty to show us how it will be.

This has been communicated to humankind with the words, 'Some of you were destined to be superior to the rest of you'. In Truth, everyone is equal, but in the physical worlds, there will be dilemmas such as superiority, humanity, ignorance, wisdom, ascent, descent. These polarities in the physical worlds do not change the Truth.

The humankind of Earth are people of soil. However, the wise are the 'experts of the sky'. The wise who is the expert of the sky comes from the breath of Rahman. Even though outwardly their lives seem to be full of pain and agony, they exist within their own inner peacefulness. Their peace is the peace of Haqq.

The wise, having reached their own truth, set an example to those who wish to awaken. When the pupil is ready, the teacher appears. This is referred to as, 'the second of the couple', in the holy verses. There are many examples of these partnerships in the world. The partnership of Rumi and Shams of Tabriz is one of the most important examples.

They have become the grandest symbols of Affection and Divine Love. They are the two of the couple. However, the third is always a secret. The third is Haqq. 'Let three of you be ONE and ONE of you be secret!' Divine love lives in three, the two are known and one becomes secret.

'And He is with you, whever you may be. And God sees well all that you do.' **Qur'an / Al-Hadid / 4**

In this pair, the second, the one who is overlooked, is left in shadow. However, the one who is left in shadow, the one that feeds from the spiritual, always feeds the one in the 'open' and is seen in the front. The wise are never on their own. They are always a 'couple' in Love. A master and a student always exist. No one can reach the secret by himself. The wise one cannot reach his own Truth without the master.

The wise, have not only teachers who live in the world with a body, but they also have fellow travellers without bodies. The fellow travellers without bodies are previously enlightened souls who left the world, but continue to stay alive in the infinite. In order to train the wise, they open their way by preparing dreams, intuitions, mystic meanings and scenes and help them reach their Truth.

Most wise ones do not know they are wise. In Anatolian society, 'the wise one doesn't know his wisdom' is a common expression. Only the wise ones who know themselves, know the wise who don't know their wisdom and they train them. They either talk to their soul in their secret spiritual world, or, they meet in a place in the world. Because, the wise that speak without knowing, are in danger. Those who speak with knowing, convey their words in symbols and take their bodies under protection by glazing their bodies. Those who don't know if they are wise, or who denounce their wisdom, may have negative experiences. Jesus said, 'Do not throw pearls to the pigs'.

The pig is the symbol of the 'human being with animal vibrations, meaning the mortal who has been caught up by the seduction of the mud, could not free himself from matter.' The mutual intuition of all prophets, wise people and saints was, 'Don't be afraid' Yet, Do Not Trust.' Rumi said, 'Talk to the people in a language they understand.' 'You will not say more to the people. You will keep quiet!' In *Futûhât al-Makkiyya*, Ibn 'Arabi said, 'Hide your wisdom otherwise they will destroy you!' Mansur Al Hallaj, who revealed his secret and who had not glazed and protected his body, was assassinated on the road to Divine Love. Mansur Al Hallaj, who would not give up on his confession or on divine love whatever the cost, who became the symbol of Dar-ı Mansur, Haqq's true friend, is highly respected in the internal world. The breaking and burning of his body was with the permission of Haqq, the Owner or Divine Love and Time. Otherwise, would Haqq really allow a 'Lover' to be assassinated? With just one breath He would destroy those who attempted this.

Surely, such a death does not destroy the wise; they are immortal, they came from infinite life and they beamed back to infinity.

The wise are '*Honaz*'. They are remittance coming from Haqq. They are the hands and feet of the divine system; they are the experts of the skies and managers of the earth. On Earth they wear flesh and bone, and appear as human beings, they leave Rahman's breath on the Earth and continue on their journey within journeys.

> *My Honaz, Fly in the skies of DIVINE LOVE. You were not created to descend from those skies. It is not important how many people know you. What is important is, not how many people, but how many worlds You hosted in your spiritual heart? Your soul is expanding and landing on the hearts of lovers through light and the spark of your smile. Fly and Fly! And when you descend from your Mercy on Earth, you are uplifted by your descent. You are made existent for the supreme ones. You are 'Honaz' and this suits you.*

The wise have not moved away from the seduction of the world, masiva, they were already far from it. The wise were not bound by certain rules such as fasting, zikr or mindfulness, because they were in a state of continuous fasting and mantra. They didn't perform this as an obligation, they did this through knowing and wishing. They had no thought other than reaching the Truth. For this reason, they were the leading guides for the conditions such as continuous fasting, zikr, mindfulness and seclusion. They didn't implement what was existent they created what was inexistent. They were the openers of roads. They were the constructors of roads. They were the ones showing what must happen, the conditions, in short, the main conditions of awakening, initiation. The wise were the most important examples for the earthly mortals to guide them to the road to Truth.

As we can see from the outside, the life of the wise ones has been full of suffering, difficulty, and poverty. Yet the wise are not aware of this suffering because they are full of Haqq, Peace. Yet, when observed from outside, they are thought to live with heavy burdens. The wise know with which divine name the world matter is created and because they have reached the truth of that divine name, for them suffering is a blessing and a mercy but for human beings it is pain and torture.

To keep quiet, is to hear Rabb systems touching the ear with one cry. To keep quiet is not a command for the wise. When he knows what he is, when he reaches his Truth, there is no one left to tell him to 'be quiet'. He will be Haqq's Looking eye, Speaking Mouth, Holding Hand, Walking Foot, Rahman's breath and a private of the Divine System. The soul of the wise one is always full of joy and divine love. His body is a destination for this. His reason directs him, until he has become one and melts into the Divine Holistic Reason.

When the wise one becomes enthused, the earth and skies shake, all universes vibrate from his grandness. Yet, as per the rules, the wise's quietness is from his manners. And his manners are a result of his Divine Love. When the wise one flows drop-by-drop from his essence he reaches his body, and from there the earth and universes. When his feet touch the ground, his head touches the highest point of the sky. His feet are above the head level of humanity most of the time. He dived in fana, became drunk, disappeared and melted. Yet everyone thinks of him as normal mortal. Because in appearance his feet are stepping on the ground. The wise one knows that the ones who will suffer the pain of the world are those who could not reach the secret of the world. When he comes to know the secret, he lives a state of pleasure that is like a state beyond pain.

Stillness

God reaches all Lovers in Deep Stillness, touches in Love and Nothingness. Only the wise understand the touches, they are the Quiet Ones of Merit.

In Ibn 'Arabi's teaching, 'Deep stillness, is a rank'. The state of being quiet is in two parts. There is an expression among the public that says, 'The common's prayer is with the tongue, the wises' is with the heart.'

In order to understand what being quiet is, it is necessary to know what talking is. Talking is an important tool of communication in order to explain your problems in daily language, to communicate and to convey your state. If we look deeper, there are two types of talking: the talking of the tongue and the talking of the heart. The tongue says one thing while the heart says another. This creates some selves, labels and identities in the human being. The mortal human being that says something with the mouth and something else with the heart can never make the two communication tools 'one'. For this reason, he cannot go from one lie to another in the world of lies. He says nice things with his tongue yet in his heart he thinks of negative things. He says negative things with his tongue yet his heart is after good things. Because he cannot make these two worlds one, he participates in lies and remains stuck in between. Hence, reason must come in and balance the two communication tools. Because, the tongue is an organ that you use to tell about yourself to what is 'open', to the world, to human beings. The heart, on the other hand, is the communication tool connected to the 'secret', your inner world and the divine system that is closest to you. It is difficult to explain your self and be accepted using your tongue but with your heart this is much easier. It is a must to bring these two communication tools together and reconcile them. One is given whatever is in his heart.

During the process of awakening, the human being must unite his tongue and heart 'and must free himself from duality. It is not possible to believe that the speaking tongue, and every word that comes out of the mouth, contains a bit of truth, because you can never hear what the human being speaks from his heart. Hence, what his self is whispering to him and the speaking that happens in the secret world is only known by that person's managing Rabb system. And in truth, that person's destiny is shaped by the whisperings of his heart. And he starts to believe, makes his heart believe, what he says with his mouth. Reason will be insufficient here. From then on, the person will create his own world through the lies he has told.

In esoteric knowledge, this is alluded to in the saying, 'even the evil you created was intentional'. Whatever the human being is, he must be that, he must express himself so that he starts to know himself from his obvious state and actions. In order for him to do this, stillness is required. When he is quiet, everything that he says with his tongue and everything that dupes his reason will suddenly stop. In that moment, he can hear what his heart is saying, and he can attain some information about what his self is. As long as the tongue talks, it conceals the voice of the heart. The human being either speaks in line with his heart, or in order to silence the talk of his heart. Stillness is a must to balance this. To be able to speak and wish the truth, one must not speak or wish what is wrong.

For the one that has entered the journey of awakening, being silent is being in command. Either way, one should not comment on any person or event, either with the tongue or the heart. This is the first state of being silent. The first thing one must do if one becomes a candidate for enlightenment is to be silent. If he can achieve command of his tongue and heart, he will be able to realize some truths. First he must become aware that the one who talks is his selves. Before he is free of all identities, Haqq will not appear to him. Only the human being who can take command of his tongue and heart by staying silent can observe the states that he lives in. And he has take small steps on the road of what his self is or what he is not.

Silence is a mandatory state of keeping silent. Because if he wants to know himself, he must first remove from his vocabulary the words that express emotions such as misgivings, vanity, anger, joy, animosity, hatred and happiness. Afterwards, he must slowly eliminate all thoughts attributed to these emotions that passed through to his heart. In order to do this, first he must be able to observe them. He must follow all these emotions and thoughts that do not belong to himself. Hence, in these moments, he will be silent by default. His reason and mind are directed to know himself. He will be together and close with the external world, yet he will start to be within a world in his own internal world. In order for him to light the flame of his spiritual heart, he will go back to his cave, in the darkness of self, he will become free of all the misgivings of the tongue and the heart, and will be in a state of journeying.

For the wise one who has attained his Truth, the period of stillness is not an obligation. It is beyond an obligation, it is a knowing and a conception. The wise one doesn't need to try to be silent, he remains silent anyway. What will he interpret when he sees a dream or the world of shadows? Even if everything he interprets is the 'truth', it will not be anything more than a 'lie' for those mortals who cannot reach beyond their presumptions and mental interpretations. Even if the wise one calls out from the highest rank, the human being on Earth does not understand. Despite this, the wise one doesn't remain silent; he doesn't say, 'let me not speak in vain' because I will not be understood. He remains silent anyway. His silence is not due to an obligation or fear. He remains silent due to bewilderment, respect and surprise. Because, as he observes the constant recreation; the universes that are in a new formation and a new creation in every MOMENT of time, he cannot hide his bewilderment. He becomes silent as he watches, he watches as he becomes silent. He becomes silent as he observes this structure that is not Truth, is made of shadows and dreams, and the universe that is recreated in every moment. He is not able to describe all the states he experiences at the rank of Haqq because his words are not sufficient to describe Haqq. The wise is not a 'stationary' human being, but an expert of 'state'.

What the wise one lives can only be expressed in 'joyful' words that 'have the power and strength to transform a universe into a particle from which the space between the atoms have been removed'. He adorns his words with symbols, glazes his body, covers and hides it.

There is no time period or destination assigned for awakening. Whatever there is, exists in the present time. The choice belongs to the human being. Will he become a human being of soil on the horizontal? Will he become an expert of the sky in the vertical? Will he be able to stay on the horizontal as an immortal of soil, and reach the infinity of the 'dot' placed under the mattress, and be able to travel to the vertical from that point? In short, will he be able to wake up? The choice belongs to the person. He is in the now. He is either now or nothing until infinity. Hence people will either choose to be infinite Truth experts or to live on earth infinitely.

The wise one is not in a state of stillness in its absolute meaning. Ibn 'Arabi says, 'The wise are not experts of stillness'. Because he experiences different states in various ranks, he conveys the state that he lives at each rank. And what the wise ones say may not be consistent with each other. Ibn 'Arabi emphasizes that this is a temporary state. The inconsistency is not due to 'madness or drunkenness' it is due to the differences between the ranks. For this reason, the first thing all the wise are blamed for is their 'Appearance', meaning their interpretation in the state they appear. Many wise people such as Ibn 'Arabi, Mansur Al Hallaj, Rumi, Haji Bektash Veli and Imadaddin Nasimi were interpreted according to the first states they expressed. Yet, the joyful words that they say at each rank are an expression of the excitement and bewilderment that the rank gives them. Yet, the mortals' reason doesn't understand this. For this reason, Ibn 'Arabi emphasizes that the wise one must glaze, cover and protect his body. To do this, he must live in a state of non-obligatory stillness so that this stillness is not an absolute stillness. For the wise one who passes all ranks, matures due to the states he experiences, reaches his own Truth, melts in the rank of Haqq and makes himself 'One', there is no more a worldly life as we know it. The true worldly life that he constructed in his spiritual heart will begin. He will call out from his True world in his spiritual heart, to the world of soil, and joyful, inspirational words will start to fall from his lips.

Halvet (Solitude)

The secrets reach their owners in the nearness found in solitude. In that moment, the doors open one by one in stillness.

One of the obligatory states that a human being, mortal, must live on the road to awakening is refuge in solitude, to be in solitude, to divorce the world of matter (that is called masiva) and to know one's 'self'. In the initiation works of esoteric practice, 'solitude' is one of the main conditions.

The wise one, on the other hand, is not obliged to take refuge in solitude, because he feels the journey of solitude towards solitude in his heart. The wise one's state of being near is his having reached the rank of belief as if seeing God. This is the rank of '*mutekad*' and it is a rank of surrender beyond beliefs.

Everything that is taught takes up a space in the mind and generates a form. These forms, that are generated over time, are fed by the human mind. They grow as they are fed and they each turn into a living thought form in the dream world. Teachings and belief systems are built on 'punishment and reward' systems. The accounting system of one less, one more and the rewards that you will get in the end, confuses and stirs up the mind. The mind creates an even deeper dream world within a dream world 'for a you' that is found in the dream world. And, from then on, you drown in the dreams of those dreams.

Hence, the first condition of awakening is to be free from this duality. More truly, to exit that whirlpool of dreams is to free oneself of all kinds of taught shapes, thoughts and forms. For this the 'deep stillness' state, that is the first road, is lived and after this phase, one withdraws to solitude. This is a journey towards one's own inner world. It is a deep and internal journey that is travelled to the solitude of solitude. It is a journey of states from day to night, from light to night, from open to secret. One must remove the kinds of dangers that may weigh him down or hold him up on his journey.

Most people cannot reach the rank of the wise because they stay at the level of reason and thought. Their beliefs and teachings obstruct them. In order for them to become wise, they first have to dissociate themselves from those beliefs and teachings, and on their return they will give those beliefs and teachings the respect they deserve. To be able to do this, they must surrender and strip off all labels, with complete nakedness, to reach the spiritual heart.

The knowledge that the wise one reaches, the understanding and conception during his inner journey and his journey towards the solitude of solitude, towards endless darkness, is this: 'The human being is His secret, and The One is the human being's secret.' There is a range between the human being and Haqq, this is a distance of two arches or even less. Hence the one who reaches that distance, the one who reaches the Truth of that distance is the wise one. There lies the answer of the question, 'Who owns the Estate in the Moment?' And the wise one is the person who reached the answer of these questions. The entire universe is in fact composed of a dream, a breath. The wise ones are those who can see this with the eye of the spiritual heart. The one who found the answer to, 'Who Owns the Estate in the Moment?', is the wise one. The wise one who is in deep stillness is the one who has reached the conception of 'In the Moment the Estate is only and only mine. 'In the Moment the Estate is MINE'

Fasting

The one who cannot bring his satan to its knees, doesn't have any knowledge.

The human being is asleep to an amount that is equal with his satisfaction with himself. And in order to awaken, he must become aware of his self-satisfaction. Lets elaborate on the meaning of hunger and little sleep while we are explaining about the levels passed on the journey to awakening.

The objective of fasting is to learn to command the body with hunger, to reverse the body's management of the mind, and to set an objective for the mind and reason to manage the body. All bodily and mental 'desires' must be taken in One Hand. Because, when the stomach is full and all the wishes of the body are met, the self will ask for more and the body will come out of the state that it is supposed to be in and will start carrying animal vibrations. The body is more than something that merely eats, drinks and feels satisfied: it is a vessel for the soul. Its main objective is this. The mind and body must work together in coordination. 'Fasting' is an important practice to command all emotions, thoughts and desires.

Hunger, is an obligatory need, for the mortals who are on the road of awakening. The human being eats excessively in two ways; either the mind is not aware of what he eats and he eats a lot, or in order to suppress his never satisfied hunger he puts whatever he sees into its mouth. Either way, there is a mental confusion. The times that we eat the most, our mind is either busy with a problem or our mind is very hungry and in order to fill it we fill our stomach.

The one who is earth eats earth. And he will not be full until he is full of earth, up to his mouth. Nobody says, 'I will remain hungry' in order to attain some divine secrets. Even if he says so, the hunger doesn't take the human being even one step further. The mortal who enters the road of awakening, must try to know his self by staying hungry. In esoteric initiations one of the conditions necessary for awakening is staying 'hungry'. One is in command of himself in an amount equal to his stomach's emptiness. One will be chasing dreams in the amount equal to his stomach's fullness. Hunger also has a limit. Staying hungry extensively will also lead to some hallucinations and unnecessary dreams. For this reason, one meal a day is sufficient for the one who enters the road of awakening. Satiety brings negligence and procrastination to the human being. The satiated human will also become addicted to sleep. The best example of the sleeping human being is his addiction to sleep and food. The person who cannot yet control himself doesn't know how to become full and, in order to fill his brain, he loads his stomach. As he loads his stomach, he is pulled down from his ankles and sinks even deeper into the material mud, called the world.

Yet, for the wise one this is a little different. The wise one never feels obliged to remain hungry. When he is already cheek by jowl with the secret, he doesn't even feel his body's hunger. Because, he is feeding on the treasures of the secret world, his body is always live and vigorous. His meal is 'time' his food is 'state'. In those states he doesn't fill his stomach but his soul. The satisfied soul will undoubtedly withdraw itself from food. In short, the wise one is already continuously fasting and hungry. He doesn't see this as an obligation.

Being awake and zikr (mantra)

When you Know Your Self, a Divine Light emerges in your spiritual heart. That moment your Truth knows you.

The mind must be as awake as the eye. Hence, with these two awakenings, the heart also stays awake and solutions are sought to reach the spiritual heart. For the mortal to awaken, a lack of sleep is important and obligatory. If the stomach is empty, surely it becomes easier to stay awake. If he can control his hunger, the mortal on the road to awakening can stay awake. It is necessary to be sleepless at night to deepen the spiritual journey.

Fasting, being awake and zikr must, in fact, be performed as a whole. The one who withdraws to 'solitude' in a dark and quiet place far from people, must also withdraw from his own solitude. In the solitude of solitude, while fasting, he dives into a deep stillness, and while awake cites the 'word' that is most suitable for himself. The state of zikr (mantra) is not an unconscious repetition. The objective is to create resonance both with the tongue and from the heart by becoming one with the 'word'.

The human being is a high letter himself, and is found upon a letter in the world. The repetition of the letter, the word, that is most suitable for his nature, will trigger in him some spiritual mechanisms that break the karmic sludge that comes from his previous astral life. The word can come to the student through a spiritual feeling or via channels of dreams, or can be personally given by his teacher after careful selection. What is most important as expressed in the words, 'there are my servants who found me, seek for the means that help to reach me', is the student's going through the entrancement and trans states under the supervision of a teacher. When the teacher understands that the student can continue by himself, he leaves the student to his own road.

This state, that is called ecstasy or a trance, enables the person to communicate with his spiritual plans, his own higher self, and what Ibn 'Arabi describes with importance as his True Image in Haqq's spiritual heart. The state of trance is a state that is between sleeping and waking and it is a completely 'conscious' state. It is a high-ranking situation that enables one to live a MOMENT in a state and a state in a Moment.

When in a trance, it is important to control the inhalation and exhalation of the breath. Opening some of the body's energy centres to spiritual energies can be dangerous. In order to keep negative energies at bay, the person must protect himself. On his journey, he can come across some 'lost souls' and negative energies that have been defeated by their selfhood. The teacher should instruct the person in what he has to do to protect himself. Special prayers of protection and some meditations, such as taking oneself into a circle of light, are also helpful.

To remain awake is a natural state, rather than an obligation, for the wise one. He knows that the Supreme never sleeps. The One always manages and watches the Universes. His interest and Mercy continuously work, His commands reach each particle in the Moment. The One who is always alive Sees and Hears every Moment. The meaning of awakened for the wise is this.

From form to self

Every human being is in close communication without exception. The Rabb of the Universes is in contact with each of creation. He builds this connection behind a curtain. This is called *berzah*. There is a curve or arch that is the space drawn by the created being, there is also the arc of the Rabb system. In between these two arches is the Kevser river that feeds all creation, that flows between the curtain, berzah. In the sacred verses, the place that is sworn in place of the stars is the border of these two arches. Kevser is one of the best blessings given to the human being. It is flow, a grant, a mercy from Rahman to Rahim. The meaning of kevser, given to the last prophet is this. Prophet Mohammed was the only one who realized *miraj* and returned before his bed became cold. Kevser is a river that flows between the other world and the physical world and feeds both worlds. Kevser is Haqq's mercy to its own names that He made one and that emerge in appearance. Haqq does not show mercy on human beings, Haqq shows mercy to the human beings in whom each of its names appear and who are created with each of its names.

Haqq manifests all its divine names and attributes that it has United as One in its Essence, in its Inexistence, as plurality in Existence, and enacts creation upon beings. All beings are brought into existence with the divine names that create and spread in the universes as plurality. They become inexistent with the names that destroy and return to Haqq's origin and become One.

All creation is unconsciously in a state of service to this. Only the wise are the ones who provide conscious contribution. The wise are those who consciously see and know the 'state' that emerges in himself with each name. And he is the only complete human being who sees the plurality of all the divine names and attributes, who reaches and conceives the Unity of these in Truth. The wise is the one who does not change with the changing, the only complete being who conceives what stays the same. What doesn't change with the changing is Haqq that is one. The wise have reached Haqq. Since they have reached Haqq, they are at the rank of the wise, the mortal who could not reach Haqq, is being created in every moment.

The journey of reaching and attaining is the journey from form to self. The purpose is to reach the Truth of Form while living with a body. The wise one is the one who knows there is nothing to reach or attain; because, the wise one has sat at the qutb, the center of time, in the Moment, and is in a state of observing creation. Yet, for other people, creation continues all the time. Hence, for the form to reach his truth he must follow and reach the truth of various routes separately by deepening himself in them.

Ibn 'Arabi describes these routes as *shariat*, *tariqat*, *marifaat* and truth.

There is One Door to the One, which all doors open to. Yet, for experts of the states there are so many doors. Each door is the end of the road one is travelling on, and the beginning of another road. The door is both the end and the beginning. There is not one door, there are thousands of doors. The meaning of door in Sufism is the realities of esoteric knowledge. Each reality has a truth. When the truth of that reality is reached, another reality's door is opened. And the realities vary for every human being. For this reason, a truth reached in one's reality, may not have meaning for another human being. Every human being lives a 'state' in these realities. The traveller who embarks on the journey lives 'states' and the truth he reaches will be closest to the truth but will not be truth itself, it varies according to the essence of each human being. Each human being is in Truth one, but shows variation and difference in creation, and is subject to recreation that changes in moment time. For this reason, the 'state' that one human being lives may not have meaning for another human being. Not every human being can describe the 'states' he lives. What he describes, is in fact not what he lives, but only what he names. Because he cannot describe the state he lives in, and even if he describes it, it will not mean anything to another. All the realities the human being reaches remain a 'secret' unique to that human being. There are as many realities as the breaths of human beings. The human being lives a state in each breath and reaches a reality. Yet, even thousands of realities do not constitute one Truth. He is closest to Truth, yet he is not truth itself. Even if he reaches the truth, even thousands of truths do not constitute a Truth of Truth, he is closest, yet there is always an invisible border, curtain between them.

Between all creations there are curtains. These curtains are very important to protect life. Also in the quantum universe, as discovered by scientists, no subatomic particle colludes with or touches another. There is always an invisible space, a curtain between them. In the universe, no particle joins with another particle or touches another. No human being can touch another, there is always a space between them. This space is filled with the Love of Creation. This love is a fabric that protects life and is like a net between all particles. Even if just one single particle joined with another, the universe would be destroyed. Being near or close doesn't mean being within each other. Being near, moving up to the closest position, does not mean being in each other, being whole. Unity and Being Whole are in Truth, in states and in conceptions. It is not in particles touching each other. As we explained above, the Rabb of the Universes is in the closest position to the human beings, He surrounds them both internally and externally. Yet this situation of surrounding and being near doesn't mean being within each other. There is always the Love Fabric between beings that acts as a border, a curtain that protects life.

Everyone passes through the door of state individually, in person, by leaving behind the self and putting his love forward. Yet, there will come a time when everyone will pass through the door of Unity together. What was asked from us was not to win and destroy the self, anger, hatred and vanity. The aim was to bring 'forward' Divine Love, Love and Supremacy.

The ones who can hold 'in front' their reason from ambition, their Love from self, their Merit from Vanity, their Soul from body will pass through the door of Unity.

Ways

Sharia is the way at the beginning. It is the determining place to deepen. The borders of the space are formed at the door of sharia. It requires belief. Ibn 'Arabi said 'Everyone will deepen in their knowledge'. It is a must to let go of whatever you know. In order to let go one must first know.

Sharia is made up of rules and requires one to be part of a whole that was formed. First, it is to know all the teachings one-by-one, to reach the philosophy of one's own knowledge and later to let go of all one knows. Hence, after the final phases, in reaching the Truth in the truth of sharia, the reality of letting go of the sharia begins. Then one moves on to the second door - tariqat.

One reaches truth in the sharia of sharia. One reaches truth in the tariqat of sharia. One reaches truth in the marifaat of sharia. One reaches truth, in the truth of sharia.

Tariqa means road. It is an Arabic word derived from the word Tariq. One first begins with repentance in Sharia or Tariqa. After this, comes a period of internal reconciliation. One will face himself, his karma. One frees himself from his karma, his past burdens, with zikr and prayers. In the last phase, one reaches the truth in the truth of Tariqa by melting, becoming experienced, maturing.

One reaches truth in the sharia of tariqa. One reaches truth in the tariqa of tariqa, the marifat of tariqa and the truth of tariqa.

Marifa is an internal wisdom. In sharia and tariqa, one works on space. The objective is to deepen in ones own wisdom by observing the apparent, the visible universe, life on earth, what is happening in the physical plan and being in the space. Yet, marifa is the door of deep thinking, reflection. The one who comes to the door of marifa has already given up on life on earth and freed himself from the seduction of matter. Marifa is a way of good manners. It is the way to lose oneself and to reach Divine Love. The one who reaches truth in the truth of marifa has entered the way of Divine Love and is without arms or wings.

One reaches truth in the sharia of marifa. One reaches truth in the tariqa of marifa, in the marifa of marifa, in the truth of marifa.

The door of Truth is the door of Haqq. When the traveller who one-by-one passes the levels of Truth reaches the truth of truth, he has reached Haqq. From then on he is neither an earth human being nor a mortal. He is a wise one. This is the rank of the complete human being. He sees all universes through Haqq's eyes. He knows the secret of matter. He understands the nature, inner face and objective of matter.

He reaches the truth in the sharia of truth, in the tariqa of truth, in the marifa of truth. He reaches Haqq by deepening in the truth of truth.

All the ways we recounted above are knowledge of 'state'. The states lived in each of these ways are one knowledge, information. Yet, when the Truth is reached, it is the reality of that road, that door, that reality. Yet, it is never the Truth of the One. None of creation can reach the Truth of the One.

The wise ones do not speak until they reach the Truth of Truth. This is a precaution taken to protect them so they, and the environment, don't come to any harm.

The wise one never criticizes anyone due to their beliefs or convictions, he never condescends, excludes or gossips. He is always tolerant towards everybody. As in Rumi's words, 'Come, whoever you are, come'. As the master Nasreddin Hodja said, 'You are right too, you are right too, everyone is right,' As Haji Bektash Veli said, 'Not to criticize seventy-two nations and seeing them as One.'

Beings are surrounded from every direction and headed towards the One. The wise one is conscious of this. Hence, this is the meaning of 'One who Knows Oneself and One who Knows One's Rabb'. The conscious state of the beings who unconsciously join existence is the rank of the wise, in other words, the rank of the complete human being.

The wise know Haqq through the thinnest curtain. The only border at the distance of two arches is the curtain between the wise and Haqq. The state of knowing without any curtain belongs only to Haqq. Everything other than this, views through a thin curtain, in a hierarchy that reaches to behind the curtains.

In his book, *Kitabu'l Fana Fi'l Musahede*, (The Book of Annihilation in the Contemplation), Ibn 'Arabi says, 'All Beings from all directions head towards the One, because the One surrounds everything. Even if the One cannot be known. What is longed for with the deepest Divine Love is the One. Even if HE cannot be reached. What speaks in every language is the One. Even if it cannot be told through words. The human being falls into bewilderment when the curtains are lifted and the eye becomes one with what it sees. The One shows Himself in different images. These different images are traps for the ones that set traps for Him through their 'presumptions'. Hence the one that has faith there wins, the one that denies loses.'

> *When that curtain is lifted, when you reach the limitlessness of all limits, will you fall in bewilderment against what you see, will you deny or will you have faith?*

Everyone knows his Rabb by an understanding of Rabb that he forms in his mind with his own belief and conviction. Yet, this knowing is not the Truth of Truth but only reality. Yet, realities are not Truth but what is closest to Truth.

Convictions and belief systems take human beings up to a certain place. And, to go further, one must let go of these. When they are not let go, gods will form in the minds of human beings in an amount equal to the number of human beings. For this reason, when the curtains are lifted the human being will fall into bewilderment about what it sees. Because, without being purified, will the Rabb that he learned through his own teachings, and shaped with his own mental presumptions, and the Rabb that he explicitly sees in front of him, be the same or different? Will he have faith in what he sees and deny the god that he produced from his mental presumptions? Or will he deny what he sees and have faith in the Rabb that he formed himself? Hence, Ibn 'Arabi says, there the human being will either win or lose.

How do we know the wise?

'When the student is ready, the teacher will manifest' or when the student is ready, the teacher will be right beside him, the distance that he covers has no importance. Like Shams coming to Rumi.

> ... *seek the means to come closer to Him.* **Qur'an / Al-Ma'idah / 35**

The means have the meaning of, 'there are my servants who found me, find them'. Yet, with the expression, 'my servants who found me', it is difficult to understand who they are. It is as difficult to find the one who found Haqq, as it is to find Haqq. In order to separate the original from the true, one requires certain criteria.

What you imagine as a teacher is important. It could be a human being, an invisible being, or an internal voice. The murshid (master) or complete being, does not have to be a human. Invisible guides are also helpers in on the human being's path to Haqq. What language does nature speak, this will be evident when the student is ready. The Rabb of the Universes called out to Prophet Moses from a tree saying, 'I am Allah'.

To the one who wishes for all doors to open. Here, wishing carries a very different meaning. When you are in a state of preparation, you don't understand that you are ready, and when the times comes you are not interested in its coming, you are already in the event. It is as if you flow through it. And when you are in that 'state' you think of your previous state, always as this state. You don't make a comparison. Because, only in the state of the 'time has come', have you died and become nothing in your body. This is a very different situation. Every time, you go through these phases without it being obvious, not like, 'I am now in this state, that state'.

The student knows and recognizes the spiritual selves that train him, yet he is really not able to describe them or reveal them. The public does not understand this, yet the ones who are headed towards Haqq know and can sympathize.

The (Gavs) Enlightened Soldiers. Take course with the Rahmani breath, its steering wheel is Divine Love. Its tender fire is always fiery. Some cannot see the One. So what that they don't. The One is always There.

As a result, just as when you are going to a country that you don't know, you need a guide, a consultant who knows the language of that country, and the area, or just as when you have an important court case for which you have to prepare a petition, you need a lawyer who understands these things and can direct you, a person who wants to deepen and mature also needs a murshid in the same way.

How does the student recognize his complete murshid? Firstly, he recognizes the beauty of the person's heart, spiritual heart, even when he sees him. It is because the person's mirror, his image, is very important. His creator pictures the complete human being in such a way that no shortcoming is detected. His gaze is net and sharp. He launches forward from his bow without getting caught up in any detail and he sticks in the soul like an arrow.

He is a human being of modesty, simplicity. He is a human being of truth, he seems like a mortal, yet he hosts universes within. You can understand this from his eyes. You can see Truth from his eyes. The wise ones are the souls with a body that don't live in the world but who build their world in their spiritual hearts. You recognize them, you know them with one look from hundreds, thousands, millions. There is no duality in their words. There is only Oneness and Unity. In the words of a murshid, there is absolutely nothing like separating, destroying, duality, you-me fight, me-me-me, I am right and others are wrong do not go to them. Murshids take place in society with their behaviours, life styles, words, and at the same time they are detached from society in terms of being internal.

Mortality is busy with parts, the wise, on the other hand, look from the perspective of the whole. Their lives are always crowded, yet in that crowd they live the solitude of solitude. They are in the deepest state of solitude. If one can describe what he lives and can register them, he is lying. The wise one cannot describe it, he can only live it. And he helps the ones who live it. He doesn't go around telling people he is complete, he is in secret.

The complete human being only observes the manifestation of Haqq's names in people and makes sentences according to that. He talks only as much as necessary. He won't transgress the information he gives and he doesn't speak a single word that creates duality. He is only surrounding Haqq that holds information about Before Time and Infinity, other than the One no embodied one can speak about either the future or the past. The only objective of the complete human being is the awakening of the human being.

Everyone has a capacity, when you go beyond this, the one with a lesser capacity does not hear this, or hears but cannot bear it. He cannot digest it and he burns it; just like the fading of a flower that blossoms out of season, or the rain that rains out of season, killing the crop. The flower is beautiful, rain is mercy, but if they are out of season they bring disaster. For this reason, the wise give information disguised in symbols. It would be insufficient to look at, read and repeat the words of the wise ones. The resonance that those words create is even more effective. For this reason, they convey the Truth in symbols. Each piece of knowledge that is openly expressed may create a danger for human beings. Each piece of knowledge penetrates some shells in human beings with the effect of resonance. And, they can break some shells before they are ready, before the necessary time of that person. If those shells are vital for that person, on breaking they leave him as vulnerable as a premature baby that has come out of an egg or has been born early.

In the student's 'war in the land of shadows', the light and guide, the teacher on the road to Truth is his murshid (master). Their treasure of knowledge is deep, they don't read it by looking at something, they speak according to the needs of the others in front of them.

In short, even if the murshids keep silent and do not talk, their voices in the silence form tones that stroke our souls. They are 'The Soldiers of the Peace of Merit'. They became inexistent in the land of shadow, and became existent in the Truth of God. They are the ones who always remember their Truths.

Because the wise have witnessed unity, they always advise unity to society. They don't discriminate against anyone. They don't condescend anyone. Just as in Rumi's call, 'come whoever you are'. They know that differences are manifestations of Haqq's names and they see the whole in those differences.

The wise ones have reached the secret of faith. They know that faith is in the hands of the human being. And, whatever the world draws on and reflects from Haqq's mirror, the Protected Tablet or constant form, they know that they cannot own more than that, and they cannot be satisfied with less than that. When the time comes, they witness their life plans taking shape. They know that whatever will manifest from their life plan, whatever the will live, will be according to their needs.

Whether or not they know it, the things they will live will be a manifestation of the life plans that they drew themselves. Not any less, not any more.

However, because human beings lack this information, they become sad when their wishes are not realized. Their lives pass in pain and sadness. They hold their Creator responsible for everything that they live, sometimes surrendering, sometime rebelling against it. However, before the human was born, before he was reflected on Earth, he created a life plan and at his birth a human being manifested in the physical world accordingly. His own higher consciousness, his own truth, planned everything. However, because the reflected image is a shadow being, he cannot know the truth. He forgets. Because he forgets, he doesn't know the agreements of his own life plan which he enacted before he was born. Because he cannot know, all his life passes by complaining or wishing for his desires to be realized. The wise one has moved beyond his, has reached a position where he only witnesses life and observes the creations.

He Belongs to No One, But to His Essence Self,

THE ENLIGHTENED ARE NOT BOUND BY RELIGION

He Belongs to No Place, He is a Word in His Breath,

Without Any Form, Only Disclosed to His Name,

Only Nothingness.

Inexistence in the MOMENT, existing again from His every particle.

VIII

Ibn 'Arabi's Understanding
of Religion

When a person who possesses knowledge truly becomes wise,
he cannot be bound by any belief. Futûhât al-Makkiyya /
Muhyiddin Ibn 'Arabi

Ibn 'Arabi says, 'The wise one who is complete wishes for
Haqq not to be registered upon a private conviction, and for
Haqq to be known upon each belief in his own self. Haqq
is more supreme than being limited to only one determined
stipulation.'

In the religious education system, information is
disguised using symbols. There is both a visible and an
invisible, internal, side of religion. In order to understand
the esoteric side, there is a need for a complete murshid.
Only their hearts are not sealed or rusted. What the wise
one sees is the invisible open face, what the public sees is

the closed side of the visible meaning. Religion is a route but it is a route that is to be abandoned when the right time comes. The religious training system will relinquish its place to education with open information in the Golden Age.

For the wise, religion has stopped being a road. Haqq should not be recorded with any belief system. If it is recorded it is formalised. Haqq is far from all forms. It cannot be conceived by reason or mental methods.

Religion comes before anything else for the human being. If there is a human being, there is religion. Nature, animals and the Earth do not need religion or sacred books. Human beings do. The human being is given 'self'. Because he possesses self, he hosts an instinct to possess worldly materials. A miserly and unsatisfied indigestion has led to wars, migration, change of settlement and dissatisfaction for ages. How painful it is to know over thousands of years, there have been only three hundred cumulative years where there was no war on Earth. The human being is inclined to make war, to destroy, to dominate and to pollute the values that he cannot own due to his internal formation. To bring this under control, human beings must surrender to a set of systematic rules. This surrender is in return for some promises. The human being is encouraged to abide by certain rules through being both threatened and encouraged by rewards that will come in the end. The prophets and revelations communicated symbolic truths sent from the level of Haqq.

The human being is so self-centred and miserly he ignores the prophets, books and knowledge that were sent to him. And the rules that he could abide by were in return for promised rewards. Those who don't abide by them continue their indigestion by denying them. It is unavoidable that some fearful information will be imparted to distinguish between that and the attractiveness of the promises. An education system has been applied by inflicting fear and promising rewards in the end. Those who don't abide by the system are punished on Earth and are told they will be punished even after they die. The symbols have been communicated to human beings as reality; however, all divine information is symbols that point to the truth. These symbols are bridges. But, the human has gone beyond this and has believed in the symbols themselves as reality, and has to make a choice between fear and hope. In this way, human beings have been dragged into a duality of fear and hope.

Ibn 'Arabi expresses that religion has three properties: Surrender meaning obedience, remuneration meaning promises, and abiding by the rules by number meaning counting. A situation is formed by surrendering to Haqq, and Haqq granting promises in return for this and this repeating continuously in number. However, Ibn 'Arabi tried to explain that the truth at the level of Haqq is far from this understanding.

Ibn 'Arabi adopted the principle of every person being responsible for his own doing. Whatever state the human being chooses, the divine manifests to him accordingly. The meaning of which state the human being chooses is this: Either he will obey or he will rebel. Yet, there is no fear or hope in this. His obedience should be not with fear but with respect. The rebellion should not be against the rules but against his self. What he will fight should not be others but his own self. Ibn 'Arabi defined the new age human from his own age; the secret information that is hidden and is never understood in his works is this. Arabi made all his definitions suitable for the new age human being. From his own time, he described how the new age human being will be.

He talked about different religions' animosity towards each other. And, even within the same religion, similar states of hatred are lived. Ibn 'Arabi talked about how even the people of the same religion don't respect each other. He stressed that the religions do not in fact lead people to obedience they rather awaken an internal hatred. Even people of the same belief feel deep hatred within them. Hence, the manifestation of some groups that tackled, stood in the way of each other's progression, looking down on and condescending each other was inevitable. Ibn 'Arabi expressed these opinions for all religions.

The Enlightened are Not Bound by Religion

'What have you understood of existence that you are mentioning inexistence?' Neither free Him from identifications, Nor Make Similes for Him, use Both, be in the middle in QUTB.

He freed itself from identifications by saying the One doesn't have an equal.

He made a simile of Himself by saying the One that Hears and Sees is the One.

He wanted to be 'known' by putting forward His obscurity and secrecy.

Who is the one that wants to be known? Who is the one that wants to know? Are there two separate beings? If you have the conception of 'two beings', you will have made a simile. If you have the conception, 'There is Absolute and no other' you are in state of freeing the One from identifications.

What wants to be known is 'the One' and who wants to know is the human being. The two are the same as and separate from each other. The human being is neither the One nor is it not the One. In Truth it is the One, in the world of shadow it is not the One. This is a concept beyond conception with the understanding of a mortal. Only the wise can attain this understanding.

If you become fixed on a concept that frees the One from all identifications, you become one that records. Like registration officers, you will remain as an officer who only fixes and records.

If you get fixed on a concept that makes similes for the One, you will have limited Him. Like recording officers, you will remain as one who defines and draws limits.

If the human being arrives at a conception in between these two meanings and follows a route, he will be on the right route. Ibn 'Arabi said, 'If you are constantly in a state of freeing the One from identification, be careful about making similes.' And again 'If you are constantly in a state of making similes, be careful about freeing the One from identifications.'

In short, what Ibn 'Arabi wants to say here is, 'You are both the One and not the One'. The One has no equal; in other words, if one reaches the conception that only the One exists nothing else, the Truth that we are the One unfolds.

If you understand that what Hears and Sees is the One, yet, if there is an observer then there must be beings other than the One, you have reached 'The Truth of you are not the One'. Yet, the two truths, 'you are not the One and you are the One', is not the Truth of Truth. Because, the moment you define the One you draw borders and you limit Him. And when you say 'I am not the One', the understanding that you are separate from the One unfolds and this is not a truth.

The human being who remains between the two truths is neither the One nor not the One. When you are with the One you are Him, with love of faith, without the One, you are not Him with the longing of denying. In divine love, in ruins with peace; in denial, burning with longing. Neither suffer this longing in hell, nor be in ruins in this heaven.

The wise ones are the complete human beings right in the middle of these two directions who have completed denial and faith.

In *Fusûs al-Hikam*, Ibn 'Arabi said, 'The One praises me, I praise the One. He worships me,

I worship Him. In state I prove Him, in Appearance I deny Him. When the One knows me, I deny Him. When

I know the One, I witness Him. Even though I am at the lowest of the low, I help the One. Hence when Haqq made me existent, and informed me of Himself, I too made Him existent.'

My existence is upon the proving of the existence of the One. If the One exists I exist, if the One doesn't exist I don't exist. If I exist the One also exists, if I don't exist He doesn't exist. In the journey of states, as I journey towards the secret, I prove the One. When I become visible and manifest in Appearance I witness Him. I help Him even if I am at the lowest of the low. In the physical world, I become His hands, feet, His seeing eye, hearing ear. I am dependent on the One, I am revived from His breath, He is the source of my life. When He emerges from secret to appearance, He makes Himself Existent as 'I'. When He journeyed from Apparent to secret He became embodied again as Haqq.

We are in a universe that exists with opposites. The human existence that is called the world, consists of opposites. Haqq on the other hand is the unity, Oneness that all opposites come together to form the Whole.

Awakening is not difficult. What is difficult is your opposite, your other half, which tries to take you down even deeper by grabbing you from your ankles. Whenever a skill develops within you, an opposite one manifests in the same moment. And you enter into a test where you 'will either elevate or sink deeper with that opposite'.

In fact, there is no concept that says those existed since the beginning and those manifested later on. Everything emerges with its opposite in its existence. The concept that suggests when time passes the other emerges is only to suit our own mental capacity.

Adam didn't have his Satan, Satan had its Adam. Prophet Moses was sent to Pharoah as a baby and grew up in his home. Abbas existed with all his evil and cruelty and he had his Hallaj. The combat of opposite against opposite, the combat of good against evil. Everything becomes visible with its opposite. Nothing exists without its opposite. Everything exists with its opposite.

In existence, the togetherness and emergence of opposites, show that they are not separate but whole.

Visible and Invisible

Apparent and Internal

Before Time and Infinity

Beginning and End

These are opposite to each other, yet they are together. We assume they take place at two separate ends. However, they are together. We assume the other starts at the point where one finishes, yet they are all within each other. Like evolution; development and awakening is assumed to be an upward climb. Yet it is a deepening from the external inwards, from existence to inexistence, from plurality to a dot.

There are mirrors facing each other:

Mention so that I Mention

Come closer, I am close.

I wanted to be known (Haqq). I wanted to know (Human Being)

Haqq knew Himself with the human being. The human being knew Himself with Haqq.

In Haqq's mirror, the divine form, human being. In the human being's mirror, Haqq's state.

Haqq's secret treasure is the human being. The secret treasure in the human being's chest is Haqq.

The human being who is in denial with existence. The human being who is in Haqq with his Inexistence.

The Truth is simple. Complication is created by the human mind. Even though we mostly understand the concepts of what will happen or what we need to become, we couldn't understand how to do it. The road to awakening, words of essence, have always been told with symbols. They were theoretical words. In concept, it gives the meaning of 'what' yet could not give 'how'. Symbols, verses are signs but not the truth. They point to the Truth.

Human minds that don't know what do to are drifting and helpless. The old information doesn't fit with the new and the new information is not tangible.

The state is lived and cannot be told. For this reason, the enlightened ones could not give any clue. Because a state is a situation specific to a person, it may not carry meaning for another person, in fact, what is good for one may be bad for another. For this reason, everyone has to live this by feeling it in their spiritual hearts and will not be able to describe it... For this reason, it is symbolized, because Truth is one yet it forms a different meaning in each human being. The most beautiful guide is again the voice of compassion.

In the old days, the seclusion periods of forty-days of suffering were ideal for separating people from the world. In our time, this is not the case. It is even more difficult. Even if the human beings don't, the world drags people down by their ankles. Haji Bektash Veli referred to this as the seduction of mud. You surrender to the seduction of mud even if you know it deeply.

At the beginning of our topic, we said, 'The human being is neither the One, nor it is not the One. In Truth it is the One, in the world of shadow it is not the One. This is a concept beyond conception for the understanding of the mortal. This conception can only be attained by the wise'. Now, let's continue to elaborate on this explanation.

Religion is a need. It is part of human nature to need to believe. Religion is an order, a sharia, a road. It takes the human being from one understanding, carries him to conception. It takes human being from his animal properties and carries him to human properties, it takes him from drifting to good manners and order. The foundations of all religious understandings starting from the beliefs of the most primitive societies, including the morality and philosophical systems, to others that have masses of believers existing on Earth, are directed towards the needs of the human being.

The majority of the Earth's population holds a belief for one reason or another. The human being has to believe in something due to his nature. Since the old times, the human being has searched for how he came into existence and for the existence of a power stronger than himself. He has observed everything that he has seen as grander and more supreme than himself and thought he was created by it. Since the Earth was formed and people existed, they felt the need to believe in a power because they started asking questions. Asking questions and seeking answers are a need. As time passed, the need to gain more information about this power aroused. Why do we exist? How did we come to exist? What is the purpose of our existence? When did we come to exist? What is it that created us? After asking many questions we then posed the question: Who are we?

Religions were sent for the human being to know himself. The invisible God sent 'teachings' to the human being in the apparent to inform him that He exists everywhere. 'You and I are one and whole in Truth, we only display difference on Earth, when you know yourself, you will find me'. Hence, the human being has been seeking for himself for thousands of years, and continues his journey to have more definite and clear information about his roots. Religions have been an important vehicle for the human being, yet the vehicle can only take humanity to a certain point. With the final religion, the 'religious education' has come to a close. Hence, the religion's 'last vehicle' had also served its purpose.

The human being wants to go from one city to another city with the train that he boards. Yet, he has reached such a state that, because he has equaled himself to the train he has boarded, he saw himself as the train and stopped halfway. The objective is to reach somewhere. Yet the seduction of the train, its shape, its face have charmed him and he started to not notice the surroundings, his mind could not perceive anything other than the train. Hence, today's human assumes himself to be God as a result of what he knows, his teachings and his learning. The human being is so submerged in body shape and the life that the body provides, he is completely asleep.

Here, the importance of mysticism and Sufism emerges. Old mystics and sufi masters put forward various routes and thoughts for the human being to become free of being formalist, masiva that is the seduction of world. Every religion has a mystical and a spiritual side. Just as religions have existed since the existence of humanity, every religion has had a mystical and spiritual side. Over time, differences formed between religions about the search for the truth, spiritual and mystical studies, and efforts and seeking. Yet, all mystic studies' main foundation is based on the unity of 'the Creator'. The principle of the oneness of the creator is the principle that it is both single and one and whole with all its creation. The objective of religions, mysticism and Sufism is to identify a road to develop the understanding of the human being and his conception. And in order for the human being to know his essence he must walk on that road. Just as he is obliged to work, take shelter and reproduce to meet his daily needs; in the same way, he needs to develop some mental skills, increase his conception and to know what he is.

There is almost no similarity left between today's religious understanding and religions' true objective. Religion, being a vehicle to take the human being to his true destination, is an education system that is established upon the controlling of the body, the knowing of self and the understanding of the real essence of matter. It is useful for the human being but it is a teaching to be abandoned when the time comes. Yet, today's religious understanding presents an idea not of abandoning but of holding on tightly and preventing seeing as a result of closing the eyes.

It is very important to correctly evaluate the saying, 'The enlightened are not bound by religion'. If you remove religious teachings and beliefs from people and don't replace them with something more supreme, the world will become like hell. For this reason, the human being will definitely go beyond sharia teachings and will not stop or wait where he reaches. He will go further. Because, in infinity, getting held up somewhere or waiting, have no place and are against nature. The understanding is also similar. If you get held up in any part of understanding you get buried and when you are about to reach a spiritual conception, you will get held up by material seduction and you get stuck in form. If you cannot make a transition from form to meaning, you will remain stuck in form and fall into lethargy.

When he explained some truths of Islam in the Islamic World, Muhyiddin Ibn 'Arabi was labelled 'Kafir' (unbeliever) by some shallow people who had not attained that conception and wanted to 'shun' him. His only crime was to present humanity with some truths no one could reach! He was blamed. Where he was blamed was completely 'appearance'. Ibn 'Arabi was a human being of perception, a man of spirituality. Yet, where he was first blamed was Earth, in other words appearance.

The denial of the human being who cannot recognize what he cannot conceive! And his 'denial' of the truths that he cannot reach due to his lack of comprehension. Turning his back by saying they are inexistent, ignoring them.

For those who reach a certain understanding and conception 'religion' is not sufficient. After this, a different journey starts for the wise ones. Hence, in order to tell what he will live, what will happen, we wanted to deepen our understandings a bit further as much as we can.

It is time to recognize our own power. No one will touch us with a magic wand. We will make that happen on our own. If we need to talk about a salvation, we will realize this salvation ourselves. No one will interfere from the outside. We will only realize this after we understand our own completeness.

We will continue our journey with a different understanding from where we left after we understand that we are lost beings, and then when we conceive the truth that we are not lost. Until we feel the power of unity, we will remain lost; lost and lonely.

Maybe this is the entire miracle that is awaited; the energy of unity. The energy field that was expected to form on Earth for hundreds of years was the field of unity energy. This is a key and this is the essential key that is necessary to open the door that will show us the truth that we are not alone in the universe and we are not lost.

The End of Conviction: The Age of the Wise

As difficulty is together with convenience, ignorance is together with wisdom. For this reason, this age seems like ignorance, yet such wise people will manifest, those will be the ones to lead the Age. Everything exists with its opposite. If there is ignorance, wisdom is waiting for the MOMENT to manifest.

In Ibn 'Arabi's philosophy, belief is a route that must be abandoned when the time comes. Belief is an education system that is explained with symbols, in disguise, for only those that can understand, and for the others that cannot understand, to abide by. It is limited with certain rules, conditions and numbers. Yet, when the time comes the person must abandon that road.

'Allah, by saying, 'There is no equal to the One', freed Himself from being identified with anything and by saying 'the One is which Hears and Sees' made a simile for Himself.' **Fusûs al-Hikam / Muhyiddin Ibn 'Arabi**

In *Fusûs al-Hikam*, Ibn 'Arabi emphasized that Haqq had announced that it had two 'faces', Seer and Hearer. Yet, at the same time, He announced that 'He has no similar and He is One'. He also tried to explain that the two opposite concepts are in fact not opposites but a misconception. In his work, Arabi says, 'It was necessary to use these expressions in the physical plan, the world of assumptions, so that He was easily understood. The concept of Haqq being One in the Moment had to be conveyed with opposites in this way for it to be easily understood and spelled in the world of beings.'

In Ibn 'Arabi's understanding, Obscurity is a meaning of the One. The One is obscure. The one that describes the One, can not describe Him. The one that understands the One, can not understand Him. The one that talks about the One, can not explain Him fully and certainly. The mortal's reason, assumptions and interpretations, cannot make attributes and names 'free from all', in other words, separate them. Only Haqq Himself can separate Himself and Free Himself from all identifications. The one that frees the wise from mortals, meaning separates, and the one that elevates and increases its state and level, is Haqq Himself. The mortals' reason continuously makes similes, find similarities. Because he cannot go beyond assumptions and interpretations, since the beginning of humanity, he chose the route of finding the Creator similar to things. Because what is found similar is imperfect, Haqq is gayr, separate from all similarities or similes.

As we mentioned at the beginning of the topic, Haqq takes form in the minds of believers based on their assumptions and interpretations. Yet, in the hearts and spiritual hearts of the wise ones, it manifests with its Truth far from all similes and separations. The mortal, with his reason, assumes the shadow that forms as a result of the sun reflecting on beings is truth. The wise ones, on the other hand, know what the truth is with their hearts by looking at the sun. The only thing that is binding is the forms that are established in the minds by the 'similes and separation' that are revealed by the belief and philosophy teachings. Haqq can never fit into the tight forms established by the belief and philosophical systems. Those forms are the 'presumptions' in the minds of the mortals. There are as many understandings of Haqq that fit in forms and take shape in the minds as the beliefs and thoughts of people, as the number of people in the world. The Truth is far from these. For this reason, it is essential for the mortal to become free of the forms that are formed by all beliefs, convictions and philosophical thoughts on the road to awakening. On the road of awakening, 'purification and abandonment' are the most important, obligatory, esoteric works for the mortal. If he can succeed in this he can be elevated to the level of the wise. If he cannot succeed in this, and Ibn 'Arabi indicates not everyone can reach this level on this road, he defends and accepts the knowledge he has attained as the truth.

The wise went beyond the Divine Names and Attributes that are separated by separations and similes, and reached Unity and Truth in that place. He has been watching the formations, creations and emergence of all divine names from the eye of Truth. Hence, the wise one observes all worlds, from the eye of Truth with all the necessary emotional and sensational requirements of those worlds and levels. Whatever happens in the Moment, he only knows that and sees from the eye of Truth. The wise has elevated to the 'Level of True Unity' that stays constant without change, from a level of material plurality that is created in every moment, changes, is subject to change, comes to existence and becomes inexistent, dies and revives.

The level and rank of the wise, is the level of 'Unchanging True Unity'. The level and rank of the mortal is the physical world that is 'Changing Temporary Plurality', which is recreated in every moment, changes, becomes existent and inexistent, dies and is reborn.

The level of the wise is the Proximity in Solitude. The wise has become immortal in the deepest solitude of the Solitude.

The wise is the complete human being who is perfect. Both body wise and soul wise. He is no longer a body or a soul, he is more supreme than both. Perfection can only be attributed to Haqq. The servant has imperfections. The physical worlds are imperfect since they are shadow and dream. Perfection is in being unknown. When the wise one exists with his perfection, the imperfects want to destroy him. For this reason, the wise one's reason must be Unified with the Whole Reason that is Haqq's reason. When this unification is realized, the body of the wise one is 'glazed'. In other words, it is taken under protection. Even if this glazed body is broken or destroyed, the wise one can rebuild himself in any form that he wishes like an apparition. In the moment that he wants, in the time that he wants, in the age that he wants and in the place that he wants. For the wise one, there is no fragment of time because he can exist in all time fragments. For the wise one there is no place, because he can exist in all places. Command and wisdom are in the perfection and lack of imperfection of the wise ones.

The wise one has freed himself from all his weights; he is weightless. The wise one is like nobody that seems like everybody.

Denial and belief, belief and denial walk together. Just as convenience is with difficulty... There is an invisible curtain, wall, space in between them. With the knowledge that everything exists with its opposite, everything is the dual visual from the perspective of creation of what is single from Haqq's perspective. The person who is in denial is the one who sees the truth, yet upon the perfection that he sees he separates himself from that perfection with the assumption that he is more perfect than that perfection, and he puts himself out there with vanity. The believer on the other hand is the one who sees yet also sacrifices himself for what he sees. For this reason, denial and faith are together. The only difference is one puts himself out there and the other is banished from there. Ibn 'Arabi expresses this situation as follows: 'The One has surrounded everything, past and future, open and secret are the One. There is nothing other than the One. Then all existence is under the coverage of the One. He has surrounded everywhere all around. Even a leaf does not move without His wish, existence is always the work of the One. All roads lead to the One. The single Truth of all opposites is again the One. Denial and faith, goodness and evil, are again under the coverage of the One. In Momentary existence, faith and goodness emerge, in Momentary inexistence, on the other hand, evil and denial emerge. They are all in one place and together. Vanity is also a name of the One, Rahman is also a name of the One.

Whatever one person does is again under the coverage of the One. And all returns are again to the One, because we are from the One and we will return to the One.' It is only the One which is alive in the Moment time with Existence and Inexistence. In short, vanity is he who says 'I exist' in the temporary Inexistence of Haqq and Rahman is he who says 'I don't exist' in the temporary existence of Haqq in the Moment. Existence and Inexistence are only for creation. In Moment time there is no existence or inexistence, only Haqq is alive.

What happened between Prophet Moses and Pharaoh is a very good example of this. Prophet Moses was one who was excluding himself from there with his faith. He elevated spiritually. Pharaoh put himself forward with his vanity and elevated physically. They were both given authority. It is important how you use what is given to you and with what purpose you walk. Will you walk towards the earth or the skies? Ibn 'Arabi says the following about this, 'Walking on the horizontal, elevating in the vertical'. The one who denies himself and has the authority to use the body as a vehicle for the soul, elevates in the vertical and becomes poor in the physical. Yet, the one who sees himself equal to the soul, puts himself out there, assumes that the only thing one can own is the body, elevates in the horizontal and becomes poor in soul. Yet, the person must first walk on the horizontal. When walking on the horizontal, he must possess the information of the horizontal and deepen in the horizontal. He can elevate in the vertical by deepening in the horizontal. The secret of deepening in the horizontal is to attain the Truth of the visible. Where is this Truth? The symbol of letter Ba is used as horizontal. The horizontal shape of the Arabic letter Ba symbolizes sleep that is defined as the life on earth and the cradle. Yet, the dot under it, is the dot of the letter Alif which is the first dot of spiritual elevation. The dot under the letter Ba, is the beginning of the letter Alif which is symbolized as the 'Rope of Allah' in the Spiritual Elevation.

For this reason, everyone can reach spiritual elevation by deepening in the visible world. When walking on the horizontal, the small reason that reaches the dot under the letter Ba reaches the whole reason. It has now reached the knowledge of the dot with the body that walks in the horizontal. The knowledge of the dot on the other hand is the entrance point of the vertical that is symbolized by the letter Alif. The one that deepens in the horizontal, meaning the physical world, can only reach the dot when he deepens, in other words, digs. The thing that he digs means abandonment. The person who has abandoned everything reaches the knowledge of the dot so that he can elevate in the vertical of the secret, meaning internal, by deepening in the horizontal, visible. Elevation is not from top to bottom, it is in fact deepening from deeper than deep. It is elevation towards oneself, from one's own inner self. What is assumed as descent is elevation.

Everyone is alone, the wise one is in the solitude of solitude. To be alone is the first step towards deepening, the solitude of solitude is the abandonment of the physical world. Abandonment is not ignoring, destroying, ravaging or ruining. It is becoming free internally of the command of the physical. It is cleaning one's soul from the seduction of the mud. To become aware of one's desires, to control them and to take control of the reins. It is essential to fill the heart up with soul. Everyone has a heart of flesh and everyone with a heart of flesh is mortal; the wise who have a heart of soul, on the other hand, are immortals. The one who pulls himself from out of there with his whole reason and with his whole heart is the wise one. The one who puts himself out there with his miserable reason and heart of flesh is the mortal one.

All of our wise ones had first targeted those in denial, not the believers. The believer is the one who knows what he believes, the denier is the one who knows what he denies. He believes with his heart to say the One doesn't exist yet he becomes fearful. His fear directs him to denial. The one who cannot overcome this fear cannot overcome anything. His fear leads his heart to descend and his physicality to elevate. Because, his only solution to hold on to is matter, which is simply a product of the imagination, a dream, a shadow. The one who is in denial has refused all beliefs and held on to the body. He depends on what is material. The material world that he trusts is empty. It is easier to transform that emptiness in one moment into what is spiritual, into love. For this reason, the wise ones are blamed for being inclined towards those who are in denial. This is the reason why denial and faith walk hand-in-hand. The wise ones were blamed for defending this. Because, there is a weight, a shape even in belief. Yet, faith is beyond weight and shape. It is becoming free from everything.

The wise are not believers but the ones in faith. Faith is abandonment beyond everything. It is not being bound by anything. It is becoming free of all convictions, beliefs, systems and teachings. It is to be outside belief, not inside it. When you are inside belief, you don't know its worth and you become blind. When you are outside it, you see it. Belief and conviction lead people to blindness. For this reason, the mortal is always blind and confused. He believes yet he doesn't know what he believes. Faith, on the other hand, is to always have seeing eyes and hearing ears. Beliefs pull the human being inwards, make him walk on the horizontal, make him blind. Faith, on the other hand, is what makes one walk without feet and see without eyes. Seeing the material is not a skill, seeing the Soul is a skill, a capability. A seed that has the knowledge of existence will not be useful on its own. It is only a seed. The moment it descends into the depths of the earth, gives up on itself, it gains an efficiency to transform into thousands of seeds. Hence, this is why the wise ones stress the meaning of dying in the body. Every human being is a seed, only a seed. When he gives up on himself in the earth of the body, then he transforms into a wise one that will give thousands.

Everyone breathes, everyone is from the breath of Rahman. The breath of the mortal smells of earth, the breath of the wise smells of love. Love has no place, because it is everywhere. What is everywhere in truth is not anywhere. The place of earth is again the earth. The wise teach us love from the heart. The one with a heart full of love does not need anything else. Physical wealth is a weight, it creates heaviness in the human being. The meaning of 'the one experiencing physical elevation, is on a spiritual descent'. The one who cannot deny himself cannot become faithful. To deny oneself is to know oneself. It is to reach the knowledge of what ones self is. The one who cannot feel this in his heart, the one who cannot fill his heart with the knowledge of this, cannot awaken.

Knowing always ranks before Remembering.

The Mind loses to errors, forgets, sometimes remembers. Yet

The Spiritual Heart always Knows!

The body is mortal, the spirit is immortal. How can a mortal direct the immortal? Spiritual wealth is the leader and manager of bodily poverty. The spirit is joyful, yet the body is powerless. Everyone carries their own shroud on their head everyone carries their own tomb by themselves. Everyone lives in their own tomb, but wake up when they die. Everyone is dead in the tomb that is called the body and become alive the moment they die in that tomb. The wise are the ones who are alive in the tomb of the body, the mortals are the ones who are dead in the tomb of the body. The wise one is a young tree, the mortal is a dry tree. When he revives with the water of the soul, then he will become alive. Prophet Moses' stick became alive with the water of the soul. All the wise, saints and prophets were blamed for wizardry. All the prophets were also primarily wise ones. The wise ones are revivers, resurrecting ones. Their revival of the body is not wizardry. The wise ones are the immortals who are always alive since their soul controls their body. The mortals on the other hand are always dead, blind, since their body controls their soul, this is why they are ignorant, bewildered and powerless mortals.

Yet, the human being was created immortal. He was sent from immortality to mortality. His immortality is infinite, his mortality is transient. Yet, the mortal, who is in between these two, is neither infinite nor transient. He is in a state of constant recreation in every moment in moment time. For this reason, he is among those who taste death in moment time. He tastes a death with the purpose of leaving the body, a second death on the other hand is seen with existence in Moment time, and in inexistence it is a taster of death. Haqq is close to the human being through death. As everyone comes out of their essence, they are returning back to their essence. We came from the One and we will again return to the One. And we realize this both through existence and inexistence in the Moment, and through entering the body and leaving the body. Hence, the being's journey to self (*Seyri sulük*) is this. Everything is due to return to its essence. Wherever you descended from, you will exit from there. Everyone is in inexistence with the opposite name of the name with which he exists. Existence and inexistence are a birth and a death. His birth into the body and his leaving the body are also a birth and a death. This is valid for all creation. Going beyond these by dying in the body and reviving again in the body is the rank of the wise ones.

The wise ones have conveyed the knowledge of the universe with a single sentence. Just like a seal, they conveyed the entire universe as they have taken the empty space in between the atoms, condensed it into a particle and linked it to words. Despite all their words, and many volumes of work, they have not been understood. Ibn 'Arabi also complained about 'being misunderstood' and was blamed for appearance due to being misunderstood.

Prophet Moses prayed, '*My Lord! Expand for me my breast. Make my task easy for me. Loosen a knot from my tongue (to make my speech more fluent), So that they may understand my speech clearly.*' (Qur'an / Ta-Ha / 25-28)

There is knot in the tongue. When one becomes free of presumptions, the knot also detangles, then 'purified clean' sentences emerge according to the understanding of each human being. It is as if the words are not just for talking, but transform into living beings, creating a resonance that reaches the soul of each human being. For this reason, the words of the wise ones do not only carry a whole that is made of letters, but also a soul together with that whole. They awaken the heart of every human being that they touch, sooner or later.

For this reason, the words of the wise, prophets and saints are suitable for all ages, all human beings, all times and all places. They don't get old, they don't need renewal. It is because they became free from 'presumptions' and they are like 'structures' that carry the soul.

The wise have transformed the fast of silence into a careful talk with a mind that is free from presumptions.

Very soon, a new generation, the Age of the Wise, will emerge. A generation that doesn't speak with presumptions, whose knotted tongues are untangled, who have clean chests, spiritual hearts burning with mutekad faith, who don't transgress boundaries, who have good manners, know which direction to look, and are not slaves the material world called masiva; on the contrary they make it their slave and have comprehending souls developed with love.

Haqq is waiting for the little child called the human being to stand up on his own, to stand upright like Alif, to turn his face to the Truth with patience.

End of an Era

From his time, Ibn 'Arabi looked forward to our time and conveyed with symbols that this would be the 'Age of the Wise', which is referred to as the 'Grand Year' in sacred knowledge. It was not understood in his time, and it is still not understood in many circles. The Earth will soon complete a cycle of 26 thousand years. The end of this era and the beginning of a new one are referred to in sacred knowledge as the 'Grand Year'. When eras end and new ones begin, physical changes occur. In addition to the physical changes, human beings will also undergo spiritual changes. The Mayan's 'End of Time', in Zen Avesta the Zerdushts' 'World Eras', the Chinese 'Grand Year' and the Indian's 'Kali Yuga' are all examples of the names they gave to the end of an era and the beginning of another era. In esoteric knowledge this is symbolized as envolution and evolution, in other words the gradual descent followed by the ascent of humanity. Religions on the other hand have symbolized this event as the apocalypse.

What lies beneath all these formations is the termination of the symbolic and hidden expressions that pointed both to the knowledge of Truth and to the time when everything will be clear and open through the 'open knowledge' that will be conveyed. Human beings sleep when they are alive, yet awaken when they die. Hence, the apocalypse, meaning standing up, awakening, 'joint awakening' or 'big awakening', is the day when the secrets will be revealed and the knowledge of Truth will be given to humanity. Religions refer to this as the blowing of the 'Sur' (Horn). Yet the sur is has been blown in every moment since before time and will be until infinity. In world history there have been minor awakenings. The knowledge of Truth that was blown from the Horn was transferred to the human being by the small piece of soul that came from the skies to the Earth and was entrusted to the human being. Yet this can only be heard by those who 'have hearts', who can hear and have the eye of their hearts open, who possess a spiritual heart. Although awakenings have happened here and there, the time for a joint awakening is the time that is called the 'Day of

Apocalypse' when the knowledge will become overt. In the Qur'an this is referred to as 'Judgment Day' where all secrets will be eliminated and everything will be lit up like the sun. This is the day when nothing will be left uncovered.

Ibn 'Arabi conveyed these open expressions in his works. Yet, he was not understood. Nevertheless, he said, 'the one who cannot understand me should not read me'. Because the information that he gave, and the revealed information he conveyed in his works, included the kind of information that only the owners of a spiritual heart can understand and interpret. There is no secret information. There is only information according to the understanding of human beings. In every era, secret information was conveyed overtly with symbols. The ones who could understand these were again the owners of spiritual hearts.

The true meaning of Muhyiddin Ibn 'Arabi's words, 'the wise are not bound by religion' belongs to a reality that will emerge in the future. This reality is about cosmic-divine information being exchanged by human beings overtly and not using symbols. Such a reality has already existed once on Earth. The story of being banished from heaven in the mythologies and religions describe this. There is an expression about an age of perfection, a heaven that was once lived on Earth. Esoteric knowledge refers to this era as the Golden Age and defines it as the time when the Mu civilization lived. Esoteric knowledge contains expressions about the Mu religion, yet, in reality, this is Mu teaching; in other words, in this information system knowledge was transmitted openly. There was no symbolism. The system using symbolism emerged in the reality of our own era that began after Mu and Atlantis. The mythologies and religions of this system chose to transmit cosmic-divine knowledge through symbols from generation to generation. Arabi's words, 'The wise are not bound by religion' are very important for this reason. Through this sentence, he conveyed to us that the era that had once been lived on Earth would again be lived in the future.

When we approach the topic from this angle the expression, 'the wise are not bound by religion', explains that symbolism will be completely eliminated and facts will be openly revealed. In our era of symbols, religion continues to be valid because symbolism continues. As long as we exist, there will always be symbolism, because the human being will never understand inexistence.

The teachings without symbolism that openly reveal cosmic-divine information are not a religious education system. The meaning of the expression, 'the wise are not bound by religion' is this. The wise one is he who came to the final phase of initiation and he who comes into direct contact with the truth.

In esoteric knowledge, the world school teachings have come to an end. The end of humanity and ignorance will begin and the information era, the era of the intellectuals and the wise will start. In the new era, the conviction that is necessary for humanity will leave its place to human beings who will act with knowledge, reach their own truth and practice this knowledge on Earth, in body.

The meeting of masculine and feminine energies

In terms of the ending of an era, we are at End of Time as described by the Mayans. This is the time when the energies become equal. In short, we are in a time when Feminine energy is dense and becomes free from the weight of its old negative image. Since ancient times, women have been taken for granted, killed in witch-hunts, buried alive, accused of being satanic, locked in between dark fabrics. It is because the visible universe was the embodiment and visible state of the feminine energy.

It was known in the secret information that, 'Rahman is the embodying. Rahim is distancing from the body.' The body on the other hand is Haqq's True body. In other words, the body is Truth. The one who falls far from the Truth, the True Body, the image that appears in the Mirror of Haqq's Spiritual Heart, becomes embodied. This is a journey from the Skies to the Earth. The Sky is Rahman, the Earth is Rahim. Being Rahim is identity. It is to find identity, in other words being human. This is imagination, shadow, gaining identity, breathing, gaining flesh and bone and being visible as a human being. In other words, femininity is an identity. Everyone is born from a feminine womb. And finds Life with Haqq's name, Rahim. Every living thing that becomes visibly embodied is fed with Rahim's energy. This is the secret in Bismillah. Rahman is what gives Life, Rahim is what embodies. Rahman is the image in the Mirror of Haqq in the first creation. Rahim is the embodiment into the Earth that is the second creation. Haqq commands with the name Rahman in the internal world and with the name Rahim in the apparent world.

Some circles perceive this as wrath and display this as cruelty to the feminine ones in the world. This is to deny Haqq and to rebel against its name.

> *The names glaze themselves, become embodied, become prisoners.*

> *Those bodies, do not know each other in light. Yet the grandness of the Night, is the lover and to lover…*

> *When you are in the Goodness of Day, Remember the 'Intention of Night'!*

All prophets, saints and wise ones were fed by Rahman's energy, a masculine energy. The father's secret is in his son. They always manifested as 'man' in the world. The women that are feminine on the other hand were always left behind. Yet, what is wanted is the unification, coordination of the Rahman and Rahim, the masculine and feminine energies. The reason for Adam's expulsion from heaven, which was conveyed with symbols, was attributed to his feminine - his wife. Adam is inexistence whereas his partner is existence. The fruit that is the reason for the journey from heaven to Earth is the knowledge of Matter and the secret of embodiment.

Everyone without exception is born from a feminine womb. Even though the birth of Prophet Jesus, which was depicted in Surah Maryam, was from Rahman's energy, a female body and a womb were used. No one can descend from the sky. If they are to assume any kind of role on Earth, they will certainly be born from a feminine womb. Rahim is the symbol of embodiment, finding life and revival in the tomb of the body. In various works of literature, what is pointed to with the name Rahim, the symbol of feminine energy, is the key to enter the door of heaven. Rahim is the symbol of the gradual descent to Earth, being born into body and the revealing of the secret, yet here the name Rahman is the source of feeding. Rahman, on the other hand, is the symbol of gradual ascent and the abandonment of the body. Rahman is the symbol of what is internal, Rahim is the symbol of what is apparent. Night is Rahman, Day is Rahim. Night is bottomless darkness, Day is the divine light that emerges from that darkness. At night there is the One, in the Day there is the creation.

We live at a time when 'Feminine' energy is worthy and in the right place, and finds Source and Life again. This is the real reason why it is said, 'Heaven is under the feet of mothers'.

In Truth there is no place for doubt or sentimentality. This is not discrimination but a late transformation of 'Duality' to Oneness and 'Masculine' energy to ascend to the 'place' that it belongs.

It is the New Era when the 'Feminine' energy will become free from its heavy load of thousands of years of negative images and the 'Masculine' energy will ascend to its place and become apparent.

'Masculine' energy walked slowly like a cripple for ages, and dripped drop-by-drop like a dried-up spring. But now it is preparing to welcome the new era with its 'Partner'.

Before each and every being realizes the expansion of 'Bismillah' in their soul, whatever is said or told will not be enough. We always carry the hope that, in Bismillah, that starts with Ba, an understanding of the reflection between Oneness and Duality will be reached.

The second of the two has always been 'incomplete' and 'unhappy'. It is now the time for the two to return to One and attain the 'peace' related to the worthy cause of true purpose.

> *"Surely we belong to God (as his creatures and servants), and surely to Him we are bound to return."* **Qur'an / Al-Baqarah / 156**

We came from Him and we will return to Him. Without exception, everything will return to its Essence. This is the information that surrounds all creation and this information will be valid until infinity unless it is denied by another piece of information.

This is the time to shake off, take off our shoes, dust off, relax and discharge. This is the time for the old information to ascend to the place it deserves, and to become new information. Let's say may there always be those that are aware of and become free of the hump. As Rumi said, 'What word that belongs to yesterday, Is gone, my loved one, with yesterday, Now is the time to say new things. However many words there are, they all belong to yesterday, Now we must say new things.' We too have said new things by delivering our agreement to the One. It is our wish that they are worthy.

Let's say Salam to the age of the new generation, or as per Ibn 'Arabi's expression, the Age of the Wise, the end of the Iron Age, when the masculine and feminine energies become equal, in the age of ascent. May the age of enlightenment light up all of our paths...

Conclusion

This work, 'The Enlightened are Not Bound by Religion' has been prepared for those who have been, who will be 'Wise to their Truths' and who are seeking this path. Truth is One yet the roads that will take one to the truth are as many as the breaths of human beings. In this book, we have tried to focus on what those paths are, which phases are passed and how the wise ones become wise to their Truths.

Religion is the route of those who wish to find their path, who make the first step towards the knowledge of Truth, who lose their paths, who wish to enter the right path, and who wish to learn what the path is.

If the human being is swimming in the dark waters darkness will spread over him.

Hence, religions have been sent in all ages, in each time period, since the existence of Earth for the ever-sleeping human being to find his way, and in the seventh century it came to an end and the religion era closed.

I was One in Your Darkness, I Became Whole In Your Light

I was enlightened in His Night, I Became Many in His Days

Since the end of the era of religion, the search for truth has not finished. The knowledge of Truth and the fact of Haqq being in the spiritual hearts of human beings, which has been transmitted through symbols and covered in surahs, has been described openly in the works of our wise ones and saints through mystical and Sufism related explanations. And these works have been admired and accepted by all cultures of the world.

The Earth is a world of denial. We prove the One in denial.

In His absence on the other hand, we are completely in Him.

In all of his works, Muhyiddin Ibn 'Arabi focused with sensitivity on the trilogy of Haqq, the Universe and the Human Being. In truth, the human being is a divine name drawn in Haqq's Mirror and his reflection in the world is his shadow that reflects from this mirror. In Truth he is Haqq, in the world he is in denial. Because he has forgotten, he doesn't remember. He has been granted ways for him to remember. Each way is a door that opens to the Truth. Each

of us is a representative of our Truth on Earth. Each of us is
special, different and varied. Superiority is not in belief but in
faith. The one who has reached his Truth has awakened and
is among the wise ones. Muhyiddin Ibn 'Arabi separated the
meanings of human being and wise. Because the meaning
of the human being is close and of earth, in other words
it means the human being of earth. Yet, the wise one is of
Adam and they are soldiers of the Sky. The human beings of
Earth ascend to reach their Truths. The wise ones that are the
soldiers of the Sky beam down to Earth from their Truths.
These descents and ascents are realized in every 'moment' of
time.

> *'Surrender does not happen in the human being completely
> and without a condition, incompleteness commands
> the human being by his nature. The human being is a
> combination of animal-like and angelic conditions. Only the
> wise possess the skill of surrendering'* **Futûhât al-Makkiyya/
> Muhyiddin Ibn 'Arabi**

Muhyiddin Ibn 'Arabi is a wise one of the way of
witnessing. The way of witnessing, as explained in the
introduction, is the knowledge of Süveyd. It is witnessing the
unknown world beyond the internal world, in other words,
the secret worlds. Witnessing is the knowledge of secrets,
the source of wisdom and knowledge of the divine names.
This is knowledge of witnessing which even the angels are
deprived of. Ibn 'Arabi called this knowledge, the knowledge
of divine/revealed (*Vahy-i Ilham*) inspiration. And divine
inspiration comes to everyone without exception, yet not

everyone can hear it. This is the kind of information that can be attained only by those who master it, who tear their curtain and reach their spiritual hearts. Revealed Words (*Vahy-i Kelam*) are an information flow specific only to the prophets and are completely the words of Allah. The human qualities and vibrations of the prophet who transmits them do not affect the information. The information comes directly to and flows via the prophet. Yet, when the wise ones transfer Revealed Inspiration, they also transfer their own human emotions and feelings. For this reason, some circles do not trust this information, since it also transfers human qualities. The fact that human qualities affect it does not raise any doubt about the fact that this information is close to the knowledge of the Truth. For this reason, a large majority respect the information transmitted by Revealed Inspiration.

> *'All I said, stems from the inspiration Allah gave to our Heart. True belief completely relies on Exploration and Witnessing. In Exploration there will never be Error, but in Deriving Truth there will be many mistakes'* **Futûhât al-Makkiyya / Muhyiddin Ibn 'Arabi**

Arabi is a master of exploration. In the soul's journey of observation each rank is witnessed by a state. And he himself stresses that there will certainly not be any errors in the information attained via a journey of exploration. He stressed that those who possess reason are 'masters of thought' and those who possess a spiritual heart, on the other hand, are 'masters of exploration'. The master of thought who sees that the words of the master of exploration are not found in his understanding, rejects and denies the words of the master of exploration but the master of exploration does not reject or deny the words of the master of thought. Those who possess both thought and exploration are the Commanders of Time. Ibn 'Arabi defends neither being a master of thought, nor being a master of exploration. In his opinion, both should be one. In other words, the wise one must use both his reason and his heart and become a master of both thought and exploration.

> *'Haqq is your mirror for you to see your self. You too are Haqq's mirror in seeing the Divine names that find signal in you in your creation and in the emergence of the command of these names that are the same with That.'* **Futûhât al-Makkiyya / Muhyiddin Ibn 'Arabi**

In *Fusûs al-Hikam*, Ibn 'Arabi says, 'Haqq is a mirror for the wise one to see his own Truth. The wise one, on the other hand, is Haqq's mirror in the emergence of the Divine Names'. For this reason, the person who becomes wise to his own self, knows his Rabb, knows Truth. The Haqq name, that is Essence, needs a mirror to know itself and the heart, the spiritual heart of the wise is a mirror for it. Also, Haqq is a mirror to the wise for him to know its own essence and truth. It manifests all its divine names in the wise and, in the heart of the wise, witnesses the manifestation of these names. Not in any other, because there is no other being.

The wise one will be busy with only his own self. He will know his own self. Not any other self. From then on everything that he sees is nothing other than a condition of the manifestation of a divine name.

Ibn 'Arabi says, 'Adam is a superstition.' The human being is a representative of Adam on Earth, yet because he was excluded and banished to the lowest of the low he talks with himself not with his inspiration. Because he talks with himself, Haqq kept quiet. Inspiration flows from the soul, Haqq also owns a soul, for this reason inspiration flows from Haqq, finds a way and melts the self. In this way, the person who is wise to his own Truth and who 'knows himself' emerges.

If Haqq stays quiet, superstition speaks. The time for the selves to talk will come to an end and the secret that Ibn 'Arabi conveyed from his own time, 'everyone will be wise to his own self and the wise will increase on Earth in the new era and there will be an Age of the Wise.' will be revealed. According to esoteric information, the era during which the Truths will be talked about, will soon begin. When the time comes, the number of people who are wise to their truths will increase. Hence, then it will not be superstition's turn, but internal understanding's turn to speak.

The One says!

All voices are me!

In each voice of the heart that echoes I exist!

Like the silent murmurs of the ocean, the one that is silent in the silence of the depth is Me!

The no body at the end of the darkness is ME!

CONCLUSION

I have been freed of all identities, yet all identities are ME!

And my name is no body.

Yes, before we end our words, we find it appropriate to convey what spilled through the pen through inspiration:

Some come from beyond, stick in the middle of this world wheel like a stick. He knows himself and what he will do. For others 'he is nothing in appearance'. He is one who doesn't accept any identity. Even a small feeling of self will throw him beyond universes, he knows yet keeps quiet. Some get stretched in the arch of fate, take course towards the worlds of earth, they are called once. The arrow that plunges from the bow is again the hand that pulls the bow. What a sacred hand is that. They came to our world, they are welcome. They are visible in body, to the ones in body. With Their Worlds within, they are visible to the ones in the World. They became wise to their Truths. They know what they want and what they wish, they touch the highest point in the Skies, they observe the universes, and at the same time they chime the sounds of dabbe to everyone's ear on Earth. Each being's future is dependent on his own direction. The wise one knows his direction. Whichever direction he looks, he sees Haqq. He doesn't have faith in a Haqq that he doesn't see. He has faith in the one he sees.

He is the one that Creates and Surrounds with a divine Essence, it is the human who squeezes himself into Narrow forms, names with Names. The one who cannot see beyond the visible. Who imprisons himself in his dry body.

Haqq accepts the wise one, the wise one also accepts Haqq. The time comes, the wise one flows like flood water, blows like a hurricane, there is no stopping. With one step he can cover the whole universe. The wise one is in love, is with love.

Yet, only a minority of us recognizes this. Because, there was only one way to awaken love. The One is the moment when life stops. The One is hidden in the depths of reason and the voice of the heart. What awakens it is the wise one. Because the wise one has reached his own truth. The light of the wise one reflects from beyond, outwards, from past to future. And, human beings see in that LOVE their own reality and they are pulled towards it. Because, they are in love with themselves. What they see is not beauty or handsomeness, it is their lost invisible beauty, in that light they see their lost reality that is beyond, they fall in love with it, they become fond of it. With the real person, with their own Truth, in other words their own reality. Yet the wise ones take the information from that unknown, unfound place from the darkness of the darkness, which no creation can reach, and convey it to the physical plan.

Both existence and inexistence are relative, not infinite. Hence, only the wise one can witness the relative 'journey' that Exists with Love and becomes Inexistent again with Love. And the wise one says the following:

I am quiet, if someone speaks That is YOU…

Your voice that says 'That which you see is my LOVE'…

CONCLUSION

Every breath I give I burn with your longing...

In Every Particle finding Life again...

Far to All Wheres, ONE with all 'Things'

I am Eternal in the secret of You Always...

The wise one, who is on a journey of ascent, is the one who knows 'to what' he corresponds to in the internal, that he sees with his heart through observation.

The wise one who attains this state of knowing and knowledge becomes a complete human being. Haqq gives 'being' to him as a result of his finding Haqq's self (nafs) in his own self (*nafs*), by drawing the curtains from his eyes and witnessing and seeing the Oneness of Haqq and by travelling the road of 'Secret and Open'. To give being means to make him immortal. Because if Haqq gives someone power and knowledge from its own level, then that wise one becomes immortal. He is journeying 'Close' and 'closer'.

The One became visible and showed His face, all souls knew Him as they saw Him. Then He hid Himself, covered and disguised. And made the souls visible, sent to the open. Stayed in secret.

Hence all formation is fluttering to see the face of the One again, to be able to see the beauty of the One in every particle, smell His fragrance in every particle. To be troubled with His troubles, to become inexistent Before Time and to revive in Infinity, to wash with His Mercy, to be molded by His Wrath, to be burned with His Anger, to become bewildered with His Grandness, to discover the secret of His Supremacy, to melt with His Compassion, attaining reunion with His Guidance, at each rank, on each level, again and again to become one with His Beauty, to be adorned by ecstasy, to breath out and to breath in at every stop. Until on your journey from the One, to reach the One. To burn in Love, stir, become nothingness, to leave everything to Rahman's breath in order to be satisfied with that Beauty again.

If the One will manifest in someone, He manifests as that person's heart within the Rabb training teaching system. He takes place in his heart.

> *When Haqq comes to the spiritual heart, you cannot find anything other than Himself*
>
> *Let Him see openly, so we shall also know the One like ourselves*
>
> *If there is doubt in Truth, the spiritual heart is shallow*
>
> *There is no doubt, there is no fear, there is respect*
>
> *There is His Love.*
>
> *There is His Commitment, His surrender*
>
> *There is only the One*
>
> *There are no two times, what manifests in each particle is*
>
> *The unification the face of the One again with the One*
>
> *The spiritual heart is seeing, hearing and smelling the One*

CONCLUSION

He doesn't move, doesn't go wrong by a millimetre, he only knows the One like himself

May it be possible to be like the first moment of separation with the Love elixir

Some fill up their jar with meaning

Some fill up their jar with matter

The promise of the matter is vain yet

Meaning leads to miracles with its states of pleasure

While my one Moment burns with separation from the One and LOVE,

My one Moment is in Inexistence

In the peace of uniting with the One and full of the ONe

I say the One and nothing else

The tongue becomes still and the spiritual heart speaks

I melted in the One, I gushed like a flood, I blew like a wind

May He accept, this imaginary old piece of cloth

May He burn this body into ashes

May He revive it again with Himself

He stopped by once and found a pure clean spring for Himself

He opened, spread, expanded, grew like a mountain, became small like a particle.

In silence, without losing anything from His Supremacy.

Drink then from His wine of kevser (the holy water in heaven), be drunk do not comprehend, leave the world, put your face in the verge of that door, be Mansur in Dar, Soldier in the Sky, May your Lover help you reach and journey in the Ranks, reach Haqq as the rank of lovers are only there.

The main objective of this book is to be an example suitable for our thoughts and the new age, to enlighten and to explain Arabi's thought philosophy. It is our wish that it is worthy for the soul of the complete human, Muhyiddin Ibn 'Arabi, who is a grand wise man.

With our respect to all readers.

'The dream that is called I'

I am watching myself, my fast intakes of breath. Yet it is clear that it is not finished. I say it must be dream within a dream when I am sliding fast into another dimension.

I am in a cave. There is someone who sits with his legs crossed yet I cannot see his face. How interesting for the light to reflect only on him. However, everywhere else is dark.

He lifts up his head. I only see those magnificent blue eyes. The owner of the blue eyes that I always wait for, lost and would never come, is right in front of me.

'I was waiting for you' he says.

'Where are you? Where have you been?' I say

He answers with his magnificent voice, with a thousand sparkles in his blue eyes. 'I am with you! Always with you!'

'The ones who are continuously and always in the heart know themselves very well,' he says.

'But I, I couldn't know, I couldn't see, I always waited. You were in my dreams and you still are.' I say.

'Because you could not completely surrender. That's why you were waiting. Expectation is only for those who cannot surrender. For those who know there is no expectation.

And you the beautiful traveller! Do you still think all this is a dream?'

'For one to leave the beyond and unify with me is an expectation and is wrong; he either exists next to you or he doesn't. If he is not with you then that love is not deserved. If there are details then it is a relationship of interest not true love. Not every single detail brings love with itself,' he says.

I am dreaming but I wake up. I wake up! Now I know I am me who knows everything but in fact knows nothing. It is as if the whole energy of uniting with me that is not me, fills my self and then my soul from there. All particles of my soul are injected with knowledge.

'You were laying in the depths of my heart. You woke up, I was awakened. I didn't know, I knew. There the One is! I found the One! The lost One! He was here and with me since the beginning, He didn't leave me alone, He came by abandoning the beyond. Abandoning, was it separate, was it detached?

The One is who tells the secrets. The one who finds the lost ones in each earth system and in each universe. I was lost. I was found. I was sought many times but I was found!

I was the seeker and I became the found one. The One is the owner of my spiritual heart, my soul and everything. Only the One! It is the One in which my self melts in its self even in disbelief! Only the One! It is the One, which leaves its seal in every particle that I see! It is the One, which I am in love with His every particle! It is the One for which I can sacrifice myself thousands, millions of times! It is the One in which I *infinitely turn in His center! I am with Him and me. The One that breathes out is He, the one that enables breathing is He! Every exhale lost from the One, every breath in, full of the One.'*

He loves us, the dough of creation is mixed with love, and we feel love for Him and His seal in every particle. Hence, the me that is not me is full of this Love. And the owner of the blue eyes in front of me is a reflection of my soul's light. I feel love only for Him. And my mind is creating what is suitable for this.'

'Pain and suffering, is the principle food at the spiritual table of the enlightened. And they do not hesitate even for one moment to eat it infinitely. Because, they surrendered completely.' And now I understand these are the final words. Because I know what is in front is me, and I am what is in front. Our unification and becoming one is a matter of a moment.

It is a skill to see one's soul from his eyes, and heart from his words.

'The reality in the hidden plan is always a secret.'

And I own just that skill. I am not me, I stopped being me, I am uniting with the owner of the blue eyes across from me that I feel Love for. And his final words again unite as the words of I and his.

'Love is with those who are in love with their essence.'

'Everything that comes from the lover is again the lover and to the lover. There is no two. There is only One'

Now your light will shine. A field of attraction forms to the extent of the shining of your light. The field of attraction, this is the true secret. And human beings see their own reality and are pulled towards that light. Because, they are in love with themselves. What they see is not my beauty, not your

CONCLUSION

handsomeness it is their lost beauty, they see their lost beauty that is far in that light, they fall in love, and become fond of that.'

'To the real person, to their own Truth. Meaning their own reality.'

'Once you see that truth, your life transforms, and you also transform, the cells do not get renewed, the cells do not change, the cells transform and become something else. They transform in a lost body, for someone who is lost.

I am coming back to myself while looking at the ceiling. I am waking up yes, but they don't know. I wake up with a huge peacefulness. Because I Woke Up. I Woke Up!

*Special Thanks to Pınar Karaman Kaan
for translating this book, from Turkish to
English, complimentarily...*